J. R. R. Tolkien

GUIDES FOR THE PERPLEXED

Bloomsbury's Guides for the Perplexed are clear, concise and accessible introductions to thinkers, writers and subjects that students and readers can find especially challenging—or indeed downright bewildering. Concentrating specifically on what it is that makes the subject difficult to grasp, these books explain and explore key themes and ideas, guiding the reader toward a thorough understanding of demanding material.

Other titles available in the series include:

Kafka: A Guide for the Perplexed, Clayton Koelb
Joyce: A Guide for the Perplexed, Peter Mahon
Modernist Literature: A Guide for the Perplexed, Peter Childs
Postcolonialism: A Guide for the Perplexed, Pramod K. Nayar
Science Fiction: A Guide for the Perplexed, Sherryl Vint
T. S. Eliot: A Guide for the Perplexed, Steve Ellis
Woolf: A Guide for the Perplexed, Kathryn Simpson

J. R. R. Tolkien

Toby Widdicombe

BLOOMSBURY ACADEMIC

LONDON • NEW YORK • OXFORD • NEW DELHI • SYDNEY

BLOOMSBURY ACADEMIC
Bloomsbury Publishing plc
50 Bedford Square, London, WC1B 3DP, UK
1385 Broadway, New York, NY 10018, USA

BLOOMSBURY, BLOOMSBURY ACADEMIC and the Diana logo are trademarks
of Bloomsbury Publishing Plc

First published in Great Britain 2020

Cover image © iStock

A catalogue record for this book is available from the British Library.

Library of Congress Cataloging-in-Publication Data
Names: Widdicombe, Toby, 1955–author.
Title: J. R. R. Tolkien/Toby Widdicombe.
Description: London, UK; New York, NY: Bloomsbury Academic, 2020. | Series:
Guides for the perplexed | Includes bibliographical references and index.
Identifiers: LCCN 2019010342 (print) | LCCN 2019015023 (ebook)
| ISBN 9781350092150 (epub) | ISBN 9781350092167 (epdf) |
ISBN 9781350092136 (hb: alk. paper) | ISBN 9781350092143 (pb: alk. paper)
Subjects: LCSH: Tolkien, J. R. R. (John Ronald Reuel), 1892–1973–Criticism
and interpretation. | Tolkien, J. R. R. (John Ronald Reuel),
1892–1973–Themes, motives.
Classification: LCC PR6039. O32 (ebook) | LCC PR6039. O32 Z8957 2020 (print) |
DDC 828/.91209 [B] –dc23
LC record available at https://lccn.loc.gov/2019010342

ISBN: HB: 978-1-3500-9213-6
         PB: 978-1-3500-9214-3
       ePDF: 978-1-3500-9216-7
      eBook: 978-1-3500-9215-0

Series: Guides for the Perplexed

Typeset by Integra Software Services Pvt. Ltd.
Printed and bound in Great Britain

To find out more about our authors and books visit www.bloomsbury.com
and sign up for our newsletters.

To Page
You had me at blue-plate special

CONTENTS

FOREWORD

I have written many books in my academic career. This one is special to me, however, and not just because Tolkien is so supremely important as a literary figure. There are more personal reasons. When I was ten or eleven, my school in Oxford put on a musical version of *The Hobbit*. This will have been in 1965 or 1966. I had read that novel a year or two before, but I had not encountered Tolkien's masterwork. In the musical, I played a minor role as a member of the Spider Chorus. Yes, there was such a thing—and I was dreadful. Tolkien himself came to the production and met us all backstage after the performance. As I remember, he was avuncular and charming and kind enough to say encouraging things about our efforts and to shake each of us by the hand. You don't forget those moments, particularly when you follow them up by reading *The Lord of the Rings* and being utterly captivated by it. And then it turned out that Tolkien was my family's neighbor in Headington (he lived one street away) and that his son Christopher and my father were both academics at the same Oxford college for several years.

So, this book is special to me because I feel as if I am paying Tolkien back for his kindness so many years ago by trying to explain to others the wonderful and alluring complexity of his work.

ACKNOWLEDGMENTS

This book would not have been possible without my students, who made the teaching of Tolkien's works a true joy. So, I have to thank the following for making this book what it is, and this is only a partial list: Aaron Acuna, Vincen Avichayil, Molly Bailey, Alex Bako, Frances Basketfield, Matthew Benice, Ian Cady, Edmar Carillo, Deb Castillo, D'ana Castro, Elise Chadwick, Elizabeth Chadwick, John Chenault, Alicia Clement, Erika Coker, Patrick Czyz, Kira Decker, Michael DiBattista, Crystal Dietz, Marijna Donker-Haverman, Kathryn Dufresne, Danielle Essary, Eric Flanders, Robert Foran III, Adam Foutch, Alec Garcia, Josh Garcia, Toni Godes, Kara Griffith, Heather Guthrie, Tiffany Hancock, Jonathan Harvill, Mitch Hoback, Jacob Holley-Kline, Joe Hopp, Justine Jackson, Kjol Johnson, Alex Jones, Ben Kraft, Andrew Krause, Apsen Knight, Elizabeth Kronz, Megan Linton, Samantha Mack, Katie Mansfield, Stacy McAfee, Rory McAllister, Kjersti McElwee, Megan McIlmail, Robyn McKerley, Andrew Mullins, Julia Murakami, Cameron Murray, Dan Murray, Paige Nelson, Aurora Newkirk, Jessie Overton, Lori Paajanen, Katie Pace, Elizabeth Pearson, Sarah Reeves, Chris Richardson, Tania Rowe, Josef Rutz, Myra Scholze, Tyler Smith, Tony Stevens, Antoinette Street, Zach Tate, Jonathan Wagner, Sarah Ward, John Warren, Chelsea Wentland, Richard Whitney, Connor Younce, and Jason Yurman.

You kept on asking questions, and I tried to answer all of them as best I could. Here I try to answer them a little more fully.

I would also like to thank my editor at Bloomsbury, David Avital, for always believing in the project and trusting that I could get it done during a peripatetic sabbatical, and my copy-editor, Liz Hudson, for doing a beautiful job with a difficult manuscript.

Introduction

It is common with books that briefly discuss the lifetime literary and cultural achievements of J. R. R. Tolkien to begin by citing his popularity based on polls that judge readers' tastes and interests. Such plaudits most frequently take the form of "writer of the century" or some similar form of words. It is also common to cite Tolkien's founding importance in the genre of fantasy, a genre which along with science fiction is the overwhelming favorite of so many readers. I will take as a given the truth of both views: yes, Tolkien is extraordinarily popular and important and influential. What such an assessment masks, however, is that Tolkien is also difficult to come to grips with in a fundamental way. We can read and appreciate *The Hobbit* (1937) and *The Lord of the Rings* (1954–5) for example. We can work a little harder (perhaps *a lot harder*) and appreciate *The Silmarillion* (1977). Yet, the questions that remain after acknowledging Tolkien's stature as a literary figure are, perhaps, the most important questions in Tolkien studies. How are the pieces of Tolkien's legendarium related? How is Tolkien's legendarium connected to the rest of his output as a creative writer? How could one man produce academic and creative work that is so remarkably insightful and so varied? And how, finally, are the works published during Tolkien's lifetime connected to those that were published posthumously?

How do I know that these are the questions that concern readers? Because these are the questions that my students always have when I teach courses in Tolkien. Regardless of whether I teach Tolkien as a writer of fantasy or as one of the great writers of the twentieth century, these four questions routinely come up. This book is my effort to answer these four questions and one more (which runs as an undercurrent through the classes in Tolkien that I teach): What are the themes in Tolkien's work? Tolkien does show persistent preoccupations in his work, and this book will also illuminate those.

The first chapter of this book looks at Tolkien's life in relation to his work as a creative writer. Here my purpose is to highlight some key facts of Tolkien's life as a way of using the life to illustrate and explain the art. Tolkien's difficult and disrupted childhood; his love of invented languages; his Roman Catholicism; his capacity for close friendships; his service in the Great War; his extended courtship of, and later marriage to, Edith Bratt; his achievement of first-class honors at Exeter College, Oxford University; his long and distinguished career as a professor at Oxford University—all these play out in his fiction in fascinating ways that help us to read the map of his legendarium.

The second chapter is concerned with the complex gestation of the legendarium itself, with its false starts (in *The Book of Lost Tales Parts I* and *II* (1983; 1984)), its excursion into children's literature (in *The Hobbit*), its crowning achievement so long in the making (*The Lord of the Rings*), its complicated backstory (*The Silmarillion*), and the numerous pieces of the puzzle published after Tolkien's death in 1973 by his son Christopher, who dedicated himself to editing and presenting all of his father's literary work in wonderful detail. And once the genesis and development of the legendarium is clarified, the relation between that set of fantasy works and Tolkien's other works of children's literature and of academic enterprise needs illumination also, as any reader who simply picks up some of Tolkien's work may not comprehend the connection between the two without some background knowledge.

The third chapter looks at Tolkien's languages. It begins from the premise that Tolkien created his fantasy world of Middle-earth as a means to set off (as a setting does a ring) his fascination with languages and with invented languages in particular. I will not present a detailed discussion of any one language (Elvish, for example) but will, instead, show how Tolkien's love of language suffuses the entire legendarium and, indeed, almost all his published work as a creative writer and academic. It is the one constant in all he did, and part of what I shall do is to show how early this fascination shaped him as a thinker and writer.

The fourth chapter is given over to Tolkien's meticulous treatment of time in his work. Tolkien worked painstakingly on the chronology in the Appendices to *The Lord of the Rings*, and that effort is manifested throughout the legendarium in his creation of the Four Ages as well as his depiction of the world before time began (as outlined in *The Silmarillion* and elsewhere). Three points are emphasized in this chapter: the depth of Tolkien's world derived in part from the omnipresence of time; the moral landscape, in which good is always at battle with evil, is only ever seen as an almost infinitely vast conflict; the differences among the peoples he creates derives in large measure from their relation to time. The complicated fit between precisely depicted, specific events and the backdrop of millennia against which those events are played out, between the macrocosm and the microcosm, requires elucidation.

The fifth chapter focuses on the peoples or, better, species with which Tolkien filled his created world of Middle-earth. Tolkien talks of the Valar and elves and men and dwarves and orcs and, most famously, hobbits. Each species is further subdivided historically or geographically or linguistically or politically into different and distinct groups. There are beings, too, who play crucial roles in the legendarium (the wizards and the Nazgûl) as well as singletons: Beorn and Tom Bombadil.

The sixth chapter examines the dominant themes of Tolkien's legendarium, both those that I consider significant and those that other scholars have emphasized. My intent is to offer a sort of thread through the labyrinth of Tolkien's artistic achievement. I do so in part because students of Tolkien's work find the identification of themes a tremendous help meet in understanding his created world.

The book concludes with an afterword and three appendices. The Afterword discusses the recent publication of *The Fall of Gondolin* (2018): what it reveals about the legendarium and what it means for the work to be the last by Tolkien (father and son). As to the Appendices, the first is given over to a set of tables illustrating the sources for Tolkien's mythology in Anglo-Saxon and Middle-English, Scandinavian, Celtic, and Germanic literature. To these tables I add two more: the sources Tolkien used from earlier fantasy literature and other important but miscellaneous sources that do not conveniently or precisely fit into the other tables. This appendix gives the general reader an understanding of Tolkien's sources in enough detail to make experiencing or studying the legendarium richer and more satisfying. The second appendix focuses on how Tolkien's world has been depicted on film: from the cartoons of the 1970s and early 1980s through Peter Jackson's three films devoted to *The Lord of the Rings* (2001–3) and the three on *The Hobbit* (2012–14). My focus is on understanding how and why the films diverge from the books. The third appendix offers the reader a list of texts for further reading along with some suggestions about future directions for Tolkien studies.

This study in the Guide for the Perplexed series is not, of course, the first introduction to Tolkien's work. It is, however, different from its precursors in that it's deliberately responding to particular questions that puzzled or curious readers will likely have. It is also a different sort of book about Tolkien than many others because it begins from the assumption that Tolkien's work matters so much not just because it is beautiful and artful and sustaining but because its message is urgent. At root, Tolkien's legendarium depicts again and again and with great variety the elemental struggle between good and evil in the world. It is unfashionable in this postmodern age to talk about such supposedly naïve concepts. It is even odder (in the opinion of some) to believe that good and evil exist as entities. And yet, we are alive now in a world in which three great forces are in play, and the outcome of the struggle could not be more profound as it is a matter of life and death for many of us if not for all. The first is the conflict between a worldview founded on the nation-state and one founded on globalism. The second is the conflict between secularism and religion. The third is the conflict between those who see climate change as presenting a genuine threat to everyone on this planet and those who see climate change as either a fiction or as unimportant or as not human-made (or some combination of these characteristics). And these conflicts are being played out in an arena where many countries (among them the United States, Russia, and China) have the capacity to wipe out humanity forever just by entering a few lines of code and pushing a few buttons. To this struggle, Tolkien adds a deeply mythic voice calling out that good can triumph over evil but can only ever do so temporarily. He shows again and again in his fantasy fiction that good must be ever-vigilant against evil. To millions he is profoundly convincing. His voice matters deeply, more deeply perhaps than the voices of politicians and leaders who have failed persistently and inexcusably to solve problems which are are solvable though global in nature, problems which deep down and in the dark hours of the night we all know exist. His voice matters, too, because he speaks with such beauty and conviction and intricacy. This book is my effort to explain that wonderful voice.

1

Tolkien's Life and Art

Tolkien's life can be summarized in just two paragraphs, largely as a succession of dates.

John Ronald Reuel Tolkien (known as "John Ronald" or, more familiarly, as "Tollers") was born on January 3, 1892, in Bloemfontein, South Africa. A younger brother (Hilary Arthur Reuel Tolkien) was born in February 1894. His father, Arthur Tolkien, died in February 1896 when Tolkien was barely four years old. Between 1900 and 1911, Tolkien went to King Edward's School, Birmingham. His mother, Mabel Tolkien, died in November 1904, so Tolkien was brought up by a guardian, Father Francis Xavier Morgan, chosen by his mother. In 1908, Tolkien met his future wife, Edith Bratt. In 1910, Tolkien was awarded an exhibition (a partial scholarship) to Exeter College at Oxford University. Between 1911 and 1915, he went to Exeter College and graduated with first-class honors in English language and literature. In 1915, he was commissioned in the Lancashire Fusiliers regiment. In March 1916, he married Edith Bratt and between July and November of that year he saw action in the Great War (1914–18) at the battle of the Somme. Also in November of that year, he was invalided out with trench fever. He saw no more action in the war. In November 1917, his oldest son, John, was born. In 1918 and 1919, he worked for the *New English Dictionary* (what would later become the *Oxford English Dictionary*).

And now his academic career began. In 1920, he was appointed Reader in English Language at Leeds University, and his second son, Michael, was born. In 1924, he was appointed Professor of English Language at Leeds University, and his third son, Christopher, was born. In 1925, he was elected Rawlinson and Bosworth Professor of Anglo-Saxon at Oxford University. In 1929, his fourth child and only daughter, Priscilla, was born. In 1937, *The Hobbit* was published. In 1945, Tolkien was elected Merton Professor of English Language and Literature at Oxford University. In 1954–5, the three volumes of *The Lord of the Rings* were published. In 1971, Edith Tolkien (née Bratt) died from complications from an inflamed gallbladder. She and Tolkien had been married for fifty-five years. On September 2, 1973, Tolkien died at the age of eighty-one from an acute bleeding ulcer.

A life described in fewer than two dozen dates.

The first question that perplexes so many readers of Tolkien's extraordinary work is this: How did someone who led an apparently ordinary life (birth, education, career, family, death) create something as remarkable and beloved as the legendarium? The answer to this question is both an easy and crucial one with which to begin any study of Tolkien's life and work. However, the question itself stems from a profound misunderstanding of the life, a misunderstanding that begins with the first (and only authorized) biography of Tolkien—written by Humphrey Carpenter and titled simply *J. R. R. Tolkien: A Biography*.[1] It was first published by George Allen & Unwin in 1977, only four years after Tolkien's death. The misunderstanding begins early in Carpenter's work. Before he gets to the biography proper, he begins with a description of meeting Tolkien in 1967 at Tolkien's house in Headington, just outside Oxford. There, he reduces Tolkien (despite *The Hobbit* and *The Lord of the Rings*) to "the archetypal Oxford don, at times even the stage *caricature* of a don" (2000: 14). That misunderstanding is to think or imagine that Tolkien's life was ordinary or uninteresting or dull. Carpenter repeatedly depicts Tolkien's life in this way, as "dull and uneventful" (2000: 162). Later biographers have adopted the same reading of Tolkien's life. So, for example, almost a quarter of a century after Carpenter's book came out, Michael White, in *Tolkien: A Biography* (2003; originally published in 2001 as *Critical Lives: J. R. R. Tolkien*), talks of Tolkien as an "obscure professor" with "in many ways, [a] completely unremarkable, almost plain" family background (2003: 10) and a "conventional" life (122).

Before answering the crucial question of how someone such as Tolkien could have created the legendarium, it is necessary to counter this widely held but mistaken view that Tolkien led an obscure and humdrum life. I'll do so by rehearsing again the facts of Tolkien's life, but this time it will not be in the form of a succession of dates but as a brief discussion of the life that lies behind those dates.

Tolkien's father, Arthur, died when John Ronald was just four years old. His parents were already physically separated, with his father remaining in South Africa and his mother now living in England. His mother, Mabel, died when Tolkien was twelve. So, Tolkien lost both of his parents before he was even a teenager. No one who has not been orphaned can comprehend how deeply unmooring and confusing having no parents can be as one grows up. His mother, Mabel, chose in 1899 to switch from Protestantism (her father had been a Methodist and later became a Unitarian) to Roman Catholicism. The consequence of this decision was that she was ostracized by nearly all her family and went from being a poor mother with two children (surviving off the interest from her late husband's capital in Bonanza Mines and the largesse of her brother-in-law) to being nearly destitute. She moved her family from place to place based on cost and proximity to Catholic churches: from her family's home in Birmingham to Sarehole (a village just outside Birmingham); to slum housing in Mosley (a suburb of Birmingham); to a small place near King's Heath Station; to a small house on Oliver Road (both in Birmingham). At one point, because she had been hospitalized for complications from diabetes, her two sons (John Ronald and Hilary) were separated and went to live with different members of her extended family. Then when they were all reunited it was in a sub-let in Rednal, Worcestershire: just a couple of rooms in a tiny cottage rented by the local postman from its owners, the Oratory. So, before John Ronald was a teenager, he had experienced real poverty in the days before there was any idea of a welfare state.

After his mother's death in 1904—she was only thirty-four—Tolkien was placed under the formal guardianship of her priest, Father Francis Xavier Morgan. Now Tolkien lived with his stern and unloving and widowed maternal aunt, Beatrice, in the Birmingham suburb of Edgbaston. Morgan, however, realized that such an environment was not conducive to growing up happy, and so, in 1908, he moved the two brothers into one room in a large house owned by some friends of his, the Faulkners. By the age of sixteen, then, Tolkien had moved almost ten times from one temporary arrangement to another: sometimes with his mother (before she died young) and brother and sometimes without. In almost anyone,

that would breed feelings of acutest uncertainty about at least four
of the foundation stones of life: security, modest material wealth,
shelter, and affection.

When Tolkien moved into the Faulkners' house in 1908, he
met there his future wife, Edith Bratt. She was almost three years
older than him, very attractive (as her photograph attests (photo
5: Carpenter, 2000, p. 144–5)), an orphan (like Tolkien), and
illegitimate. In a sense, they saved each other from the material and
social deprivations of their lives until that time. However, Tolkien's
guardian, Father Morgan, found out about their relationship and
forbade his ward from seeing her again until Tolkien came of age (at
that time, twenty-one)—in part because she was distracting Tolkien
from his studies and in part because she was not Catholic. Father
Morgan also moved the brothers out of the Faulkners' house to
lodgings nearby. Tolkien took his guardian's command seriously—
because he admired him and because Morgan supported him
financially. Tolkien did not see or communicate with Edith between
early March 1910 and January 3, 1913. By the time he did talk with
her again, Edith had become affianced to someone else (George
Field, the brother of one of her school friends, Molly). It took a
train trip to Cheltenham (where Edith was now living) and a lot of
talking back and forth before they finally agreed to marry. Father
Morgan reluctantly but politely accepted what was almost a fait
accompli. John Ronald and Edith married in March 1916, but only
after Edith had converted from Protestantism to Catholicism and
been received into the Roman church in January 1914. Tolkien's
relation to religion was, then, a fraught and complicated one.

In the meantime, Tolkien's education prospered. While at
King Edward's School, Birmingham, he became a member of an
intellectual and bookish clique of several senior boys: the "Tea Club
and Barrovian Society" (TCBS). This group was extraordinarily
influential in his life; his friendship with the members of the club,
Christopher Wiseman, Rob. Q. Gilson, and Geoffrey Bache Smith
(often known as GBS), proved formative in his long life. He won
an exhibition to Exeter College at Oxford University in 1911 and
graduated with the highest degree possible (first-class honors)
in 1915. In a sense, then, his intellectual achievements and their
certainty compensated for all the ways in which as he grew up his
life was anything but certain and secure. With that achievement
behind him and his love for Edith sealed by a wedding, he went off

to war, and between July and November he took part in the battle of the Somme. It is impossible to exaggerate how awful the Great War was for those who fought. For Tolkien, the Somme was so appalling as to be almost beyond direct description. He simply said that trench warfare was an "animal horror" (quoted in Carpenter 2000: 91) and war itself an "utter stupid waste" (75). History records that in the five-month battle, the Allies advanced just six miles across a sixteen-mile front at the cost of 650,000 casualties. Of Tolkien's three best friends from the TCBS, only one survived: Christopher Wiseman. Rob Gilson died at La Boiselle on July 1 (the first day of the battle of the Somme) and GBS on December 3 from injuries caused by shrapnel. Tolkien himself was fortunate indeed to be invalided back to England in November 1916 for the rest of the war with trench fever (a potentially fatal infection carried by lice). It was during his long convalescence that Edith sang and danced for him in a wood near Roos in Yorkshire, a magical moment that was transformed into a central moment in the myth of Beren and Lúthien.

After the war, there was the job at the *New English Dictionary* and the spectacular rise to the eminence of an Oxford professorship at the remarkably young age of thirty-two; there was the long marriage and four children; there was the sustained effort to balance his love of creative writing with his academic work and his family life as sole breadwinner and devoted father. As I suggested earlier, it has become accepted as a biographical fact that these were dull and ordinary years in Tolkien's life. They were not, for several reasons. First, the marriage of John Ronald and Edith was a complex and difficult one in part because of his preoccupation with his work, in part because of her shyness around his academic colleagues and friends, in part because of his idealizing of Edith, and in part because the relationship was founded on coercion. Tolkien had forced Edith to convert to Catholicism when her social roots were in Protestantism, and she had been about to marry someone else when Tolkien came back onto the scene just in time. Second, it was an extraordinary achievement to continue his creative writing when either a strictly academic career or family life would have been enough in itself for most mortals. Such focus had its consequences, however, and in this case the result was that Tolkien and Edith led rather separate lives. Third, as a professor, Tolkien was sometimes criticized by his colleagues for not producing enough strictly academic work, yet at the same time he managed to win a remarkable number of disciplinary and curricular battles while at Oxford. These may seem rarefied as skirmishes to the general public, but when you are in the midst of them and you care about the outcome they are not. And then there is that wonderful inscription on the headstone the Tolkiens share at their gravesite in Wolvercote Cemetery:

Edith Mary Tolkien, Lúthien, 1889–1971
John Ronald Reuel Tolkien, Beren, 1892–1973.

Above all things, that inscription enshrines idealism as well as love and hints at the complexity of the relation between life and mythology for Tolkien.

And how does this life, then, inform his art? Tolkien himself wrote this deeply moving comment about his married life (to his son Christopher in 1972), shortly after Edith's death:

For if as seems probable I shall never write any ordered biography—it is against my nature, which expresses itself about things deepest felt in tales and myths—someone close in heart to me should know something about things that records do not record: the dreadful sufferings of our childhoods, from which we rescued one another, but could not wholly heal the wounds that later often proved disabling; the sufferings that we endured after our love began—all of which (over and above our personal weaknesses) might help to make pardonable, or understandable, the lapses and darknesses which at times marred our lives—and to explain how these never touched our depths nor dimmed our memories of our youthful love. For ever (especially when alone) we still met in the woodland glade, and went hand in hand many times to escape the shadow of imminent death before our last parting. (Tolkien 2000: 420–1)

What this moving statement suggests is that the legendarium is very much a substitute for autobiography, with Tolkien expressing himself "about things deepest felt in tales and myths" (that is, putting his most important life experiences into creative narrative) rather than in conventional autobiography. This letter also suggests that his life was not the dull and routine existence it is conventionally argued to have been. For example, on at least one occasion, it can be gleaned from his published letters that Tolkien suffered a nervous breakdown in the first part of 1938. For this he was given the standard treatment at the time: absolute rest.

So, how could someone such as Tolkien produce the wonderful and haunting legendarium (principally *The Lost Tales, Unfinished Tales* (1980), *The Hobbit, The Lord of the Rings, The Silmarillion, The Children of Húrin* (2007), *Beren and Lúthien* (2017), and *The Fall of Gondolin*)? The cheeky answer is that it is hard to imagine anybody else doing so. Tolkien worked on his legendarium from 1913 or 1914 until his death sixty years later. That shows tenacity of purpose as a natural characteristic especially as Tolkien was not a professional creative writer but an academic. He had, then, to sandwich into that stressful, salary-paying occupation the creating of his mythology in the early hours of the morning night after night, year after year, decade after decade. Tolkien had tremendous difficulty finishing anything because (among other reasons) he was such a perfectionist. The appendices to *The Lord of the Rings*, for example, show how much more he would have tinkered with the epic if only the publisher and its deadlines had allowed him to. *The Silmarillion* in its condensed and fragmentary form shows how much he had to say if only his life had not been cut short, and yet his inability to finish *The Silmarillion* in the eighteen years between the publication of *The Lord of the Rings* and his death in 1973 suggests less diminished energies than it does perfection writ large across this most ambitious piece of his legendarium.

The legendarium is the means to create a society and a history and a culture to give literary expression to Tolkien's invented languages, particularly Elvish. Language first; story after. As Tolkien put it: "mythology is language and language is mythology" (2016a: 96). Only a philologist could imagine such an arrangement. Tolkien was an academic linguist for thirty-nine years (1920–59) and a philologist by inclination long before he became a professor. He was a lover of language ever since he first saw, as a boy of nine, some coal trucks on the railway sidings at the bottom of the garden at the King's Heath house, coal trucks with Welsh place names such as Nantyglo, Senghenydd, Blaen-Rhondda, Penrhiwceiber, and Tredegar. To Tolkien, and to very few others, would such words speak movingly. And to only Tolkien (as an undergraduate at Oxford) would two lines from Cynewulf's Anglo-Saxon poem

Christ dazzle as much if not more because of how they *sounded* rather than because of what they *meant*:

Ēala Ēarendel engla beorhtast
ofer middangeard monnum sended. (*The Christ of Cynewulf*, ll. 104–5)

Yes, "Ēarendel" may be glossed as a bright light, but what else does it mean? Only a committed philologist would have spent a lifetime finding out. It is also surely accurate that only someone as committed to his career *and* to creative self-expression would have been able to produce not only the legendarium in all its variety but also academic books and articles of importance when first published and even now. The list of such academic works is a long one, but primary among his notable academic works is his 1925 edition—with E. V. Gordon—of *Sir Gawain and the Green Knight* (2nd edn, 1967), his 1936 seminal essay on *Beowulf* titled "Beowulf: The Monsters and the Critics" (1997), his 1939 lecture "On Fairy-Stories" (1997), and his 1962 edition of the *Ancrene Wisse*.

If one turns from his character and achievements to his life considered more directly, it is possible that Tolkien's orphaned childhood (with his father—far away in South Africa—dying when Tolkien was only four) may plausibly be seen as the source of repeated father figures sometimes high-handed or abusive or evil in their behavior (Gandalf, Saruman, Elrond, Denethor, and so on). It would be surprising, too, if Father Morgan's efforts to quash Tolkien's romance with Edith Bratt did not show up in his mythology. One need think only of the efforts of Lúthien's father, Tinwelint/Thingol to prevent Beren from furthering his romance or of Elrond's attempts to dissuade Arwen from choosing a mortal life with Aragorn to see how life may be re-expressed in art.

It is also startling that the legendarium rarely includes complete functional families, or, to put it another way, it is remarkable how often the legendarium includes fragmentary familial groupings at a time (the early to mid-twentieth century) when nuclear families were thought of as the norm. And Tolkien could not have looked to Edith for some model of normative family life, for she herself was an orphan and illegitimate as well. So, there are Galadriel and Celeborn without offspring; there is Elrond without a wife and with only a daughter with whom his relationship is contentious; there is

Denethor mistreating his two sons, Boromir and Faramir, by putting unreasonable expectations on them both; and there is Frodo who has no living parents and so is adopted by Bilbo. And this list could be extended to include other Tolkien-created orphans, in one case outside the strict scope of the legendarium: Kullervo, Túrin, and Beren. Again, it is not surprising to see such narrative elements repeated, for Tolkien himself had no personal, experiential model on which he could base a family in his legendarium. He had almost no memories of his father because he had died when Tolkien was so young. His mother, Mabel, did not remarry, so when she died when Tolkien was twelve and his chosen guardian was a Catholic priest there could be no more mothers in his life.

It is also important to point out that in addition to Tolkien and Edith having no typical family life as they grew up, Tolkien's mother was largely ostracized by both her own family and that of her dead husband once she decided to become a Catholic. In a fairy tale, perhaps, she would have been accepted back into the fold by both her family (the Suffields) and her dead husband's family (the Tolkiens), but in real life that did not happen. Tolkien may have written about fairy stories as an academic, and he may have written the greatest fantasy epic in all of Western literature, but his long Middle-earth narrative is definitely not an idealization of everyday family life.

It has often been remarked, with some justice, that Tolkien has few women in his legendarium and those who do appear are rather one-dimensional. It is not hard to see why this would be the case. Tolkien idealized his mother, but she died when he was quite young and only after sacrificing so much in the name of religion. It is tempting to see her depicted in the figure of Galadriel exiled in Middle-earth by her own choice just as Tolkien's mother (by her own choice) left South Africa and returned to England without her husband. Tolkien was saved by his future wife, Edith, and she becomes idealized explicitly and famously as Lúthien.

In addition to having few female role models within his immediate family, it is also the case that Tolkien was educated in the privileged English school system: King Edward's School, Birmingham, and Exeter College, Oxford. That system was, at the time when Tolkien was being educated, all male and not co-educational. Then he went into the army for two years: again all male. Then he was an academic for forty-five years: again nearly all male. He didn't

write that much about female experience because to him it was
largely terra incognita, with Mabel Tolkien and Edith Bratt Tolkien
performing roles (mother and wife respectively) rather than being
representatives of the gender. He didn't write that much about
female experience, too, because the Scandinavian mythologies he
treasured persistently privilege male over female life. Indeed, in one
text in Tolkien's legendarium, *The Hobbit*, women do not appear at
all; and when they do appear elsewhere they are nearly always seen
in relation to men and not as independent agents: Éowyn, Arwen
Evenstar, Rose Cotton, Goldberry, and so on. The great exception
is Galadriel, for her husband, Celeborn, is a mighty elf but (by
Tolkien's choice) so much less engaged in the action than she is. It is
interesting to speculate that Tolkien was aware of this characteristic
of his writing and satirizes it in the story of what happened to the
entwives. Treebeard misses the entwives, but cannot find them. The
ents and the entwives grew apart long before the present time of
The Lord of the Rings, then they led separate lives, and then the
entwives disappeared in the Brown Lands.

And there is the matter of Tolkien's Catholic faith. There is no
organized religion in Tolkien's legendarium and no mention at all
of God. This statement often leads to some version of this question:
How could and why should as devout a Catholic as Tolkien avoid
Christian references and allusions in his work? There are several
explanations for the absence of Christianity in the legendarium.
First, Christianity as such may be absent, but the first two sections
of *The Silmarillion* ("Ainulindalë" ("The Music of the Ainur") and
"Valaquenta" ("Account of the Valar")) constitute a creation myth
analogous in form to the Book of Genesis and in intent to Milton's
Paradise Lost. Second, the theme of the struggle of good and evil
(which is one of the most important in the whole legendarium) is
spiritual although not distinctly Christian. Third, Tolkien himself was
no fan of allegory; he preferred the idea of "applicability" because
while the former emphasizes (as he saw it) the power of the author,
the latter emphasizes the power of the reader. Allegory would involve
an explicitly Christian message; applicability would allow readers to
apply the religious and spiritual message of the legendarium however
they wished. Fourth, Tolkien was a believer in sub-creation, a concept
he introduced and defined in 1939 in his essay "On Fairy-Stories"
(1997). There he argues that God is the creator and any creative
artist can only emulate that first act of creation.

Finally, it is possible that Tolkien was sufficiently ambivalent about his own experience of Catholicism that he would have had no wish to feature formal religion in his fiction. It was his mother's choice of Catholicism, after all, that caused great hardship to the family between 1900 and her death in 1904, and yet it was Father Morgan (Tolkien's appointed guardian) who enabled Tolkien to get an education that allowed him to fulfill his intellectual ambitions. It was Catholicism that became so central to his life, but it was also Catholicism that caused the first major rift in his relation with Edith Bratt when Tolkien required that she be accepted into the Catholic faith before they could be married. It is worth turning briefly to a letter Tolkien wrote to his son Michael in 1965 in which he rehearses his relation to Catholicism in explicitly autobiographical terms—an unusual rhetorical turn for him. For Tolkien, Catholicism is associated, too, with the two most important figures in his early life—his mother and his guardian—and in terms that are markedly ambivalent, for they are associated with the most sorrowful times in his long life. In the letter, he begins by recalling the end of his mother's life as she died alone and in terrible poverty. Then he thinks of his guardian, Father Francis Morgan. Tolkien admits to meeting many terrible Catholic priests but considers Father Morgan a fine man who taught him so much about love and forgiveness (Tolkien 2000: 353–4). For Tolkien, the underlying reason for religion (specifically Catholicism) not being part of his legendarium is that his experience of it was so ambivalent, and complicated, and inchoate. The creation of art requires distance; Tolkien may not have had that in his attitude to religion.

In order to create the legendarium in the fashion in which it has come down to us, Tolkien needed other experiences in addition to his upbringing, his education, his marriage, his fascination with languages, and his Catholicism. One such element is his service in the Great War (1914–18) as well as his vicarious experiences in World War II (1939–45) through his sons' service. It is not my intent to be exhaustive in any discussion of how much we need as readers to understand the importance of warfare in Tolkien's work, but I can at least sketch something of its consistent presence in order to describe more fully Tolkien's achievement. Biographically, it is important to remember not just that Tolkien was involved in the Great War for two and a half years (June 1916 to November 1918) and that he survived the battle of the Somme, but that he was of the generation that was young enough to have sons in the next world conflict too. When World War II broke out, Tolkien was just forty-seven and the father of two sons of enlistment age: John (born 1917) and Michael (born 1920) and another son, Christopher (born 1924), who was to come of age before the global conflict was over. Michael became an anti-aircraft gunner, and later in the war Christopher enlisted in the RAF. Indeed, Tolkien himself saw a certain kind of distant action in the war as an air-raid warden in Oxford.

So, how did Tolkien's war experience affect his legendarium? Perhaps the most important point is that his war experience and, in particular, what happened to two of his closest friends in that war stimulated him to pursue with lifelong tenacity the creation of his mythology for England. Of the four principal members of the TCBS at King Edward's School, Birmingham, two died at the Somme: Rob Gilson and Geoffrey Bache Smith. That meant that only one of Tolkien's closest friends, Christopher Wiseman, survived. The TCBS thought that they were destined for great things as a group and because of their friendship. In a letter to Smith shortly after Rob Gilson's death, Tolkien wrote (on August 12, 1916) some lines that proved extraordinarily prophetic of his own achievement. There he writes of his belief in achieving "great things" with God's help; he refers to bringing back older mythologies ("rekindle an old light") and to his belief in the struggle of good and evil. There, too, he talks of finding his voice as a writer (in the "Book of Lost Tales" and the beginning of the entire legendarium) (Tolkien 2000: 9–10).

And everything came about as a result of the TCBS being tested in the crucible of the Great War. For, it is also surely the case that Tolkien suffered massively from what is now called survivor's guilt. While Gilson and Smith died, while almost all of Tolkien's Company B of the 11th Lancashire Fusiliers was annihilated at the battle of the Somme, Tolkien was invalided out with trench fever, and that fever persisted almost until the end of the war and allowed him to avoid further conflict. To that survivor's guilt and the wish to do something to compensate for the death of two of his most beloved friends must have been added the sense of destiny Tolkien would have felt deeply emphasized in one of Smith's last letters to him before he died of wounds on December 3, 1916: "if I am scuppered [die] tonight ... my dear John Ronald ... may you say the things I have tried to say long after I am not there to say them, if such be my lot" (quoted in Carpenter 2000: 93–4).

And how as far as narrative is concerned does Tolkien's experience of war show up?

First, in the omnipresence of conflict in his legendarium and in his work associated with it. We see it in the Battle of Five Armies in *The Hobbit* (goblins, men, elves, dwarves, and eagles). We see it throughout *The Lord of the Rings*, in which respect it is worth noting that Tolkien wanted the third volume of that epic to be titled not *The Return of the King* but *The War of the Ring*. We see it throughout *The Book of Lost Tales Parts I* and *II* and *The Silmarillion*. We see it in *The Legend of Sigurd and Gudrún* (2009), in *The Story of Kullervo* (2016), in his translation of *Beowulf* (2014), in the recent *Beren and Lúthien*, in his continuation of the Battle of Maldon titled "The Homecoming of Beorhtnoth, Beorthelm's Son" (with its moving depiction of the battlefield after a conflict is over) (1966), in *Finn and Hengest* (2006), in *The Children of Húrin*, in *The Fall of Arthur* (2013), and in *The Fall of Gondolin*. In fact, we see it even in his lesser and later work *Farmer Giles of Ham* (1949). Only in *Smith of Wootton Major* (1967), the last work published in his lifetime, is war not central to what happens in the narrative. Nor should we be at all surprised that war is everywhere in Tolkien's work, for Tolkien himself once wrote to his son Christopher (in a letter dated May 6, 1944) that the origins of the legendarium were his experiences in the Great War. Indeed, the earliest parts of the legendarium were written during stolen moments in his war service (Tolkien 2000: 78).

Second, we see warfare showing up in different ways. It shows up in massive armed conflict (Nírnaeth Arnoediad or the Battle of Unnumbered Tears, for example). It shows up in physical locations such as the Dead Marshes northwest of Dagorlad and near the borders of Mordor. It's there that, in *The Lord of the Rings*, Frodo has that extraordinary moment when he sees a dead face below the water and reaches out to it. It is hard not to see Tolkien's own experiences of trench warfare in such a moment, for one of the grotesque ways in which a soldier could die in a trench was by slipping off a duckboard and drowning in the water and the mud that were the bane of the common soldier on the Western Front. In a letter to Professor L. W. Forster written on December 31, 1960, Tolkien comments that the episode in the Dead Marshes and the journey to the Black Gate (or the Morannon) were based on his battle experiences on the Somme (Tolkien 2000: 303). Warfare shows up, too, in verbal echoes at crucial moments in the legendarium. For example, in *The Fellowship of the Ring* when Gandalf faces the Balrog on the Bridge of Khazad-dûm in the Mines of Moria, he tells it three times: "You cannot pass" (Tolkien 1994a: 322). (That statement is surely an intentional echo of Robert Nivelle's famous comment directed at the Germans in 1916 after their assault on Verdun: "Ils ne passeront pas!" ("They shall not pass!").)

It shows up, too, in what many see as one of the most moving but puzzling relationships in the entire legendarium: that between Frodo and Sam. To some, the relationship reeks of class privilege and homoeroticism, but when read correctly it represents Tolkien's tribute to the relation between batman (Sam) and commissioned officer (Frodo) that was a remarkable feature of the Great War. The batman was a common soldier and (among his other responsibilities) he had to look after the officer to whom he had been assigned so that the officer could spend his energies less on everyday survival and more on the vital role of leading his men. By analogy, Sam ministers more and more as the narrative of *The Lord of the Rings* goes on to Frodo's physical needs so that he can focus on his "leadership" role: destroying the One Ring in the Cracks of Doom. Long after his combat experience in the Great War, Tolkien wrote: "My 'Sam Gamgee' is indeed a reflexion of the English soldier, of the privates and batmen I knew in the 1914 war, and recognised as so far superior to myself" (quoted in Carpenter 2000: 89).

The legendarium is recognizably and straightforwardly the work of Tolkien in other respects too. One, which is sometimes reduced to a veneration of the Inklings as the paradigm for *all* writing groups, is Tolkien's "clubbiness". Tolkien was gregarious in groups dominated by male discourse and was very successful in such an atmosphere, as his effective and radical revision of the English curriculum at Oxford University shows. This characteristic appears most famously in the legendarium, of course, in the creation of two fellowships crucial to the success of their appointed quests. The first occurs in *The Hobbit*. There the narrative begins with the creation of a company of thirteen dwarves, a hobbit, and a wizard: Thorin Oakenshield, Fili, Kili, Balin, Dwalin, Oin, Gloin, Dori, Ori, Nori, Bifur, Bofur, Bombur, Bilbo Baggins, and Gandalf. Their intention is to go to the Lonely Mountain and take back Smaug's treasure. The second occurs in *The Lord of the Rings*. There the narrative pivots on the creation at the Council of Elrond of the Fellowship of the Ring and its nine members: four hobbits (Frodo, Sam, Merry, and Pippin), two men (Aragorn and Boromir), one dwarf (Gimli), one elf (Legolas), and one wizard (Gandalf). Their intention is to help Frodo to destroy the One Ring in the Cracks of Doom. Tolkien's own life was rich with such groups. The best known are the TCBS (a group of four: Tolkien, Christopher Wiseman, Rob Gilson, and Geoffrey Bache Smith) and the Inklings (with a nucleus of seven: Tolkien, C. S. Lewis, Warren Lewis, R. E. Havard, Owen Barfield, Charles Williams, and Hugo Dyson). The first group met from 1911 to 1916. The second from about 1931 to the mid 1950s. But there were other clubs too. The Stapledon Club (at Exeter College), the Viking Club (at Leeds University), and the Coalbiters (a group founded by Tolkien and open to Oxford dons interested in reading the Icelandic sagas). This last group was usually six or seven strong: Tolkien, George Gordon, Nevill Coghill, C. T. Onions, John Bryson, C. S. Lewis, and R. W. Dawkins. It lasted for a couple of years in the early 1930s until (logically and naturally) all the sagas were extemporaneously and orally translated by the group, and so it dissolved.

If we move briefly away from the legendarium to include some of Tolkien's other works, then, once again, the question that catalyzed this chapter's development—"How did Tolkien create his extraordinary world?"—is simply answered. No one but Tolkien could have done it. So, his life as a devoted father is the source for his children's stories (for example *The Hobbit, The Adventures of Tom Bombadil* (1961), and *Roverandom* (1998)) because they began as oral tales told to his growing family and then showed up in different ways in the legendarium itself. His life as an academic is the source for *Farmer Giles of Ham* (with all its philologist and Oxford in-jokes) and *Smith of Wootton Major* (an allegory of the battle between literary theory and philology with an indirect connection to the legendarium in its concern with the world of Faerie) as well as his published talk "A Secret Vice" (about the creation of constructed languages, a "hobby" directly connected with the many languages in the legendarium).

Two more issues need to be raised at this point. Each contributes to the confusion that many readers encounter when they read or study Tolkien. Each is less directly connected than my earlier discussion with the reading of Tolkien's work through the lens of his life, so I have left my analysis of them until the end of the chapter. The first is the matter of naming. The second is the incompleteness of his legendarium.

Whenever I teach Tolkien's works to students, the question of character names comes up because students find the plethora of names confusing and sometimes, frankly, annoying. I offer them a partial answer by saying that such variation in names is a feature both of myth and epic, for the more important characters are the more meaning will accrete to them, and that accretion will often take the form of contextual renaming. One sees this in *The Odyssey* and *The Iliad*, for example. That satisfies my students to a degree, but it ignores the particularities of Tolkien's twentieth-century re-creation of a mythology for England. So, we may take an obvious, interesting and straightforward case: Aragorn, say. When Aragorn introduces himself in *The Two Towers* to the Rohirrim, he runs through his names by way of self-definition: "I am Aragorn son of Arathorn, and am called Elessar, the Elfstone, Dúnadan, the heir of Isildur Elendil's son of Gondor" (Tolkien 1994b: 423).

That's a long list, but he is also Strider and Estel and Thorongil and Aragorn II and King Elessar Telcontar and Edhelharn and Longshanks and Wingfoot and Envinyatar. So, the protagonist in Tolkien's major epic has at least fifteen names attached to him. This is no small matter, for as Carpenter points out in his biography of Tolkien, naming was crucial to him:

> It is impossible in a few sentences to give an adequate account of how Tolkien used his Elvish languages to make names for the characters and places in his stories. But briefly, what happened was this. When working to plan he would form all these names with great care, first deciding on the meaning, and then developing its form first in one language and subsequently in the other; the form finally used was most frequently that in Sindarin. However, in practice he was often more arbitrary. It seems strange in view of his deep love of careful invention, yet often in the heat of writing he would construct a name that sounded appropriate to the character without paying more than cursory attention to its linguistic origins. (Carpenter 2000: 102)

The naming of Aragorn follows this pattern with some names being Elvish (Elessar and Edhelharn) and some simply appropriate (Strider and Longshanks). The reader or student of Tolkien need merely decide to use one name for clarity (say, Aragorn) and then explore the ways in which Tolkien elaborated on one name and for what reason(s).

So much for Tolkien's polished work published during his lifetime. Another instructive and clarifying strategy applies to his incomplete works in progress. The generalization is that with his fragmentary works the reader should look for the ways in which the myth itself evolves. A useful example of this development is Tolkien's *The Story of Kullervo* (edited by Verlyn Flieger). Kullervo is also known as Kuli, Sake, Sākehonto, Honto, Sāri, and Sārihonto. His father (Kalervo) is also known as Talte, Taltelouhi, Kampa, and Kalervloinen. His uncle (Untamo) also goes by Untamoinen, Unti, Ūlto, Ulko, and Ulkho. A plethora of names indeed. Now, some of this elaboration comes from Tolkien's source (the Finnish collection of folk tales called *Kalevala*). That is, Tolkien was simply following a beloved model. Some of it, however, comes from Tolkien changing his mind about naming practices as the project (his retelling of one of the stories in *Kalevala*) progressed. In this case (as distinct from the case of Aragorn), Tolkien never finalized his names as *The Story of Kullervo* is incomplete. As Verlyn Flieger points out, Tolkien "began by following *Kalevala* nomenclature, but in the course of composition changed to his own invented names and nicknames" (2016b: xxi–xxii). *The Story of Kullervo* itself exists as only one incomplete manuscript with numerous revisions and re-revisions and rough plot summaries. Among the pages of the manuscript is a wonderful insight into Tolkien's working practices: MS Folio 6 (41–3). MS Folio 6 is a "List of Names," and this list presents some three dozen of them along with equivalents and explanations as well as a couple of important strikethroughs. The lesson from examining Tolkien's creative practices is this: for readers, clarity and understanding come from practicing patience (as Tolkien never rewards a superficial look) and from coming to understand the long process of sub-creation that resulted in the legendarium and all its associated stories.

The second matter somewhat less explicitly attached to Tolkien's life is the fragmentariness of his legendarium. There are personal reasons for the incompleteness of his creation: he had a hectic life as father and husband and academic, without taking into account his ambitions as a creative writer. So, his writing was pushed to odd moments of free time and a great many late nights and early mornings spent struggling with the enormity of his vision. And he was a procrastinator, too, and a perfectionist, and an inveterate reviser of his work—frequently beginning again and again from scratch. He termed himself in a letter to Caroline Everett in 1957, "a notorious beginner of enterprises and non-finisher, partly through lack of time, partly through lack of single-minded concentration" (Tolkien 2000: 257). These personal reasons have obscured another explanation, and one which offers a way out of the maze of different versions of so many of the pieces of the legendarium. In an Appendix ("The Evolution of the Great Tales") to his edition of *The Children of Húrin* (2007: 269–82), Christopher Tolkien mentions no fewer than ten times the incompleteness of his father's legendarium. Again and again and again he talks of his father abandoning his plans, and then he renders a judgment: that his father "failed of his purpose" when "grievously, he stopped and never went further" (Tolkien 2007: 280). I do not deny that Tolkien's legendarium is unfinished and its "Great Tales" incomplete: *The Children of Húrin* is incomplete; *Beren and Lúthien* is incomplete; *The Fall of Gondolin* is incomplete; "The Tale of Eärendel" (1984: 252–77) is little more than notes toward an ending. Any student of Tolkien's work sorrows at the fact.

There are all those autobiographical reasons why this should be the case. However, I would suggest that one of the ways in which the confusing aspects of his incomplete legendarium may be better understood is to see their fragmentariness as precisely matching the qualities of the very myths he admired so much and endeavored to emulate in his efforts to create a mythology for England. In a famous letter to Milton Waldman (probably written in 1951), Tolkien offers a coherent sketch of his legendarium. He prefaces the sketch with this self-effacing comment:

Do not laugh! But once upon a time (my crest has long since fallen) I had a mind to make a body of more or less connected legend, ranging from the large and cosmogonic, to the level of romantic fairy-story—the larger founded on the lesser in contact with the earth, the lesser drawing splendour from the vast backcloths—which I could dedicate simply to: to England; to my country. It should possess the tone and quality that I desired, somewhat cool and clear, be redolent of our "air" (the clime and soil of the North West, meaning Britain and the hither parts of Europe: not Italy or the Aegean, still less the East), and, while possessing (if I could achieve it) the fair elusive beauty that some call Celtic (though it is rarely found in genuine ancient Celtic things), it should be "high," purged of the gross, and fit for the more adult mind of a land long now steeped in poetry. I would draw some of the great tales in fullness, and leave many only placed in the scheme, and sketched. The cycles should be linked to a majestic whole, and yet leave scope for other minds and hands, wielding paint and music and drama. Absurd. (Tolkien 2000: 144–5)

Nearly all of this Tolkien quite remarkably achieved. We can quibble about whether the stories of Beren and Lúthien or of the children of Húrin were drawn in "fullness" before Christopher Tolkien elaborated on them, but we do have *The Hobbit* and *The Lord of the Rings*. We do have the "large body of more or less connected legend ranging from the large and cosmogonic, to the level of romantic fairy story–the larger founded on the lesser in contact with the earth, the lesser drawing splendour from the vast backcloths." We do have the cool and clear tone and the elusive Celtic beauty. Yes, we may regret he did not complete more, but that is the way of mythologies (and epics, too). We will understand Tolkien's legendarium better, I think, if we see its fragmentariness as not just autobiographical but also as intentional.

In 1938 (shortly, that is, after the publication of *The Hobbit*), Tolkien wrote a story titled "Leaf by Niggle" (1964). First published in 1945, it tells the tale of an artist named Niggle who is painting a canvas of a tree. Much happens in the tale, but the two points I want to emphasize from the narrative are these: Niggle becomes sidetracked by trying to depict each leaf perfectly and by taking care of the many mundane things he has to do; and he does create one perfect leaf which ends up being preserved in a museum. The story dramatizes Tolkien's life in a nutshell: anxiety, procrastination, vision, achievement, fame. To this picture, I will add some comments Tolkien made about how *The Lord of the Rings* came into being:

One writes such a story not out of the leaves of trees still to be observed, nor by means of botany and soil-science; but it grows like a seed in the dark out of the leaf-mould of the mind: out of all that has been seen or thought or read, that has long ago been forgotten, descending into the deeps. No doubt there is much selection, as with a gardener: what one throws on one's personal compost-heap; and my mould is evidently made largely of linguistic matter. (quoted in Carpenter 2000: 131)

The value of reading Tolkien's work through the lens of his life (the purpose of this chapter) is that it helps to explain some of the work's complexities, to diminish the number of ways or the degree to which readers become perplexed about the legendarium by incorrectly assuming some grand disjunction between author and work. There is value to "descending into the deeps" to understand how Tolkien produced a legendarium of such exquisite and complicated and resonant beauty.

Note

1 It is interesting to observe that this misreading of Tolkien's life has very much continued into the present. In May 2019, Fox Searchlight released a biopic of Tolkien's life, *Tolkien*. Whatever its merits may be as film, it doesn't mention C. S. Lewis or the Inklings, and it has nothing to say about the crucial role of faith in Tolkien's life.

2

Tolkien's Legendarium

Five questions often come up when studying or discussing Tolkien's legendarium. What is the history of its publication? What is the history of its creation and composition? What were Tolkien's habits as a writer? What has been the role of those who have edited his work posthumously? What is the arc of its overall story? The answers to these questions go a long way toward clarifying an achievement in fantasy literature that remains unparalleled. Initially, the legendarium's overarching narrative seems fragmentary and confusing, and, indeed, it is complicated, but it has a shape and a clear, profound meaning. The legendarium as a whole rewards close attention in wonderful ways for those interested in understanding the nature of Tolkien's work.

The Publication of the Legendarium

Tolkien's legendarium is a mighty and complex achievement with two remarkable characteristics. The first is how little of it was published during Tolkien's lifetime. When he died in September 1973, only six pieces of the legendarium had been published: *The Hobbit*, *The Lord of the Rings* in three volumes, *The Adventures of Tom Bombadil*, and *The Road Goes Ever On: A Song Cycle* (1967). Of these, *The Adventures of Tom Bombadil* and *The Road Goes Ever On* include a great deal of material previously published in *The Hobbit* and *The Lord of the Rings*. By 2019, more than fifty years after the publication of *The Road Goes Ever On*, the legendarium has swelled to twenty-four volumes. Of these eighteen new books, the most important is *The Silmarillion* and the most extensive *The History of Middle-earth* series published in twelve volumes between 1983 and 1996. The other parts of the legendarium published since Tolkien's death include *Bilbo's Last Song (at the Grey Havens)* (1974 (poster); 1990 (book); revised edition 2002), *Unfinished Tales of Númenor and Middle-earth*, *The Children of Húrin*, *Beren and Lúthien*, and *The Fall of Gondolin*.[1] The spate of posthumous publication constitutes the second remarkable characteristic of the legendarium: much of it is the result of the editorial work of just one person: Tolkien's youngest son, Christopher. He has been solely responsible for *all* of the later posthumous volumes in the legendarium.[2]

It is also important to distinguish between the twenty-four pieces of the legendarium and Tolkien's other work, for some who read, say, *The Lord of the Rings* are surprised to discover how much other work Tolkien accomplished during his lifetime—some of which appeared when he was alive and some of which only appeared posthumously. So, there is the academic work: the Middle-English edition of *Sir Gawain and the Green Knight*; the translations of *Sir Gawain and the Green Knight*, *Pearl*, and *Sir Orfeo* (1975); *Finn and Hengest: The Fragment and the Episode*; *The Monsters and the Critics and Other Essays* (1983); and *Beowulf: A Translation and Commentary*. There are the stories that Tolkien created in imitation of or as continuations of Anglo-Saxon, Breton, and Scandinavian works and myths: "The Homecoming of Beohrtnoth Beorthelm's Son"; *The Legend of Sigurd and Gudrún*; *The Fall of Arthur*; *The Story of Kullervo*; and *The Lay of Aotrou and Itroun* (2016). There is the work in the fantasy genre: *Farmer Giles of Ham*; *Tree and Leaf*, which included "On Fairy-Stories" and "Leaf by Niggle"; and *Smith of Wootton Major*. There are his children's stories: *The Father Christmas Letters* (1976; revised edition as *Letters from Father Christmas*, 1999); *Mr. Bliss* (1982); and *Roverandom*. And, finally, there is Tolkien's work as an artist: *Pictures by J. R. R. Tolkien* (1979). Again, almost all of those which were first published posthumously were edited by his son Christopher. The only exceptions are *Finn and Hengest* (edited by Alan Bliss); *The Story of Kullervo* and *The Lay of Aotrou and Itroun* (both edited by Verlyn Flieger); *The Father Christmas Letters* (edited by Baillie Tolkien, Christopher Tolkien's wife); and *Roverandom* (edited by Christina Scull and Wayne G. Hammond). Finally, there is the second edition of the Middle-English *Sir Gawain and the Knight*, which is unique for having been published during Tolkien's lifetime but edited by someone else: Norman Davis.

The Creation and Composition of the Legendarium

It is often remarked on by writers and scholars how extraordinarily difficult it is to pinpoint the moment of artistic creation, and Tolkien's legendarium is no exception. So, in discussing the creation and composition of the legendarium, I will present some particular dates and crucial events in the gestation of Tolkien's fantasy, but these should not obscure a very simple fact: Tolkien's Middle-earth occupied his imaginative life from his early twenties until his death at the age of eighty-one. It is, then, the product of *sixty* years of effort—essentially a lifetime's work. That in itself goes some way to explaining why the legendarium is so dense and complex. There is a path through it, but that path necessarily simplifies the history of how Tolkien came to create his imaginative world, even as it clarifies.

Origins

The origins of the legendarium may be traced back to September 24, 1914, when Tolkien, while at Phoenix Farm, Gedling, Nottinghamshire, wrote a poem titled "The Voyage of Éarendel the Evening Star." This poem was inspired by the ambiguous word or name "Éarendel" in the Anglo-Saxon poem *Christ* (or *Crist*). The relevant lines in the Anglo-Saxon poem are these: "Éala Éarendel engla beorhtast / ofer middangeard monnum sended" (1964: ll. 104–5). Eärendil the mariner is, of course, central to the storyline of *The Silmarillion*. Famously, when his friend G. B. Smith asked Tolkien what his poem was about, Tolkien admitted: "I don't know. I'll try to find out" (quoted in Carpenter 2000: 83). He was to spend the next sixty years working out the answer, and the answer is the legendarium in all its glorious and astonishing complexity. As Christina Scull and Wayne G. Hammond remark in their *J. R. R. Tolkien: Companion and Guide* (2006): "The poem is the

germ from which the mythology evolved" but, they go on to add, it
is not "the first consciously written poem of the mythology" (1.54).
That honor belongs to Tolkien's poem "The Shores of Faery" (dated
July 8–9, 1915) and its related illustration showing the city of Kôr
(drawn May 10, 1915). Tolkien wrote under the poem: "First
poem of my mythology Valinor" (quoted in Scull and Hammond
2006: 1.70). It is even possible, indeed, to trace Tolkien's interest in
Eärendel further back to the moment when he first encounters the
poem *Crist*: Trinity Term 1913 during lectures when he was up at
Exeter College, Oxford.

It is, however, equally possible to trace an alternative beginning
of the legendarium back to another nearly contemporaneous
text: Tolkien's poem "The Tides" (December 4, 1914) and the
accompanying illustration titled *Water, Wind and Sand* (see
Hammond and Scull 1995: 45–6). Later revised versions of the
poem were titled "Sea Chant of an Elder Day" (March 1915) and
"The Horns of Ylmir" (or "Ulmo, Lord of Waters"), and the poem
becomes the song Tuor sings to his son Eärendel after the fall of
Gondolin (Tolkien 1986: 215–18). As to the relation between
the visual and the written at the beginning of the legendarium,
Hammond and Scull comment: "Tolkien's creativity worked in
advance of his consciousness, and the painter occasionally preceded
the poet" (1995: 47).

The Book of Lost Tales

Regardless of exactly how far back one can trace the origins of
the legendarium (to some time in 1913 or 1914), it is most useful
to begin a detailed study of its creation and composition with *The
Book of Lost Tales*, a work which is very complex in structure and
resistant to simple interpretation. That complexity begins with the
title itself. Unlike, say, *Unfinished Tales*, where the titular adjective
is Christopher Tolkien's addition to define the tales published under
his editorship, *The Book of Lost Tales* is Tolkien's own title and
refers to his idea that the tales were "lost" in the sense that English
mythology was lost (or incomplete in comparison to Scandinavian
mythology) and "lost" also in the sense that they are unknown to
the reader of *The Book of Lost Tales* until the central character in
the frame story (Eriol) is told them by the elves of the Lonely Isle

(Tol Eressëa). The first meaning of the word "lost" is well illustrated from a letter Tolkien wrote to Milton Waldman, most likely in 1951, in which he remarks that he could find no myths or stories from England to rival Celtic, Finnish, Greek, and Scandinavian legends (Tolkien 2000: 144).

There are other initial complexities to explain. *The Book of Lost Tales* was published in two parts in 1983 and 1984. However, that bipartite structure is an editing and publishing convenience and Christopher Tolkien's (and perhaps Houghton Mifflin's) choice. The original manuscripts (or "tattered notebooks" (Tolkien 1983: 9)) from which Christopher Tolkien produced his version of the lost tales feature no such structure. And then there is the intricacy of J. R. R. Tolkien's narrative as shown by this simple fact: Of the 682 pages of *The Book of Lost Tales Parts I* and *II*, fewer than 300 are given over to the tales themselves with the rest consisting of commentary and assorted editorial material. And that is not excessive on Christopher Tolkien's part but just a recognition of how thorny the manuscripts are. As Christopher Tolkien remarks in the headnote to "The Coming of the Valar and the Building of Valinor" (1983: 64–93): "the *Lost Tales* were written in the most bewildering fashion" (64).

The Book of Lost Tales is the starting point for the legendarium for one simple reason: it features (as Christopher Tolkien puts it), "the first emergence in narrative of the Valar, of the Children of Ilúvatar, Elves and Men, of the Dwarves and the Orcs, and of the lands in which their history is set, Valinor beyond the western ocean, and Middle-earth, the 'Great Lands' between the seas of east and west" (1983: 1). For that reason alone beyond any particular intrinsic merit, the tales matter. The two parts of *The Book of Lost Tales* feature sixteen tales and several links between them.

The Book of Lost Tales was begun in late 1916 and was largely abandoned by late 1919 or early 1920. The likely cause of its being abandoned (beyond any actual creative difficulties on Tolkien's part) was that Tolkien in the summer or early autumn of 1919 was asked to compile a glossary (*A Middle English Vocabulary*) to accompany *Fourteenth Century Verse and Prose*, which Kenneth Sisam was writing for Oxford University Press's prestigious Clarendon Press imprint. The work was very time-consuming with Tolkien's glossary finally appearing in May 1922. In the meantime, Tolkien had been appointed to a readership of English language at the University of Leeds in the autumn of 1920. Tolkien's creative interests and his academic career clashed, and, not for the last time, the former gave way.

The Book of Lost Tales is fragmentary and incomplete and inchoate in its treatment of the narrative. It appears that Tolkien thought the work when he abandoned it would have been finished with the addition or completion of six tales to take the story through the voyages of Eärendel, the march of the elves from Valinor, the defeat of Melko, and the Valar's prohibition on the elves ever returning to Valinor. The work would also have included an extended role for Eriol as protagonist in the history of the elves and the overall work's connection to England. As an indication of how fluid Tolkien's ideas for his legendarium were at this point in its creation, however, it should be noted that in 1920 Tolkien produced another outline for The Book of Lost Tales in which Eriol is named Ælfwine, and Ælfwine has a markedly less active role in the narrative than his earlier iteration, Eriol.

The Book of Lost Tales has its literary antecedents, and this point in an understanding of the legendarium matters as it should not be thought that the sort of frame tale that Tolkien toyed with in Eriol and, later, Ælfwine was utterly original. Indeed, Tolkien as a young language and literature professor would have been familiar with Boccaccio's The Decameron, Chaucer's The Canterbury Tales, the prose Edda of Snorri Sturluson, and William Morris's The Earthly Paradise. Regardless of such possible narrative analogues, the frame tale of a man (Eriol or Ælfwine) being told stories by elves who experienced the events depicted was abandoned by Tolkien as the Silmarillion story developed in later years, because it was just too complicated—and unnecessarily so, as he slowly but reluctantly came to realize. Overall, The Book of Lost Tales has much the same style as the later Silmarillion story, but it is markedly less coherent. Ironically, it is also more detailed than its descendant and so more mundane and less mythic.

The "Sketch" and the Two "Quentas"

Between the abandonment of The Book of Lost Tales (in about 1920) and the beginning (in 1926) of that which would become the Silmarillion story, Tolkien continued to work on his legendarium through prose and poetry devoted to three of his most important stories: those involving the children of Húrin, the love between Beren and Lúthien, and the fall of Gondolin. In 1926, Tolkien took a major step forward in his thinking by focusing, for a change, on the macro (the legendarium) and not the micro (the individual tales) when he created a twenty-eight page "Sketch of the Mythology," or, to give its full title, "Sketch of the Mythology with Especial Reference to 'The Children of Húrin.'" He did so, apparently, without benefit of intervening versions. Christopher Tolkien calls this "Sketch" the "Earliest 'Silmarillion'" in his *The Shaping of Middle-earth* (1986; vol. IV of *The History of Middle-earth* series) and quotes his father as to its provenance:

> Original 'Silmarillion.' Form orig[inally] composed c 1926–1930 for R. W. Reynolds to explain background of 'alliterative version' of Túrin & the Dragon: then in progress (unfinished) (begun c. 1918). (1986: 11)

Christopher Tolkien also divides the published version into nineteen sections although he admits "there is no manuscript warrant for the 19 divisions so made: it is purely a matter of convenience of presentation" (1986: 11). The most important changes by Tolkien since *The Book of Lost Tales*' version of the story are that the narrative frame (including the Cottage of Lost Play and almost all of the Eriol/Ælfwine mediating device) and the creation story and the music of the Ainur are completely absent. It is also worthy of note that this earliest version of the Silmarillion story even as a "Sketch" is finished in a way that, for example, *The Book of Lost Tales* and the later "Quenta Silmarillion" is not. The narrative here runs from the arrival of the Valar to the overthrow of Morgoth.

In 1930, Tolkien took the creation of his legendarium a step further than the "Sketch" by producing a prose typescript titled "The Quenta: herein is Qenta Noldorinwa or Pennas-na-Ngoelaidh." The descriptive subtitle runs as follows: "This is the brief History of the Noldoli or Gnomes, drawn from the Book of Lost Tales which Eriol of Leithien wrote, having read the *Golden Book*, which the Eldar call *Parma Kuluina*, in Kortirion in Tol Eressëa, the Lonely Isle" (1986: 77–8). (As before with the "Sketch," Christopher Tolkien divided the published account into nineteen sections even though such sections did not appear in the original manuscript.)

The "Quenta Noldorinwa" of 1930 is different from the "Sketch" of 1926 in four important ways. First, some of the phrasing and syntax of the Silmarillion emerges for the first time. Second, the creation of the world is briefly mentioned and the Valar are now explicitly described where before, in the "Sketch," Tolkien made no mention of either. Third, this version of the legendarium was written by Tolkien with the "Sketch" (and possibly "The Book of Lost Tales") open in front of him as he composed. In that sense, the "Quenta Noldorinwa" is a more considered and deliberate document than the earlier "Sketch." Fourth, this version of the legendarium is almost three times longer than its predecessor. Like the "Sketch," the "Quenta Noldorinwa" is also a complete narrative of the legendarium up to this point in its evolution.

Between 1930 and 1937 (it is impossible to be more precise as to when), Tolkien produced another fuller version (the fourth since 1916) of the legendarium called the "The Quenta Silmarillion." It has a subtitle, which runs: "Herein is *Qenta Noldorinwa* or *Pennas inGeleidh* or History of the Gnomes"(Tolkien 1987: 201). Christopher Tolkien comments on it as follows: "As originally written, the *Quenta Silmarillion* [...] was a beautiful and elegant manuscript" (1987: 218). Such polished work is rather unusual among Tolkien's manuscripts. The "Quenta Silmarillion" (as written between 1930 and 1937) differs from the "Quenta Noldorinwa" in several important respects. First, the narrative frame now involves a new character, Pengolod of Gondolin, as the compiler of the account with Ælfwine/Eriol demoted from creator to translator. Second, it is divided into seventeen chapters and a conclusion (where before there had been no such division). Third, it is a much longer account than the earlier version of the legendarium. As before where Tolkien produced the "Sketch" for a definite audience (namely one of his teachers when he was at King Edward's School, Birmingham: R. W. Reynolds), so the impetus for Tolkien to create a coherent account of his legendarium at this point in its development was another audience: the publisher George Allen & Unwin, which had just published *The Hobbit* to almost universal acclaim and impressive sales and was, as a result, looking for more by Tolkien in the same vein.

After the "Quenta Silmarillion" was rejected by George Allen & Unwin in December 1937, Tolkien put it aside for thirteen years. Then in 1950–2, he revised it for yet another audience (the publisher Collins), who had expressed an interest (which petered out as it happened) in publishing Tolkien's new and largely complete manuscript epic: "The Lord of the Rings" in tandem with the Silmarillion story. During this period of revision, the tale of Beren and Lúthien was completed. Then, in 1956–8, Tolkien revised the "Quenta Silmarillion" once again, this time for George Allen & Unwin, who wanted a new work by Tolkien to capitalize on the success of *The Lord of the Rings*. During this period of revision, the first chapter "Of the Valar" was separated from the rest and became a separate work, the "Valaquenta," and the character of Fëanor and the events surrounding him were significantly altered.

In addition to the development of the legendarium between 1916 and 1958, it is delightfully characteristic of Tolkien (for whom maps were another way of organizing his ideas—think *The Hobbit* and *The Lord of the Rings*) that he should have created two maps of the legendarium as it progressed. The first map (see Tolkien 1986: Chapter 4) probably dates from the time of the "Sketch of the Mythology" (i.e., 1926) or perhaps a little earlier but was subsequently much altered with the passage of the years. This map was drawn on a sheet of examination paper from the University of Leeds, and associated with it are two supplementary leaves. The map, which has a north–south axis, is accompanied by western and eastern extensions and has names written in more than one color. The second map, of Middle-earth west of the Blue Mountains, dates from the 1930s (see Tolkien 1987: Appendix 3) and was originally very carefully drawn in pen only subsequently to be covered over with numerous emendations and additions in pencil.

So, the piece of the legendarium associated with the story of the Silmarils as developed in the various versions of that story between 1916 and 1958 came—as I mentioned earlier—very largely to a halt by 1937. It is not hard to see why. In September of that same year, George Allen & Unwin published a children's story by Tolkien, *The Hobbit*, which (much to Tolkien and the publisher's surprise) became a great success, so he had to follow that up (of course) with another story about hobbits. This he eventually did (after eighteen years), and it was called *The Lord of the Rings*. It is now time to elucidate how these two works—*The Hobbit* and *The Lord of the Rings*—fit into (or were made to fit into) the legendarium as Tolkien had been developing it for so many years before hobbits *ever* became part of his worldview, for it is important to remember that when Tolkien created the hobbits they were literally a new species.

The Hobbit

The Hobbit shows many of the same features as the rest of the legendarium, and they are features that only increase the complexity of the legendarium and, so, the degree of confusion that many readers feel at times when confronted by Tolkien's overall work. First, the tale itself went through a long gestation before it was published just as did *The Silmarillion* and *The Lord of the Rings*. It is hard to be precise in such matters as Tolkien himself offered many different versions of the story's creation from initial idea to its appearance in print. It seems, however, that the story began as a tale told over several years to his children beginning in 1926 or 1927. It then began to be written down in the early 1930s so that by about 1933 the story was written down up to the death of Smaug. This long gestation period led to frequent and confusing changes of names in the narrative—again characteristic of the entire legendarium. So, at various points in the story's creation, Smaug was called Pryftan, the wizard was called Bladorthin not Gandalf, and Gandalf was a dwarf not a wizard. Second, illustrations (perhaps as many as eight) and maps by Tolkien himself were central to the story in just the same way as they were in the development of the story of the Silmarils and, later, *The Lord of the Rings*. Third, Tolkien (always busy with work and family and an inveterate and obsessive reviser) was spurred on only by deadlines and the tantalizing possibility of publication—as he was with *The Lord of the Rings* and with versions of the Silmarillion story. He finished the remaining part of the story from the death of Smaug to the return of Bilbo to Hobbiton between late June and early October 1936 because George Allen & Unwin was urging him to. Four months to completion was lightning fast for him. Fourth, there is serendipity in the history of Tolkien and his publishers. There was luck in the success of *The Lord of the Rings* (with Ace's breach of copyright leading to the success of the trilogy on American college campuses in the mid 1960s) and luck in the publication of *The Hobbit* (with Susan Dagnall, an employee of George Allen & Unwin, just happening to get her hands on the unfinished manuscript of *The Hobbit* and liking it enough to recommend it to the publisher). Fifth, and this is characteristic of the fragmentariness of the overall legendarium, when Tolkien wrote *The Hobbit* it had little or no direct connection with the rest of the legendarium he had been working on since 1916. He simply had come up with creatures (hobbits) in a children's story and then had to work out who they were and how they related to the rest of the legendarium.

Tolkien acknowledges this point himself in a letter to C. A. Furth (of George Allen & Unwin) in 1937 where he talks of "the mythology [i.e., the legendarium] on the outskirts of which the Hobbit [Bilbo Baggins] had his adventures" (Tolkien 2000: 17). Eighteen years later, as *The Lord of the Rings* was being published, Tolkien makes much the same point again to W. H. Auden (Tolkien 2000: 215). So, in *The Hobbit* there is a necromancer who is an earlier version of Sauron; there is a Shire and a Middle-earth although *The Hobbit* calls neither of them by those names; and there is a wizard (Gandalf) although he is much less powerful than he is in *The Lord of the Rings*. There are Elrond and Gondolin, the high elves, and the orcs. There is also a ring, but it was not initially the One Ring. It is simply *a* ring that Gollum had and which Bilbo Baggins came to possess through a riddle game. Its major power was that it made its wearer invisible. Yet the ring becomes so central to the narrative of *The Lord of the Rings* that Tolkien felt he had to go back and revise *The Hobbit* after *The Lord of the Rings* was published so that the stories matched. This matching work he did in 1951 (with the manuscript of *The Lord of the Rings* nearly finished). The major change is to Chapter 5 of *The Hobbit* with associated changes to Chapter 6. As revised, the ring is much more malevolent in its power over both Gollum and Bilbo, and Tolkien even added an explanation for Bilbo initially lying about the event:

There [in the 1951 revision to Chapter 5] the true story of the Riddle Game, as it was eventually revealed (under pressure) by Bilbo to Gandalf, is now given according to the Red Book, in place of the version Bilbo first gave to his friends, and actually set down in his diary. This departure from truth on the part of a most honest hobbit was a portent of great significance. It does not, however, concern the present story, and those who in this edition make their first acquaintance with hobbit-lore need not trouble about it. Its explanation lies in the history of the Ring, as it is set out in the chronicles of the Red Book of Westmarch [i.e., *The Lord of the Rings*], and it must await their publication. (Quoted in Anderson 2002: 28 n3)

The Lord of the Rings

In a letter written to Milton Waldman (probably in 1951), Tolkien explained the relation between the legendarium (the Silmarillion material), *The Hobbit,* and the nearly completed *The Lord of the Rings.* He did so in a way that clarifies what he was trying to do in a way that he never achieved again. According to Tolkien, *The Hobbit* was an independent creation that, ironically, through the discovery of the One Ring, enabled the story to be completed. The story of the Silmarils is fundamentally Elvish; *The Hobbit* is almost human in its perspective; and *The Lord of the Rings* combines the two foci (2000: 145). In a sense, *The Hobbit* was an enlarged version of Tolkien's Tom Bombadil story in *The Lord of the Rings.* Both derive from stories told to his children. However, how Tolkien used the tales is instructive: the former became the catalyst for his three-volume epic; the latter stayed hermetically sealed into a geographically tiny section of Middle-earth. Tom Bombadil appears in Chapters 6, 7, and 8 of *The Fellowship of the Ring* and is never heard from again although he is briefly mentioned elsewhere in the epic. He is the subject of a volume of poems published in 1961 and titled *The Adventures of Tom Bombadil and Other Verses from the Red Book,* but that did not give him a further role at all in the legendarium—nor was it intended to. Indeed, the volume of poems was published in large part because Tolkien's aunt, Jane Neave, asked him for further adventures of this oldest of creatures in Middle-earth, Iarwain Ben-adar as Gandalf calls him. It is, however, interesting that for a brief moment Tolkien did think of making Tom Bombadil the hero of another tale involving hobbits before thinking better of it (letter to Stanley Unwin, December 1937; Tolkien 2000: 26).

   Just as those who admire Tolkien's work are frequently puzzled by how one man could produce both *The Hobbit* and *The Silmarillion,* so they find it a stretch to connect the material in the earlier parts of the legendarium with the complete and epical *The Lord of the Rings.* Any explanation (beyond serendipity—and that is really no rigorous or adequate answer at all) needs to begin with the facts of how Tolkien and his publisher (George Allen & Unwin) responded to the remarkable and unexpected success of *The Hobbit.* Some of that I have already hinted at in my discussion of Tolkien's wise choice not to pursue any further stories with Tom Bombadil as protagonist, but the tale needs to be told more fully in order to elucidate the legendarium's meaning.

With George Allen & Unwin asking Tolkien for a sequel to *The Hobbit* in October 1937, Tolkien began by offering material the publisher couldn't use: the Silmarillion material was simply too extensive and unusual for the publisher of *The Hobbit*. *Farmer Giles of Ham* (which Tolkien also gave to Stanley Unwin for consideration in November 1937) was too slight, was unconnected with the legendarium, and did not involve hobbits. Tolkien considered (as I have mentioned) expanding his Tom Bombadil material, but rejected the idea. So, he was now required (he came to realize) to come up with *new* matter on the hobbits. What he came up with initially was something very close to *The Hobbit*: the first chapter of *The Lord of the Rings* titled "An Unexpected Party." Really, this first chapter covers the same material as the beginning of *The Hobbit*: Bilbo Baggins and a party. Tolkien ended up writing four drafts of the chapter (in a very Tolkienian way), but the material didn't start to take a turn in another direction until two unexpected twists in the plot began to emerge: one was the use of the ring from *The Hobbit* as the One Ring of Power; the other was the appearance of the Black Riders. Tolkien did not understand the identity or purpose of either when he created them. As with the Eärendil poem from the Anglo-Saxon *Crist* (which began the legendarium back in 1914) and the opening line of *The Hobbit* ("In a hole in the ground there lived a hobbit," which dated from the early 1930s), so *The Lord of the Rings* developed as an answer to Tolkien's initial puzzlement: What or who was Eärendil (the Silmarillion story)? Who or what was a hobbit (*The Hobbit*)? What was the history and what were the powers of the ring? Who or what were the Black Riders (*The Lord of the Rings*)? Tolkien also began to realize that the story of the One Ring was no longer likely to be for children and that he had found a way to integrate the story into the legendarium (letter to C. A Furth of George Allen & Unwin, August 1938; Tolkien 2000: 40–1). One may conjecture that the turn of the story toward darker and more adult themes was caused by two events: one was personal (Tolkien nearly had a nervous breakdown from undisclosed causes in the first half of 1938); the other was global (the Second World War was only a year away from beginning).

And the history of *The Lord of the Rings* between 1938 and the publication of the final volume of the trilogy in 1955 is that of a perfectionist progressing by fits and starts, as his schedule permitted, toward the book that is so revered today. There were moments when he encountered long delays in the project, most famously the narrative after the fellowship stood at Balin's tomb in Moria took a long time to emerge. At one point, Tolkien thought the book would be finished by early 1943 (after less than five years of work). However, the emergence of a new character, Faramir, complicated the epic's future development. Then it would be done by late 1946. At last, in September 1948, a first draft was completed with a revised draft completed by October 1949. At that moment, Tolkien went down a metaphorical rabbit hole when he thought that the publisher Collins might publish not only *The Lord of the Rings* but also the Silmarillion material. He thought (probably correctly) that George Allen & Unwin would not publish both works because of cost and the difficulty of finding a readership for the Silmarillion story. Tolkien only emerged from the hole in 1952 when he came to understand that Collins was no longer interested in publishing both works or, perhaps, either of them. So, he had to go back to George Allen & Unwin. That publisher was still prepared to publish *The Lord of the Rings* and to look at *The Silmarillion* for future publication. Now, however, economics emerged as an issue. For George Allen & Unwin, the cost of publishing *The Lord of the Rings* would be prohibitive, so in order to protect themselves and assuming that sales would be slight, they offered Tolkien a 50:50 profit-sharing agreement in lieu of the usual advance and royalties. It was an understandable decision, but it cost the publisher huge profits and made Tolkien a millionaire within his lifetime. The only other complexity in the history of *The Lord of the Rings'* publication is that a second edition was published in 1966—in part to correct errors that existed in the first, and in part to deal with an issue with faulty copyright in the United States.

I began this section with an acknowledgment that some are puzzled how one mind could create *The Silmarillion, The Hobbit,* and *The Lord of the Rings.* The answer is that one mind could do so by simply pursuing doggedly and—in the case of *The Silmarillion*—over a lifetime answers to basic questions of identity wherever the search took it. Above all, the history of the legendarium is the history of a non-professional writer succeeding precisely because he wanted to publish his creative work (*badly* wanted to), but publication would only ever be a part of a life balanced by academic responsibilities as a senior member of Oxford University's faculty and the care of a large family.

In essence, *The Silmarillion* covers the history of sentient life from the creation to the end of the Second Age (the Age of the Elves) with some reference to the Third Age and the One Ring. *The Hobbit* covers one short section (one brief adventure) of the Third Age (the Age of Men). *The Lord of the Rings* connects the life of the hobbits (always Tolkien's favorite subject) to the broader life of elves, dwarves, men, and wizards, and takes the story up to the end of the Third Age. However, it is important to note that the Silmarillion story as outlined earlier was strictly a story of the First Age: from the acts of the Valar to Eärendil's successful resolution of the conundrum of the Silmarils (How is Fëanor's oath to be dealt with?) and the expulsion of Melkor/Morgoth from Middle-earth.

As *The Silmarillion* was published after Tolkien's death and only with Christopher Tolkien's considerable efforts to create a coherent narrative, that book includes material that Tolkien might not have left in had he been responsible for its appearance in print, but we will never know what the book would have looked like had only the father been involved in creating it and not his son too. What we do know is the *The Silmarillion* is a compilation. The "Quenta Silmarillion" or the "History of the Silmarils" (Tolkien 1999a: 33–255) is preceded by the "Ainulindalë" or "The Music of the Ainur" (based on a manuscript created by Tolkien in about 1951) and the "Valaquenta" or "The Account of the Valar" (based on a Tolkien typescript from about 1959). It is followed by two additional works: "Akallabêth" or "The Downfallen" and "Of the Rings of Power and the Third Age." The former (which is almost the only significant *completed* material on the Númenóreans written by Tolkien) dates from about 1951.[3] The latter dates from no earlier than 1948.

To this long list of legendarium material must be added one further source: the *Unfinished Tales of Númenor and Middle-earth*. I mentioned this work at the beginning of the chapter. Now it is time to discuss its contents briefly to bring the study of the texts of the legendarium to a close. *Unfinished Tales* (which was published under Christopher Tolkien's editorship in 1980) contains two further works on the First Age; four on the Second Age; five on the Third Age; and material on The Drúedain, the Istari, and the Palantíri. In a sense it's a compendium of material edited by Tolkien's son to clear the way for his twelve-volume edition of *The History of Middle-earth* (published between 1983 and 1996). "Of Tuor and His Coming to Gondolin" and "Narn I Hîn Húrin" are concerned with the First Age. "A Description of the Island of Númenor," "Aldarion and Erendis: The Mariner's Wife," "The Line of Elros: Kings of Númenor," and "The History of Galadriel and Celeborn" comprise the material about the Second Age. "The Disaster of the Gladden Fields," "Cirion and Eorl and the Friendship of Gondor and Rohan," "The Quest of Erebor," "The Hunt for the Ring," and "The Battles of the Fords of Isen" tell of the Third Age. All are useful in their own way, but they tend only to confuse readers uninterested in becoming Tolkien specialists, for they muddy the arc of the legendarium (*The Silmarillion, The Hobbit, The Lord of the Rings*) even as they provide some useful background.

Tolkien's Habits as a Writer

Thus far I have tried to answer the first two questions with which this chapter began: What is the history of the legendarium's publication? What is the history of its creation and composition? I now need to turn to the third question and the matter of how Tolkien worked as a writer in order to clarify further the meaning of the legendarium for enthusiasts of Tolkien's mythology.

J. R. R. Tolkien's habits as a writer were, quite frankly, extraordinary and at times maddening. Most writers create a text as a first draft and then they edit that before it is published. Then they may continue to edit the text further for subsequent publication. Tolkien was in no way as methodical or linear in his work. On the contrary, as a perfectionist, a self-confessed procrastinator, and a man for whom creative writing could never be anything more than an avocation, his habits were very different and involved some or all of the steps below:

- Writing in a hand that was very difficult for anyone including himself to decipher.
- Writing his stories on any paper to hand (no matter how small), possibly because paper was scarce and expensive.

- Creating a text (often in pencil) and then rewriting the text in pen over the original penciled version before erasing the pencil marks underneath. That process presents unique difficulties for an editor bent on publishing a text founded (as they nearly always are) on authorial intent.

- Producing (sometimes) a typescript, which would bear an unclear relation to earlier handwritten material and later typed copies.

- Taking up the work again and beginning from the beginning rather than simply revising an existing work. That process creates another sort of problem for an editor: what is the provenance of related manuscripts and which has primacy as far as publication is concerned. There are, for example no less than eighteen versions of one of the chapters of *The Lord of the Rings*.

- Abandoning a work before it is finished. That choice raises yet another concern for an editor: how is one to use material that constitutes an incomplete work and/or a false start?

- Rarely throwing out any of his creative writing. That habit produces a confusing and inchoate body of work analogous to the contemporary issue with the multiplicity of digital versions of a work.

- Organizing his creative writing according to a disorganized system that made sense to him alone.

Given such complexities, it is a tribute to George Allen & Unwin (as publisher) and to Christopher Tolkien (as editor) that Tolkien's work has been presented as accurately and clearly as it has when the truth is that Tolkien's habits as a writer have not helped to clarify the legendarium for the millions of readers passionate about Tolkien's achievement.

Christopher Tolkien's Work as Editor

I began this chapter with a fourth question: the role of Tolkien's youngest son, Christopher, in editing his father's unpublished work.

My view is that Christopher Tolkien's work as editor has been essential but in some respects unhelpful. Such an assessment extends to the work of the Tolkien family through the Tolkien Trust. Two libraries in the world house a great deal of work by J. R. R. Tolkien: Marquette University's Special Collections at its Raynor Memorial Libraries and Oxford University's Bodleian Library through its Department of Western Manuscripts. Marquette has extensive manuscript holdings related to *The Hobbit, The Lord of the Rings, The Silmarillion, Farmer Giles of Ham*, and *Mr. Bliss*. The Bodleian has the manuscripts of "Leaf by Niggle" and *The Silmarillion* as well as many examples of Tolkien's academic work and the Tolkien family's papers. It is clear from secondary scholarly works on Tolkien that the Tolkien Trust has other materials (Tolkien's diaries, for example), but very few academics have been granted access to anything that might be termed personal. (There was the publication in 1981 of *The Letters of J. R. R. Tolkien*, but that is a rather slight and ambiguously edited volume.) The Tolkien family is, of course, quite within its rights morally and legally to restrict access to any or all of J. R. R. Tolkien's work, but the result of some of the primary materials associated with his life and work as a writer not being available is that we have only one privileged biographer of Tolkien (Humphrey Carpenter), whose biography is now forty years old, and only one editor of Tolkien's work on the legendarium, his son Christopher.

My experience having taught Tolkien's work to undergraduates and graduates is that this relation of son (as editor) to father (as author) is fascinating to them and problematic and a source of some confusion as the son only reveals some of the details of his role even though his editorial apparatuses are often extraordinarily extensive. Some difficulties come from his not being the clearest of writers as he gamely uses exposition to try to clarify his father's work. Yet others must arise from the closeness of a much-loved son editing the work of a revered and famous father. Take, for example, the Foreword to *The Book of Lost Tales Part I* (1983). There, Christopher Tolkien reflects on his editing and publication of *The Silmarillion* six years earlier and concludes that his decision to publish that earlier work was mistaken. As he puts it baldly: "I now think [it] to have been an error" (Tolkien 1983: 5). In one sentence and with inadequate explanation of the reasoning behind publishing the one-volume edition of *The Silmarillion*, the editor succeeds in undermining the value of the earlier work (which had achieved a significant following between 1977 and 1983) and positing the entire purpose of *The History of Middle-earth* series (in twelve volumes) upon a single editorial reconsideration. In a sense, the editor has bracketed the target: he falls short with one volume (*The Silmarillion*) and fires over the top (arguably) with twelve (*The History*).

Tolkien's Own Explanation of His Legendarium

It is obvious by now how complicated the legendarium is, although I hope I have provided an adequate and worthwhile path through it (as I promised at the beginning of this chapter). I will close with a summary of the only detailed statement Tolkien ever made about his legendarium. That statement constitutes almost the entirety of his long letter to Milton Waldman at Collins the publisher. This letter was probably written in 1951 at Waldman's request to explain how the pieces of his legendarium fitted together (Tolkien 2000: 143–61). It was written after the manuscript of *The Lord of the Rings* was finished but before it was published. It was written, then, in the full knowledge on Tolkien's part of what he had tried to achieve in his legendarium, and it explains much of what he tried to accomplish in his work as a writer of fantasy over many years. It does so very well, as Tolkien thought that the publication of *The Silmarillion* as well as *The Lord of the Rings* might be achieved if he were crystal clear about his work. I shall reduce the substance of the letter to a series of nearly a dozen points.

- Tolkien cannot remember a time when he was not creating his world of the imagination.
- Tolkien's fantasy world is a creation founded on the three pillars of language (in particular Elvish), myth, and fairy story.
- Tolkien once wanted to create a body of legend to substitute for the paucity of myth in English culture.

- Tolkien created individual stories (some detailed, some merely sketched) and then forged the links between them.

- Tolkien constructed the legendarium in such a way that it would allow others to contribute to the enterprise after his death.

- Tolkien felt when he was creating his legendarium that he was recording actual events and not inventing them.

- Tolkien's work is concerned with four issues: the relation between art, sub-creation, and reality; the fall; mortality; and the machine (and its relation to power). The last of these is expressed in the battle between the elves (who use power for art) and the enemy (who uses power for domination).

- Tolkien's legendarium consists of a cosmogonic myth (the music of the Ainur) and three ages.

- The First Age is covered in *The Silmarillion,* or history of the elves. It emphasizes the stories of Beren and Lúthien, the Children of Húrin, the Fall of Gondolin, and Eärendil the Wanderer. The focus is on the contribution to history of those who are weak and relatively powerless. The First Age ends with the defeat of the enemy (Morgoth) and the permanent loss of the three Silmarils.

- The Second Age (or cycle) occurs after the world is made anew. The elves now live on the Lonely Isle of Eressëa, and those men who were faithful to elves and the Valar are given their own island of Númenorë and granted long lives. The Second Age is taken up with the corruption of the Númenóreans by a new representative of the enemy (Sauron) as well as with the choice by some of the elves to remain in Middle-earth and, under Sauron's instruction, to make three rings of power. Secretly, Sauron also makes one ring of power to control all other rings, and he reigns supreme in Middle-earth as a result of the One Ring even as the Númenóreans grow ever more powerful. In the end, Sauron tempts the Númenóreans to try to wrest the secret of immortality from the Valar in Valinor. They fail. Númenor disappears beneath the sea. Valinor (or Paradise) is removed from mortal attainment. Only three men escape to Middle-earth: Elendil, Isildur, and Anarion. In a last alliance, men and elves combine to defeat Sauron in Middle-earth in his stronghold in Mordor. However, the One Ring is lost.

- The Third Age is concerned with working out the fate of the One Ring and is the matter covered in *The Hobbit* and *The Lord of the Rings*. *The Hobbit* focuses on the life of ordinary folk against an elevated background of nobility and heroism and the mythic. *The Lord of the Rings* focuses on Sauron's overthrow, the return of the king of Gondor, and the permanent departure of the elves from Middle-earth. The message of the epic is that life needs both the "ordinary" and the "noble," the "heroic" and the "simple" to have value and meaning (Tolkien 2000: 160).

It is surely a tribute to the density of the legendarium that Tolkien is unable (despite admirable concision) to summarize the story and its meanings for Waldman in fewer than eighteen pages!

Notes

1 *The Children of Húrin, Beren and Lúthien*, and *The Fall of Gondolin*, and constitute the fullest telling of these three crucial tales from the First Age as edited by Christopher Tolkien. They expand on the much briefer versions in *The Silmarillion*. Eärendil's successful resolution of the conundrum of the Silmarils (How is Feänor's oath to be dealt with?) seems not to have enough material devoted to it to merit publication as a separate book.

2 Born in 1924, Christopher Tolkien was appointed his father's literary executor in Tolkien's will. He graduated from Oxford University with a BA in English in 1949 and a B.Litt. in Old Norse literature in the early 1950s. He was appointed a fellow of New College, Oxford in 1961 and a university lecturer in Early English language and literature in 1964. He resigned from these academic posts in 1975 in order to devote his life to editing his father's unpublished work.

3 There are only two other completed pieces about the Second Age: "The Fall of Númenor" (which dates from about 1936) and "The Drowning of Anadûnê" (1945–6). These were left in manuscript at Tolkien's death but were later published under the editorship of Christopher Tolkien. Two different versions of "Fall" appear in *The Lost Road and*

Other Writings (Tolkien 1987: 11–35), and a third in *Sauron Defeated* (Tolkien 1992: 329–40). "Drowning" exists in four different versions, all of which appear in *Sauron Defeated* (340–440).

Students of Tolkien are surprised at the few writings by Tolkien about the Second Age. The explanation is straightforward. First, his interest in the Second Age came late in the history of the legendarium's development. He was more than twenty years into developing his legendarium before Númenor was focused on in 1936. Second, when it was created it was integrated fully into the overall legendarium. Third, it may have been as a conception limited from the beginning by being too closely tied to the Atlantis myth. Fourth, the earliest (1936) writings about Númenor came about as a result of a writers' pact with C. S. Lewis to create the sort of story each would like to read but too rarely saw in print. The result for Tolkien was an incomplete work, *The Lost Road*, with "Fall" being felt necessary to make the former intelligible. The later writing about Númenor ("Drowning"), which dates from 1945–6, was written in conjunction with Tolkien's incomplete and futuristic story "The Notion Club Papers." Tolkien's work on Númenor was not, then, central to his vision in a way that *The Silmarillion, The Hobbit,* and *The Lord of the Rings* were.

3

Tolkien and His Languages

Of all the many delights those who study Tolkien encounter, it is surely his use of languages that is the most subtle and in need of clarification and explanation. The relation between Tolkien's life and his achievements in the fantasy genre (the subject of Chapter 1) and the extent and meaning of his legendarium (the subject of Chapter 2) are both complicated in their own ways, but it is Tolkien's use of languages that mystifies more readers than any other single concern, for some of what Tolkien says is wide-ranging and for the generalist, while some is directed much more narrowly at a specific, linguistic audience.

The Centrality of Languages to Tolkien's Vision

There are other reasons, too, for Tolkien's use of languages being a challenge for many readers. Tolkien himself—as we shall see—dabbled from a very early age in creating languages. Then, it is also the case that he was a professional linguist (what used to be called, when Tolkien was alive and flourishing, a philologist or "lover of language"). Next, it was Tolkien's opinion that the use of languages (Sindarin, Quenya, dwarf runes and so on) necessarily preceded the development of a fictive society or culture that would embody that use in action. Finally, Tolkien was a fine enough philologist to leave his languages (even Elvish) incomplete in the way that natural languages are too. So, his work has a fragmentariness which some may find frustrating.

Before we get into a detailed discussion of Tolkien's use of languages in his fantasy, it is important to point out in some detail how immediate is any reader's encountering of the alien quality of Tolkien's legendarium if that reader expects her fantasy to be served up in English. If we look at his three great creative achievements (*The Hobbit, The Lord of the Rings*, and *The Silmarillion*), the evidence is stark. The third edition of *The Hobbit* (1966) begins with a rendering of the title and subtitle of the book (*The Hobbit; or, There and Back Again*) in dwarf runes. The second paragraph of its prefatory statement is largely taken up with a lengthy explanation of what runes are along with the enticing tidbit that the runes in *The Hobbit* are not the actual dwarf runes but an English representation of them, even though such English runes "are known now to few people" (Tolkien 2007a: 1). So, there's two levels of opacity here right from the beginning. Tolkien then goes on to render the runic inscription on the secret door into the Lonely Mountain, as well as the moon runes, in such a way that a reader on encountering these runes for the first time could not possibly decipher their meaning but would (presumably) be enticed to do so at some point in the future. I know that I was enticed in this way when I first encountered the book as a boy of eight.

In Chapter 1, Tolkien continues his language games by having Gandalf scratch a "queer sign" (2007a: 8) on Bilbo Baggins' front door. This sign is an extraordinarily condensed use of language which, perhaps, only Gandalf and the dwarves can interpret, for Gloin says to Bilbo:

> I assure you there is a mark on this door—the usual one in the trade, or used to be. *Burglar wants a good job, plenty of Excitement and reasonable Reward*, that's how it is usually read. You can say *Expert Treasure-hunter* instead of *Burglar* if you like. Some of them do. It's all the same to us. (Tolkien 2007a: 19)

Note three things here. First, Gloin admits that language is always evolving ("or used to be") as culture evolves. Second, Gloin divides language-users into two groups (literally "us" and "them") without explaining what the two groups refer to and how they relate to the overarching category of some or all language-users. Third, translation is a complicated act ("some of them do"). This last comment in particular matters (as the second and third sentences of the runic prefatory statement declare) since the story is in English only in order to make the narrative intelligible to an Anglophone audience. At the time of the present action in *The Hobbit*, the languages and letters were quite different from ours today. English is used to represent the languages, but there is an implicit loss of meaning or misrepresentation of meaning in such a choice.

If we turn to *The Lord of the Rings*, we see that Tolkien is equally complicated in his discussion of linguistic matters in Middle-earth. The epic begins with a Prologue that is exclusively concerned with hobbits. Relatively close to the present time of the narrative, the hobbits had undergone a linguistic transformation as the narrator explains:

> And in those days also they forgot whatever languages they had used before, and spoke ever after the Common Speech, the Westron as it was named, that was current through all the lands of the kings from Arnor to Gondor, and about all the coasts of the Sea from Belfalas to Lune. Yet they kept a few words of their own, as well as their own names of months and days, and a great store of personal names out of the past. (Tolkien 1994a: 4)

As to the hobbits' written language, that was taught to them by the Dúnedain. Yet Tolkien is intriguingly unclear about the language spoken by the hobbits, for earlier he had commented (as the unnamed narrator): "Of old they [the hobbits] spoke the languages of Men, after their own fashion, and liked and disliked much the same things as Men did" (1994a: 2). So, they use the Common Speech "after their own fashion" (whatever that may mean). However, how "those days" and "Of old" relate to one another is entirely (and deliberately?) unclear.

The elves (the noun became capitalized between 1937 and 1954) show up early in *The Lord of the Rings*: in Chapter 3, "Three Is Company." Sam is the first to *hear* the elves as he would have "dashed off towards the voices" had he not been held back by his fellow hobbits (Tolkien 1994a: 77), and Frodo is equally taken not with their appearance but with what they *sound* like. Then the narrator reinforces for the reader the quality that stood out for Tolkien in his depiction of the elves, the beauty of their language:

The singing drew nearer. One clear voice rose now above the others. It was singing in the fair elven-tongue, of which Frodo knew only a little, and the others knew nothing. Yet the sound blending with the melody seemed to shape itself in their thought into words which they only partly understood. (Tolkien 1994a: 77–8)

So, now ignorance becomes limited knowledge because of sound alone. Frodo listens to the song and then, based on that is able to tell "These are High Elves! They spoke the name of Elbereth!" (Tolkien 1994a: 78)—able to tell in part because of the name Elbereth and in part, presumably, because of their use of language.

It is also notable that Tolkien's development of his Middle-earth languages was evolutionary. *The Hobbit*, for example, made no distinction between high elves and low elves (indeed, Tolkien had not even developed such a distinction in his own mind by 1937). His sense of what a language might be good for was evolutionary as well. The elves in *The Hobbit* sing a nonsense song that the narrator himself terms "pretty fair nonsense" (Tolkien 2007a: 46); the high elves in *The Fellowship of the Ring* sing a song that delves into an important element of their own mythology: Gilthoniel/ Elbereth. And Tolkien's sense of what an audience might bear has similarly developed, for in place of runes we now have Elvish (although whether it is Quenya or Sindarin the narrator does not say): Frodo responding to Gildor Inglorion with a kindly comment "*Elen síla lúmenn' omentielvo*," with this phrase apparently being translated immediately afterwards as "A star shines on the hour of our meeting" (Tolkien 1994a: 79).

Finally, what has also developed is Tolkien's view of textual transmission—how these languages come to us as readers. For, we discover at the end of the Prologue to *The Lord of the Rings* (in a section titled "Note on the Shire Records" (Tolkien 1994a: 13–15)) that *The Hobbit* and *The Lord of the Rings* were recorded in the five-volume *Red Book of Westmarch* written by Bilbo and Frodo. The original no longer exists apparently, but there were many copies made and one in particular matters: the copy made by Findegil, the "King's Writer", in IV 172 (that is, the 172nd year of the Fourth Age) (Tolkien 1994a: 14). That copy *alone* contains the whole of Bilbo's "Translations from the Elvish" in three additional volumes, and that material *may* be what we now have in *The Silmarillion* because it was concerned solely with the history of the First Age (Tolkien 1994a: 14).

If we turn, now, to what *The Silmarillion* reveals of Tolkien's interests as a philologist, we encounter that famous letter from Tolkien to Milton Waldman (probably written in 1951) placed there at the beginning of the book by Tolkien's son and editor, Christopher, to introduce the second edition of *The Silmarillion* (Tolkien 1999). I have talked about this letter already (in Chapter 2, on the legendarium), so I will simply point out here that in the first paragraph after his introductory comments J. R. R. Tolkien focuses on language: He sketches for the reader his long fascination with languages (both as an amateur and a professional) and in particular with two Elvish languages: Quenya and Sindarin (Tolkien 1999a: xi).

The Silmarillion, after the creation myth with which it begins, is concerned solely with the Elder Days and, so, with the elves, but it is worth pointing out four important facts about this least-understood of Tolkien's works, all of which are linguistic. First, the world of Eru's thought as creator comes into being because of sound—the sound of that most international of languages, music, for it is the Ainur's music that begins the creation of the world (Tolkien 1999a: 25). Second, Chapter 3 (as with *The Hobbit* and *The Lord of the Rings*) is the locus for the elves appearing for the first time in the narrative. And as in those two earlier works (in the sense of their being published first but not created first as *The Silmarillion* predates *The Hobbit* in its imaginative creation by two decades or more), *The Silmarillion* distinguishes the elves as, first and foremost, users of language. The elves, Tolkien says, named themselves the Quendi, which means " those that speak with voices" (1999a: 49). Third, Melian (a Maia who marries the elven king, Thingol) is renowned for her song. She teaches the nightingales to sing, for "she filled the silence of Middle-earth before the dawn with her voice and the voices of her birds" (Tolkien 1999a: 55). Fourth, the most important love story in *The Silmarillion* (that between Beren and Lúthien) is predicated on three qualities possessed by Lúthien: her beauty, her dancing, and her voice (which is described as "[k]een," "heart-piercing," and capable of bringing an end to winter by summoning the beginning of spring) (Tolkien 1999a: 165).

Tolkien and Languages: Natural, Artificial, Invented

Tolkien's love of language can be seen in his background in natural and artificial languages as well as in the fecundity of his invented languages.

Natural and Artificial Languages

As a result of his mother's teaching as well as his education at King Edward's School, Birmingham, and at Oxford University, Tolkien had a thorough background in Classical languages Latin and Greek. He was also an expert in Old and Middle English and—to a lesser degree and in a self-taught way—was familiar with Gothic and Old Icelandic (Old Norse). At Oxford, he studied Welsh and Finnish, the two languages he loved the most and which were the bedrock of Sindarin and Quenya. His work on the *New English Dictionary* (later the *Oxford English Dictionary*) and his erudite "Nomenclature of *The Lord of the Rings*" (reprinted in Hammond and Scull 2005: 750–82) show that he also knew something of Old Saxon, Middle Dutch, Modern Dutch, Old High German, Middle Low German, Middle High German, Modern German, Old Teutonic, primitive pre-Teutonic, Lithuanian, Old Slavonic, Russian, Danish, French, Icelandic, Norwegian, Old Swedish, and Scandinavian. His childhood, too, gave him a smattering of Afrikaans, mainly words picked up by his mother from her time spent in South Africa early in Tolkien's life. His highly developed sense of linguistic aesthetics meant that he could not count Gaelic among his languages, however, for he found Old Irish too complicated and "wholly unattractive" (1958 letter to Deborah Webster; Tolkien 2000: 289). To this long list of languages with which Tolkien had familiarity or command over, should be added three more: Hebrew with its "beautiful but idiotic alphabet" and extraordinary difficulty (quoted in Scull and Hammond 2006: 2.468); Italian, his understanding of which was "embryonic" (quoted in Scull and Hammond 2006: 2.469); and Spanish, his command of which was "rudimentary" (quoted in Carpenter 2000: 75).

As far as artificial languages are concerned—artificial as in the product of thinkers and visionaries determined to come up with a

genuinely international language—Tolkien knew something about
Volapük (invented by J. M. Schleyer in 1879), Esperanto (invented
by L. L. Zamenhof in 1887), Ido (promoted by the Delegation for
the Adoption of an International Language in 1907), and Novial
(invented by Otto Jespersen in 1928). Tolkien's understanding of
Esperanto, however, matters most in any study of his own invented
languages because he himself in 1909 (at the age of seventeen)
used a combination of English and Esperanto in a notebook called
"Book of the Foxrook." Then, in 1932, he became a member of the
Board of Honorary Advisors to the Education Committee of the
British Esperanto Association. He wrote a letter to the secretary
of the committee in which he praised Esperanto as the leading
artificial language but counseled against trying to improve it for
fear of destroying its beauty: "the 'humane' or aesthetic aspect of
the invented idiom" and "the individuality, coherence, and beauty,
which appear in the great natural idioms" (quoted in Scull and
Hammond 2006: 2.474). Again, in any understanding of Tolkien's
own linguistic invention in his legendarium it is the aesthetic element
that should be remembered and attended to.

Invented Languages[1]

Tolkien displayed from childhood a fascination with inventing
languages, a process he considered fundamentally artistic. His
linguistic tour de force in his legendarium (especially with respect
to Elvish) is simply a sophisticated, adult version of the childhood
invented languages he loved. As a child, Tolkien developed with
Mary Incledon, his cousin, a language which they called Nevbosh
or "New Nonsense" after Mary and her sister, Marjorie, had
invented Animalic. Both Nevbosh and Animalic were based on the
English language. So, when Tolkien was about fifteen and created
a language called Naffarin, based on Spanish and Latin, it could be
seen as a step forward in complexity. He apparently also created
another invented language founded on Gothic (itself an abstruse
language).

With respect to his legendarium language of Qenya (later
Quenya, but also Ellarissa), this he began to create in about 1915—
contemporaneous, then, not surprisingly, with the beginnings of his
creation of the entire legendarium as story in *The Book of Lost Tales*.

This Elvish language was Germanic in origin and, more importantly, Finnish in its lineage. His second Elvish language, developed just a little later, was founded on his study of Welsh, and was initially called Goldogrin or Gnomish or Noldorissa before Tolkien settled on Sindarin. By 1917, Tolkien had created a lexicon and grammar for it, which he titled "I·Lam na·Ngoldathon." The relation between Quenya and Sindarin was similar to the relation between Celtic and Latin at the time of the Roman invasion (Tolkien 2000: 219).

As before in my comments on how Tolkien's fascination with language shows up in the three major works in the legendarium, so with his conceptual development of his languages: each of them (especially the two Elvish languages) evolved over time as Tolkien's sense of linguistic aesthetics evolved. Tolkien was aware of this characteristic; it mirrored the way in which his legendarium developed too. So, in *The Book of Lost Tales Part I*, Tolkien talks of the profound separation of the Noldoli's speech from that of other elves—this separation or sundering being caused by the Noldoli wandering across Middle-earth while other elves remained in Valinor. The effects of this sundering he contrasted with the lesser distinctions (linguistically) between other groups of elves: the Teleri and the Solosimpi, and the Insuir. And as one would expect with any natural language, so the two major branches of Elvish (Quenya and Sindarin) claim a common ancestor: "Primitive Quendian," which itself later became "Common Eldarin." And before Primitive Quendian, there was the language of the Valinor—Valarin—upon which the elves deliberately tried to improve.

As one might expect—since Elvish (and indirectly Finnish and Welsh) were his beloved languages—the attention Tolkien spent on his other invented legendarium languages was less pronounced but nonetheless important and—absent Quenya and Sindarin—genuinely impressive. So, the dwarves learned their language—Khuzdul—from their creator, Aulë. And again as with so much of what Tolkien created linguistically, that language proved hard for others to learn—in this case, as it was "cumbrous and unlovely" (Tolkien 1999a: 92). The fact that such a view on Tolkien's part is quite intensely subjective does not diminish the importance of such a view. The mannish languages were always diverse although ultimately derived rather distantly from the Valar's Valarin. Some men adopted the language of the dark elves; some adopted the language of the green elves; some stayed with their own language unalloyed by Elvish influence. In a later version of the development of mannish languages, Tolkien claimed a slightly different taxonomy and evolution whereby Adûnaic was adulterated by other mannish languages to become a common speech (or, more accurately, common speeches).

Of the language of orcs, as one might expect, Tolkien as aesthete has little kind to say. The orcs had no language of their own but appropriated others, "perverted" them, and diluted their accuracy with "brutal jargons" in the form of "curses and abuse" (Tolkien 1994c: 1105). The weakness of Orkish speech was that no one group of orcs could understand another. To solve this problem, Sauron developed the Black Speech of Mordor (as in the inscription on the One Ring) only—in a rare failure on his part—to have the Black Speech fail to be adopted successfully among the orcs.

Tolkien on Writing

One of the least appreciated aspects of Tolkien's invented languages is that it led him to create entire writing systems to represent his aesthetic approach. We have seen that a little already in the runic opening to *The Hobbit*. We see it, too, early on in *The Lord of the Rings* where in Chapter 2 of *The Fellowship of the Ring* the reader is presented with a transcription of the verse inscribed on the One Ring along with a translation into the common speech (or "common tongue" as Gandalf terms it). The beautiful script is, Gandalf informs Frodo, ancient Elvish, but the language is that which was spoken in Mordor (1994a 49). So, it is possible from Tolkien's perspective for calligraphy to be beautiful even if the language is foul. In that way, he echoes his views about orality: Saruman has a lovely voice, but his words after his moral fall are foul and not to be trusted.

Tolkien's earliest invented script (which appears in "Book of the Foxrook") dates from 1909, five years before he began to develop his legendarium. It was an alphabet he called "privata kodo skaŭta" (Esperanto for "private scout code") and an interesting proof of Tolkien's seeing artificial and invented languages (Esperanto and his own private scout code) as different but not separate. Remarkably for someone only seventeen, Tolkien's code mixed a runic phonetic alphabet with ideographic symbols. A decade later (in about 1919),

Tolkien invented a phonetic alphabet in cursive script which he called "The Alphabet of Rúmil" (named after an Elvish wise man) and absorbed it into his legendarium. It constitutes the oldest of the Eldarin alphabets and was notable, wrote Tolkien in 1937, for being a "final cursive elaboration of the oldest letters of the Noldor in Valinor" (quoted in Scull and Hammond 2006: 2.1126). It was also notable for Tolkien attaching a story to its creation (language first, mythology second): Rúmil did not invent the language; others who are unnamed did that. Rúmil simply codified others' creativity. And Tolkien goes further to the mythic by pointing out that Rúmil's script was later replaced by Fëanor's alphabet—and as we shall see at the end of this chapter, it created one of the most interesting arguments among elves in their long history. (Language first; mythology second.) In historical terms, that replacement of one alphabet by another in Elvish culture was complete by 1931.

As always, Tolkien emphasized the aesthetic in his writing forms as well as in his languages. That is most memorably true in the silvered moon lettering on the west gate (that is, the Doors of Durin) into Khazad-dûm in *The Fellowship of the Ring*, Book 2, Chapter 4, "A Journey in the Dark." The lettering vies with the depiction of the archway in beauty and deliberately so. For reasons that make sense to the narrative, the script that curves inside the arch is not in blocky dwarf runes (as it is on Balin's Tomb) but in Elvish, and the illustration in *The Fellowship of the Ring* makes this very clear by adding a caption in English: "Here is written in the Fëanorian characters according to the mode of Beleriand: Ennyn Durin Atan Moria: pedo mellon a minno. Im Narvi hain echant: Celebrimbor o Eregion teithant i thiw hin." (Helpfully, Gandalf provides a translation for Frodo and, indirectly, Tolkien's readers: "*The Doors of Durin, Lord of Moria. Speak, friend, and enter. I, Narvi, made them. Celebrimbor of Hollin drew these signs*" (Tolkien 1994a: 298, 297).)

Nor did Tolkien ignore runes, a form of writing for which he had great affection as we see from the foreword to *The Hobbit*. So, in tandem with his experiments in Elvish writing (Rúmil's script), in the early 1920s at Leeds University he invented gnomic letters and Gondolinic runes and (in 1937) the runic alphabet of Dairon used by the Danian elves of Beleriand, which itself became the basis for the mannish Taliskan runic series. By the time of *The Lord of the Rings*, we also have the Sindarin Angerthas (or runic alphabet). And then in the last two decades of his life, he invented a "New English Alphabet," which, quite remarkably (and here the line between artificial and invented languages almost gets erased), used some of the letters of his own Fëanorian alphabet in its creation.

Tolkien's Commentaries on Language Invention

The rest of this chapter will discuss Tolkien's commentaries on language invention, but before we get there it is important to note two peculiarities of the subject, peculiarities that have significantly affected how Tolkien's commentaries have been studied and findings presented. The first is that there is a radical distinction between linguists interested in Tolkien's languages as a locus of historical study and those who want to use his languages for the purpose of everyday interaction, between—in essence–the theoretical and the practical. The second is that the Tolkien estate, since the death of J. R. R. Tolkien, has carefully regulated the release of his unpublished manuscripts about language (indeed, his manuscripts in general), so there are those who favor the discussion of Tolkienian linguistics by chosen scholars in specialist journals such as *Vinyar Tengwar, Parma Eldalamberon, Mythlore*, and *Tolkien Studies* while others favor the release of all the remaining Tolkien manuscripts now in order for a broader community to become part of the discussion. The first view values a sort of narrowed coherence; the second a kind of democratic chaos. My approach in light of these peculiarities is to focus on simplicity and clarity by looking at Tolkien's works by date of publication rather than by chronology of creation.[2] In this way, the analysis will mirror the reading experience of nearly all Tolkien enthusiasts.

I will begin with this simple fact: during Tolkien's lifetime the theoretical discussion of invented languages could really look at only two sources: Appendices E ("Writing and Spelling") and F ("The Languages and Peoples of the Third Age" and "On Translation") of *The Lord of the Rings* and "Notes and Commentaries" in *The Road Goes Ever On: A Song Cycle*. After Tolkien's death in 1973, the picture changed radically. Now, we have a wealth of material: *The Silmarillion; The Monsters and the Critics and Other Essays,* which contains three essays published for the first time for a wider audience: "English and Welsh"; "A Secret Vice"; and "Valedictory Address"; and parts of several volumes of the twelve-volume series *The History of Middle-earth* (published between 1983 and 1996): *The Book of Lost Tales Parts I* and *II* (*The History of Middle-earth*, vols. I and II), *The Lost Road and Other Writings* (*The History of Middle-earth*, vol. V), *Sauron Defeated* (*The History of Middle-earth*, vol. IX), *The War of the Jewels* (1994d; *The History of Middle-earth*, vol. XI), and *The Peoples of Middle-earth* (1996; *The History of Middle-earth*, vol. XII). In a very important sense, then, we have a radical distinction between Tolkien's living and posthumous contributions.

For so many students of Tolkien, it is the appendices to *The Lord of the Rings* that demonstrate so well his fascination with language. One reader may look at them as a clearing-house for some of the material Tolkien would have liked to include in the narrative proper; another reader may see them as a vital source of information. They are a bit of both, in truth, but all of the appendices show the depth of thought and effort and imagination Tolkien put into them even as George Allen & Unwin became increasingly nervous about delays in the publication of the third part of the trilogy: *The Return of the King*. That degree of detail shows up in Appendix A (on royal genealogy); Appendix B (on the chronology of his legendarium); Appendix C (on hobbit family trees); and Appendix D (on the Shire calendar). Perhaps it shows up most, however, in Appendices E and F (on language), for they, combined, have more subsections to them and offer more substantive detail than any other appendices in the epic.

Appendix E of *The Lord of the Rings*

What do we learn from these two appendices in our quest to understand the outline of Tolkien's linguistic creativity? The first point to note is that Tolkien gives primacy of place to his work on "Writing and Spelling" (Appendix E) and follows that with the work for which he is arguably more famous: languages (Appendix F). Second, he again emphasizes, in the headnote to Appendix E ("Pronunciation of Words and Names"), the existence of other written languages but maintains the fiction that the original languages were earlier translated into Westron or Common Speech and that he, as author, has simply edited the original documents into English. Third, he admits as editor (and again we have that fiction) there are limits to the accuracy of his transcription and that as editor he has tried to come up with words that offer stylistic consistency. Fourth, he stresses the distance in time between the present (in terms of *The Lord of the Rings*, the mid 1950s) and the time in which the events of the epic occurred. This distance leads him to try to balance accuracy with the needs of modern readers (1994c: 1087).

After the headnote and in a nod, perhaps, to readers puzzled by the otherness of Middle-earth, Tolkien next addresses matters of sound: consonants, vowels, and stress patterns. Some of this discussion gets quite technical with talk of falling diphthongs, aspirates, and back spirants, but Tolkien is, as a philologist, obviously in his element. In a note to all this erudition, he underlines the primeval distinction between the elves (the firstborn of Ilúvatar) and the dwarves (the creation of the Vala Aulë), for Dwarvish is a language so different from Eldarin (the languages of the elves).

It is in the section of Appendix E after his talk of pronunciation and names that Tolkien provides tremendously useful information (that was otherwise unavailable in his lifetime) about the writing systems in use in Middle-earth and, by extension, Eä. In this section (on writing), Tolkien traces the development of writing back to the Eldar and then categorizes it into a broad distinction between the Tengwar (letters) and the Cirth (runes). The former were older than the latter and designed by the Noldor before their exile as they had particular skill in such matters. They were cursive and designed to be executed with pen or brush. The first Tengwar were the Tengwar of Rúmil and were pre-exile. These were supplanted after the Noldor were exiled to Middle-earth by the Tengwar of Fëanor. These came to be used not only by elves but by men as well (the Edain and the Númenóreans). By the Third Age, these Fëanorian letters became as widespread in writing as the common speech became in spoken language.

The Cirth were designed by the Sindar and were intended to be used for etched or scratched inscriptions. This use explains their angularity, but they should not be confused with Anglo-Saxon runes, for the arrangement of letters and values was quite different. The Cirth became widely known in the Second Age and were later adapted by many peoples to their own needs: men, dwarves, orcs. Both the Men of Dale and the Rohirrim used a simplified form. The Cirth underwent significant change in the First Age as they were influenced by the Tengwar used by the Noldor. These changes reached their acme in the alphabet of Daeron (the loremaster of Thingol, King of Doriath), but this alphabet was never adopted by the Eldar for cursive writing as they already had the Fëanorian system. Indeed, the "Elves of the West" (Tolkien 1994c: 1093) largely abandoned runes in favor of cursive writing. However, the alphabet of Daeron pleased the dwarves and was widely adopted by them so much so that it became known as the *Angerthas Moria* or "the Long Rune-rows of Moria" (Tolkien 1994c: 1093). The dwarves, however, made a distinction between their own language (where the Cirth were used) and the languages of others (for which they tended to use the Fëanorian system).

The rest of Appendix E is taken up with Tolkien's detailed discussion of two tables he provides: one is of the Quenya Fëanorian Tengwar; the other is of the Sindarin Cirth. The first is laid out as a set of thirty-six numbered symbols in four columns (or *témar*) of nine symbols each. The table is subdivided with a horizontal line into two groups: symbols 1–24 in four *témar* and six grades (*tyller*); and symbols 25–36 in those same four *témar* and three *tyller*. Symbols 1–24 are primary and 25–36 are just "additional letters" (Tolkien 1994c: 1093). Tolkien makes clear the table is not exhaustive as there are other "additional letters" he does not provide as well as several signs (or *tehtar*) and variants which are likewise missing. As with his earlier discussion of pronunciation, Tolkien provides a note. This note gives further information about how Quenya's standard spelling diverged from the values provided in the table as well as a detailed discussion of vowels in the Fëanorian system; a practical illustration taken from the inscription on the west gate of Moria (which I briefly analyzed earlier); and a listing of the names of the various letters (with variants): from *tinco* (or "metal") as symbol 1 to *úre* ("heat") as symbol 24. In addition to being extraordinarily erudite and not a little intimidating, Tolkien's discussion again promotes the idea that language expresses culture as well as the fiction that he is editor/transcriber/translator of *The Lord of the Rings* and not its author. So, in the eighth paragraph of the note (a note that extends for more than two pages), he recursively but usefully refers to the title page of *The Lord of the Rings*. After declaring that "There was of course no 'mode' [in the Fëanorian Tengwar] for the representation of English" (Tolkien 1994c: 1096), Tolkien then characterizes the Fëanorian letters that run along both the verso and recto of the title page not as a phonetic adaptation into English by him as editor because such an adaptation (although he could manage it) would be culturally and historically inaccurate. Rather, the Fëanorian letters on the title page are "an example of what a man of Gondor might have produced, hesitating between the values of the letters familiar in his 'mode' and the traditional spelling of English" (Tolkien 1994c: 1096). Tolkien here is showing a couple of the qualities in his treatment of his invented language for which he is rarely praised: his attention to role and context, and his humorous extension of the fiction of the epic's frame story. However, it is these qualities, I think, as much as the breadth of the canvas in his fantasy which have delighted readers for almost sixty-five years.

The second major section of Appendix E, given over to the Sindarin Cirth (or Angerthas Daeron) with Noldorian additions, offers the reader a more extended table of signs than the Fëanorian Tengwar. Instead of thirty-six symbols, the Cirth has fifty-eight numbered and two unnumbered signs to reach a total of sixty. Tolkien presents a learned discussion of the way in which Sinadarin, Noldorian, and later dwarvish elements (both Morian and Ereborian) combine in the Cirth. What this necessarily, if ironically, clarifies for the reader is that Tolkien treats his invented languages (whether written or spoken) as if they were real, creates invented languages that are as complex as natural ones, and brings his philological understanding to bear in a way that many readers would find overwhelming. As fantasy, then, *The Lord of the Rings* and by extension the legendarium are not intended to be a light or easy read.

Appendix F of *The Lord of the Rings*

Appendix F is focused not on writing but on spoken languages in Middle-earth: how they reflect distinctions among the various peoples who inhabit that world and how they present translation challenges for Tolkien as "editor" of *The Lord of the Rings*. In keeping with the hierarchy of creation in his legendarium, Tolkien begins his discussion with elves, moves on to men, then to hobbits (dearest to his heart but latecomers to his created Middle-earth), and then other races (including dwarves, who were—it should be remembered—the creation of the Vala Aulë and not Ilúvatar himself). Some of what Tolkien says here I have already referred to in this chapter, so I shall be brief.

Tolkien begins by charting the primacy of Westron (or common speech) in the West-lands of Middle-earth, and points out that English in *The Lord of the Rings* substitutes for Westron. Even among those whose first language was something other than Westron, Westron was used as a second language. This generalization applies to several sub-groups: wild men in the Drúadan forest in Anórien; the Dunlendings, the original inhabitants of much of Gondor; and the Rohirrim. Then Tolkien becomes meticulous and points out that the first two groups only spoke Westron "brokenly" (1994c: 1101). Here, again, Tolkien is presenting his invented languages as if they were natural and followed the process of growth and decay that natural languages do. In the section on the elves, Tolkien usefully distinguishes between two groups: west elves (the *Eldar*) and east elves (who lived mainly in Mirkwood and Lórien). The Eldar spoke two languages: *Quenya* (or "High Elven") and *Sindarin* (or "Grey Elven"). The former (Quenya) was no longer a living language but a sort of ceremonial "Elven Latin" derived from those who had lived across the sea in Eldamar on the "Undying Lands" and then been exiled to Middle-earth. The latter (Sindarin) was related to Quenya but spoken by those who had not passed over the sea but lingered on the coast of Middle-earth. It had been championed by Thingol Greycloak of Doriath. It had changed greatly over time so that it became very different from Quenya, and it had done so for a fascinating reason. According to Tolkien, Sindarin had "changed with the changefulness of mortal lands" (1994c: 1102), so, by implication, Quenya was unchanging because it was associated with an eternal and unchanging land.

In his discussion of men's use of Westron, Tolkien points out that Westron was a mannish invention blended with Elvish, with the language actually deriving from the *Edain* (or *Atani*) and, especially, from those who had helped the elves at the end of the First Age to defeat Morgoth. In the Second Age, the Númenóreans spoke Sindarin and Quenya but, more commonly, their language was a pure version of Westron: Adûnaic. In the Third Age they mixed with Elvish to become a sort of "ennobled" Westron (Tolkien 1994c:

1103). This Westron was spoken by the Dúnedain and varieties of it by the Beornings, the woodmen of western Mirkwood, the men of Long Lake and of Dale. In this section, Tolkien repeats some of the observations in the section devoted to the elves, a repetition that suggests, perhaps, how hastily the appendices had to be put together to meet a publication deadline. It is also worthy of note that Tolkien uses language difference to reinforce a cultural point: the mutual hatred between the Rohirrim and the Dunlendings.

When it comes to the hobbits, Tolkien begins with the simple observation that they had used the common speech for a thousand years before the present time of the epic. He remarks that hobbits never had their own language but used the languages of those they lived near and vestiges of some of those languages show up in place names in the Shire. He finishes the brief discussion with an answer to the question that had existed ever since the publication of *The Hobbit* in 1937, eighteen years before the appendices appeared: What does the word "hobbit" mean? His answer: "Hobbit" derives from the Rohan word: *holbytla*, that is "hole-builder" (Tolkien 1994c: 1104). Sometimes Tolkien could be complicated and erudite and clever; sometimes he could be disarmingly and humorously simple.

In the section titled "Of Other Races," Tolkien covers ents, orcs, trolls, and dwarves (in that order). The ents gained their love of speech from the Eldar and particularly loved Quenya but also used some Sindarin words such as *Fangorn* ("beard-(of)-tree"). The Entish language itself was unique: "slow, sonorous, agglomerated, repetitive, indeed long-winded" (Tolkien 1994c: 1104). For Tolkien, Entish is a satire on academic language: It was so complicated that even the elves had given up trying to represent it in writing; the ents themselves (as satirized academics) only used it when speaking to each other, but this secrecy was unnecessary as no one else could learn it! The orcs were known in the Black Speech as either *uruk* (warriors) or *snaga* (slaves). *Orc* itself is a Rohan word. Tolkien completes his discussion of orcs with translations of some of the orc words used in *The Lord of the Rings* as well as a discussion of the origin of Black Speech. The trolls were originally brutish and without language, but Sauron taught them some words because it was useful for him to have done so. Some trolls spoke a debased form of the common speech. At the end of the Third Age, Sauron bred a new race of trolls, the Olog-hai: fierce, cunning, able to stand the rays of the sun, speakers only of the Black Speech of Barad-dûr. Finally, of the dwarves Tolkien comments on their odd creation and, then, moves on to characterize them as craftsmen and lovers of gems. As with the elves and the ents, the dwarves have a secret language among themselves, but the dwarves' language is even more secret as their language is book-learned rather than learned from birth. Interestingly, Tolkien as ever uses the names of places and individuals as important examples of linguistic variety. He also finishes his discussion of "The Languages and Peoples of the Third Age" (although he actually ranges more widely than this section title suggests) with a new nugget of information: all dwarves have secret names that only their people know. They don't even put them on their tombstones. Here, Tolkien may be satirizing the use of nicknames by English schoolboys: Tolkien's name at school, for example, was "Tollers."

When in Appendix F, Tolkien turns to a discussion of the difficult business of translating the *Red Book of Westmarch* into English, he provocatively explains the various registers he uses in reporting speech by pointing out that not every person's Westron is the same: the hobbits speak in rustic Westron; Gondorians and the Rohirrim in a more formal and clipped way. He also remarks that everything has been translated into English except those languages "alien" to the common speech (Tolkien 1994c: 1106). It is not at all clear from context what "alien" means, but he stresses that linguistic otherness appears in place names and proper names. In this regard, Tolkien displays his lifelong fascination with the sources of proper names. He then develops this point with specific instances of the variety in Westron as a language and takes the opportunity to make an acerbic comment about mid-twentieth-century uses of language. He singles out trolls and orcs for his particular contempt, for each commits the sin of not loving language, and then Tolkien asserts that their mistreatment of language is analogous to those in the mid-twentieth century who have reduced language to the mean, the repetitive, the contemptuous, and the vulgar (1994c: 1108). Tolkien then dives into some fairly particular editing choices he made with names. He comments, for example, that Sam Gamgee and his father have names different from how he chose to "English" them: they were known to other hobbits as *Ban* and *Ran* (names which were actually short for *Banazîr* and *Ranugad*). Similarly, his beloved Shire was actually called *Sûza* in Westron. And *Sméagol* was actually called *Trân* in Hobbit and *Trahald* in Rohirrim, but Tolkien named him Sméagol with a nod to the linguistic change from the hobbit word for "burrow" (*smial*) to the Rohirrim's *smygel.*

Tolkien finishes this section of the appendix (as one might expect) with a note about three names: *hobbit, Gamgee,* and *Brandywine,* but not before he also offers a rare and specific description of the elves (by which he means both the Quendi and the Eldar) and explicitly dismisses as inaccurate the modern view of what elves (that is, fairies) look like. Tolkien's elves do not have wings and are not tiny or diaphanous. Instead, they are tall, fair skinned, gray eyed, and (nearly all of them) dark haired. However, it is with the hobbits that we shall end this study of Appendices E and F, for they were the creatures dearest to Tolkien's heart—not least, perhaps, as he owed his initial and perhaps his enduring fame to them. He has already traced the name to the Rohan word *holbytla.* Now he upsets expectation by pointing out that he may have "Englished" their name in such a way, but in fact the hobbits called each other *kuduk,* the king of Rohan called their race *kûduk-dûkan* (that is, hole-dwellers), and the Westron term for an individual hobbit was *banakil* ("halfling"). It is hard not to see Tolkien here as parodying himself as the learned academic as well as asserting his superior and prior knowledge of this fantasy world through his erudition, and that may be a good idea given his rhetorical stance as editor, not author, of Middle-earth.

The Road Goes Ever On: A Song Cycle—"Notes and Commentaries"

These notes and commentaries are on two of Tolkien's songs which Donald Swann set to music and published in 1967 (second revised edition 1976): "Namárië" and "A Elbereth Gilthoniel." They are the rather surprising source for the only extended and widely published remarks Tolkien made about his invented languages in the eighteen years between the publication of *The Lord of the Rings* and his death in 1973. Swann became a friend of Tolkien's, and it looks as if Tolkien relished an opportunity as an act of friendship to write more about the invented languages he loved so much. In particular, the notes and commentaries offer the most beautiful calligraphic rendition Tolkien ever achieved of his Elvish script (see Tolkien 1967a: 57 and 62). They really show how much of the delight Tolkien took in his invented languages was aesthetic—indeed, that adjective probably best describes what made the elves so remarkable a creation.

Much of what Tolkien spends time on in *The Road Goes Ever On* are two matters: the sound of Elvish as poetry (its stress patterns and its pronunciation) and the specifics of the grammar and semantics of the Eldar's languages. Both are intended to buttress his implicit argument that his invented languages actually existed, that they were, then, natural. With regard to the sound of Elvish poetry, he self-reflexively comments on Appendix E of *The Lord of the Rings* (written more than a decade before) and laments that his notes on pronunciation were not done there with "great clarity" (Tolkien 1967a: 63). Now, he offers that clarity at some length. With regard to grammar and semantics, he remarks that the etymology and exact meaning of the word *miruvóre* (a word which appears in "Namárië") is unknown (as are the etymologies and exact meanings of many words in natural languages) but offers some suggestions anyway. He also skirts the exact relation between Quenya and Sindarin as sister languages but asserts that the "kinship of the two languages can be observed, even in these fragments" represented by "A Elbereth Gilthoniel" (Tolkien 1967a: 65). And so, too, he dismisses any extended discussion of the grammar of Sindarin but focuses on one particular aspect: the word ending *-ath* (Tolkien 1967a: 66). He does so with the long-suffering hauteur of an editor expert in a natural language no one else knows well rather than the inventor of a language: "I have often had questions about the grammatical features appearing in the Sindarin fragments [in *The Lord of the Rings*]. There is no time for answering these. But I might mention the ending *-ath*" (Tolkien 1967a: 66). These are the last comments Tolkien offered about his languages during his lifetime, and they are delivered with a delicious archness.

The Silmarillion

Ten years passed between the first publication of the Notes and Commentaries to *The Road Goes Ever On* in 1967 and the posthumous publication of *The Silmarillion*. The Rubicon was crossed in two respects. First, Tolkien died in 1973 and, so, whatever has been subsequently published under his name has no direct authorial sanction. He may have wished to have his preparatory material published; he might have been happy with the work of his son Christopher as editor. We do not know. We cannot know. Second, everything that has been published under his name since he became so famous with *The Lord of the Rings* has a de facto mass audience, but some of the essays on language in *The Monster and the Critics and Other Essays* were only ever intended for a small academic audience. There are, then, two important questions for any reader to mull over as she considers Tolkien's creation of his languages: How much is meaning changed when something perhaps never intended for publication is published for a mass audience? How much distortion occurs when something intended for a specialist audience is subsequently packaged for a generalist or mass-market audience?

The Silmarillion contains a tremendously useful appendix titled "Elements in Quenya and Sindarin Names" (Tolkien 1999a: 355–65). It is the most extensive discussion of names before the *History of Middle-earth* series was published in the 1980s and 1990s. This appendix is, however, the work of Tolkien's son as editor and not the work of Tolkien himself. Christopher Tolkien rather understates its importance in the foreword to the first edition (1977) of *The Silmarillion* by merely remarking that he has provided a rudimentary listing of the major elements that make up those names (1999a: ix). The appendix itself begins with an agentless passive construction (Tolkien 1999a: 355) which gives no idea of the provenance of the subsequent list of Elvish and Sinadarin names and their origins and meanings. It is reasonably clear, however, that even though Christopher Tolkien created it, he must have been relying on preliminary work done by his father. So, readers have to make what they will of the value and accuracy and merit of such an appendix. The son as editor also provides a "Note on Pronunciation" (Tolkien 1999a: 310–11), but this is clearly just a summary culled from Appendix E in *The Lord of the Rings* (which had been created more than twenty years earlier by his father). It is solely concerned with Eldar names and not with the Eldar languages as such. It has some merit but only in a secondary way.

Tolkien's Essays on Language

Six years after *The Silmarillion* was published, Christopher Tolkien edited a collection of six of his father's less well-known lectures and one of his most important academic essays (on *Beowulf*). It was titled *The Monsters and the Critics and Other Essays*. The son calls his chosen grouping "papers" and asserts they "constitute a unity" (Tolkien 1997b: 1), even though he doesn't explain wherein that unity consists. It is enough here to say that among the seven are three pieces of great value to any understanding of Tolkien's use of invented languages: "English and Welsh," "A Secret Vice," and "Valedictory Address." All of them were published for a wide and general readership in this 1983 collection. Each has, however, an earlier life as lectures. "English and Welsh" was delivered on October 21, 1955, as an O'Donnell Lecture at Oxford University— just one day, that is, after the publication of *The Return of the King*. It was then published eight years later in a collection titled *Angles and Britons: O'Donnell Lectures* by the University of Wales Press. "A Secret Vice" was originally delivered to a philological society (whose name has gone unrecorded) in autumn 1931. It was then subsequently delivered to another group probably in the late 1940s and yet a third group in the late 1960s. The original title was "A Hobby for the Home," but Christopher Tolkien changed the title to "A Secret Vice" on grounds that his father had referred to the piece by that title in a 1967 letter. Christopher Tolkien also, in the Notes, updated one of the Elvish poems ("Oilima Markirya" or "The Last Ark") included in the address on grounds that it is "one of the major pieces of Quenya" created by his father (1997b: 4). It had not been published before its appearance in *The Monsters and the Critics and Other Essays*. The "Valedictory Address to the University of Oxford" was delivered on June 5, 1959, upon Tolkien's retirement from his Merton Professorship in English Language and Literature. Before its appearance in *The Monsters and the Critics* in 1983, it had previously been published in *J. R. Tolkien, Scholar and Storyteller* (1979) published by Cornell University Press and edited by Mary Salu and Robert T. Farrell. Christopher Tolkien incorporates changes made by his father to the address, changes which were not available (because they were undiscovered) at the time it was published in 1979. The provenance of the changes is unclear. All of these essays are useful in understanding Tolkien's use of created languages.

In "English and Welsh" for example, Tolkien makes a series of wide-ranging claims that help the reader of the legendarium understand the thinking behind his fascination with languages. These claims can only help us understand in a limited manner the specifics of, say, Quenya or Sindarin or the Black Speech, but they aid us greatly in comprehending the big picture. They matter because at the simplest level Sindarin has its roots in Tolkien's love of the Welsh language. The closest thing that Tolkien offers as a controlling generalization in the address is that he will talk about his career in so far as it will "arouse or strengthen the interest of the English in various departments of Celtic studies," and do so from the perspective of someone who has always felt "most particularly the attraction of the Welsh language in itself" (Tolkien 1997b: 162). Tolkien begins at the end of the first paragraph of the address by modestly pointing out how apposite is the timing of the address as it reinforces the significance of Celtic culture in the creation of *The Lord of the Rings*:

> [T]he years 1953 to 1955 have for me been filled with a great many tasks, and their burden has not been decreased by the long-delayed appearance of a large "work" [*The Lord of the Rings*], if it can be called that, which contains, in the way of presentation that I find most natural, much of what I personally have received from the study of things Celtic. (Tolkien 1997b: 162)

He continues by contrasting his own attitude to language as the "prime differentiator of peoples" with the bureaucratic love of "uniformity," a love that derives from uniformity being "very much more manageable" as "A hundred-per-cent Englishman is easier for an English government to handle" (Tolkien 1997b: 166). In this way, he obliquely suggests that the cultural and linguistic variety so central to his legendarium is as much a political statement against the modern world as anything else before he moves on to praise the Welsh, who have "loved and cultivated their language for its own sake ... and who by it and with it maintain their identity" (Tolkien 1997b: 166). In this way, the Welsh are like the elves, whose language is beautiful because they care about it while English has the "ruinous honour of becoming the lingua franca of the world" (Tolkien 1997b: 166).

The History of Middle-earth Series

In the same year as *The Monsters and the Critics and Other Essays* was first published, 1983, the first volume in what turned out to be a twelve-volume series titled *The History of Middle-earth* was published. This was *The Book of Lost Tales Part I*. For the purposes of this chapter and my efforts to elucidate Tolkien's complex invented languages, I will concern myself only with those volumes in the series that directly relate to his views on and experiments with language. In addition to *The Book of Lost Tales Part I*, those are vol. II, *The Book of Lost Tales Part II*, vol. V, *The Lost Road and Other Writings*, vol. IX, *Sauron Defeated*, vol. XI, *The War of the Jewels*, and vol. XII, *The Peoples of Middle-earth*.

The Book of Lost Tales Part I includes an appendix titled "Names in the *Lost Tales*: Part I" (Tolkien 1983: 246–73). The list of names (from Ainur to Yavanna) is important because it shows J. R. R. Tolkien (rather than his son) delving into the meaning and significance of so many names associated with the Elder Days. It enriches our understanding of Quenya and Sindarin precisely because the list is so much concerned with those two languages. The list is also preceded by a headnote by Christopher Tolkien that is at least as useful and interesting since it discusses Tolkien's efforts toward establishing a consistent nomenclature for his invented languages. Christopher Tolkien refers to two small books kept by his father, books which date from as early as 1915 (and, so, very early in the history of the development of the legendarium and contemporaneous with the Lost Tales themselves). The first book Christopher Tolkien calls the "Quenya Lexicon" and abbreviates to QL. The second is a dictionary of the gnomish language, Goldogrin (which Christopher Tolkien calls the "Goldogrin, or Gnomish, Lexicon" and abbreviates to GL). Tolkien himself had a longer title for it *i Lam na Ngoldathon: Goldogrin*, and he also provided a date of creation two years later than QL: 1917. QL is constructed around "root" words, and its contents show that with Quenya Tolkien not infrequently invented a word and then constructed an etymology for it rather than the other way around. That is, to put it simply, sometimes Tolkien's choices were aesthetic and not linguistic or philological. There is a considerable degree of uncertainty in the 1915 lexicon caused by undefined diacritical marks, so much so that QL is very much a work in progress and not an achieved lexicon. The 1917 GL is something entirely different. It contains a "remarkable number of words" and is arranged as a "conventional dictionary" (Tolkien 1983: 247). Just as with QL, however, GL is a work in progress, and both lexicons reveal a dynamic relation with the Lost Tales. Christopher Tolkien cites one example as proof: the word for "sheep" exists in three unresolved states: *mô*, *moth*, and *uimoth*.

Christopher Tolkien adds some further, useful comments to his discussion of his father's two principal invented languages (Quenya and Sindarin) at this early point in their development. First, the lexicons are very complex documents as far as historical phonetics is concerned. Second, the lexicons (and, therefore, Tolkien's thinking at this time) included very little by way of phonology or grammar. It appears that Tolkien did work on some phonological description of Quenya at this time, but because he revised that work repeatedly what he left in manuscript form is an unusable "baffling muddle" (Tolkien 1983: 247). Third, in the creation of his Elvish languages, Tolkien included both a layer of historical punning as well as providing some connections to the language he knew best as a professional philologist: Anglo-Saxon. Christopher Tolkien explicitly states that the list of names in the Lost Tales he himself provides is a synthetic and eclectic creation of his own, one that tries to remain true to his father's intentions even as it offers greater clarity than did his father. So, he "tr[ies] to present the content of the dictionaries as clearly as [he] can" (Tolkien 1983: 248) while at the same time giving "as much information, derived from these books [QL and GL], as is possible, but without any speculation beyond them" (247).

The Book of Lost Tales Part II includes an appendix titled "Names in the *Lost Tales*—Part II" (Tolkien 1984: 335–49) and a headnote markedly shorter than that in *The Book of Lost Tales Part I*. The headnote in *Part I* is twelve paragraphs long; the headnote in *Part II* only two paragraphs in length. The latter is "designed only as an adjunct and extension" to the former (1984: 335). Christopher Tolkien, nevertheless, does make two important observations in the brief headnote to *Part II*. First, that the term "Quenya" at this point in the development of Tolkien's created languages meant only the language spoken in Tol Eressëa. For the nominal and adjectival distinctions among different linguistic groups of elves Tolkien used the term "Gnomish" on the one hand and "Elfin," "Eldar," and "Eldarissa" on the other. Second, Christopher Tolkien points out that in addition to the QL and GL lexicons referred to in the headnote to the appendix in *The Book of Lost Tales Part I*, his father also created a name list to *The Fall of Gondolin* (or NFG) in *Part II*, a list which Christopher Tolkien describes in some detail on pages 148–49 of *The Book of Lost Tales Part II*. There, he (Christopher) usefully comments that the NFG is substantial, incomplete (it only covers A–L), and in places illegible. He then quotes from his father's headnote to NFG and does so in a way which stresses the frame-tale aspect of *The Book of Lost Tales*:

> Here is set forth by Eriol at the teaching of Bronweg's son Elfrith or Littleheart … those names and words that are used in these tales from either the tongue of the Elves of Kôr as at that time spoken in the Lonely Isle, or from that related one of the Noldoli their kin whom they wrested from Melko. (Tolkien 1984: 148)

Christopher Tolkien then goes on to quote from a "preface" to the first manuscript of the Tuor story (*Tuor A*), where his father comments that "the Noldoli speak a curious tongue sweet still to my [Littleheart's] ears though not maybe to all the Eldar. Wise folk see it as close kin to Eldarissa, but it soundeth not so, and I know of no such lore" (1984: 148).

What fascinates here is three things: first, Tolkien (who is after all the creator of all these languages) pretends not to be in control of them but sees them as developing in an evolutionary way; second, Tolkien emphasizes the aesthetic aspect of his created languages ("sweet still to my ears"); third, Tolkien makes a distinction between Eldarissa and (implicitly) Noldorissa, a distinction that disappeared as his ideas developed. Shortly thereafter, Christopher Tolkien quotes twice from an earlier, struck-out version of the "preface" to *Tuor A* written by his father. Both quotations matter as they indirectly make a claim about the foundational and historical importance of language. In the first, Tolkien claims "the Elves have no true names" because those who spoke Noldorissa "passed away ere ever the rest of the Eldar came from Kôr" (quoted in 1984: 149). In the second, Tolkien asserts that Littleheart "had to learn the Elfin [language] in the end, or be doomed either to silence or to leave Mar Vanwa Tyaliéva" (quoted in 1984: 149). So, if one doesn't know a language one is sentenced to the powerlessness of silence or to exile: a heavy price to bear either way. One could argue that Tolkien here is guilty of special pleading: a professional philologist arguing for the crucial value of language. Nonetheless, the argument does, I think, have objective merit. *The Lost Road and Other Writings* bears the subtitle "Language and Legend before 'The Lord of the Rings.'" Three sections of *The Lost Road* matter to the present discussion: Section V of Part II, titled "The Lhammas" (167–98); Part III, titled "The Etymologies" (339–400); and Appendix II, titled "The List of Names" (404–7).

"The Lhammas" constitutes one of Tolkien's most useful and sustained discussions of his invented languages. It deserves to be better known even though (as nearly always in Tolkien) it is complicated and evolutionary and exists in more than one manuscript. (In this case, there are three.) The essay (which dates from the mid 1930s) covers the creation and spread of languages in Valinor and in Middle-earth with an emphasis on the elves' languages. It also (more briefly) discusses the origins of the language of the orcs, dwarves, and men. Perhaps of greatest value to students of Tolkien are the three "Trees of Tongues," in which Tolkien diagrammed the relationship among the various languages as well as their origins as his sense of that relationship developed over time. Christopher Tolkien provides a useful analysis of these and other linguistic matters on pages 180 to 198 of *The Lost Road.* It is beyond the limited scope of this chapter to go into great detail about these "Trees," but I can make a few preliminary or summary comments. First, the "Trees" are accompanied by a diagram of "The Peoples of the Elves." This pairing is important as it shows how intricately Tolkien viewed the development of language, history, and culture in his legendarium. Second, the languages of all the elves derived from both the Valar as a group and from Oromë in particular. Third, the language of the orcs is inherently evil as it derived ultimately from Melkor/Morgoth. Fourth, the language of the dwarves derived from their creator, Aulë. Fifth, the language of most men derived from a complex interaction with some groups of elves (particularly the dark elves), with the orcs, and with the dwarves. The language of particular groups of men (those of the houses of Bëor, Haleth, and Hádor) was particularly influenced by the language of the green elves. Finally, Tolkien's categorization is extensive. If we look simply at the linguistic taxonomy for the elves, we can see Tolkien creating a list of languages, but a list in flux— with various competing (and subtly changing) labels, among them:

Quendian, Lindarin, Noldorin, Teleri, Eldarin, Lembian, Ikorindian, Korddarin, Ingwiqenya, and Avari.

"The Etymologies" (which probably dates from 1937–38 with some later additions from the time of *The Lord of the Rings*) is, perhaps, an even more useful (and certainly a more extended) discussion of languages by Tolkien than is "The Lhammas," but the intent is surely different. "The Lhammas" is a historical and diagrammatic account of the relation among all Tolkien's languages; "The Etymologies" is above all a certain sort of dictionary—and just of the Elvish tongues. As always with the manuscripts edited by Tolkien's son after his father's death it is the editorial headnote that helps to clarify the text itself. In the headnote to "The Etymologies," Christopher Tolkien makes several crucial points. First, Tolkien's legendarium is characterized in part by the "astounding complexity of the phonological and grammatical evolution of the Elvish languages" (Tolkien 1987: 341). Second, Tolkien's working habit of grand designs degenerating into illegible scrawl obscures the clarity of the overall design. Third, his father's conception of the Elvish languages was not set but evolutionary. Fourth, Tolkien never tried to make a comprehensive vocabulary of his Elvish languages. So, with "The Etymologies" we have a document which is the closest he ever came to a dictionary, but it is actually "an etymological dictionary of word-relationships" (Tolkien 1987: 342). "The Etymologies" itself runs from "Ab-, Abar" to "Yur-" and has as far as possible been conservatively standardized by the editor.

"The List of Names" is a much thinner piece than "The Etymologies," for it occupies only three pages where "The Etymologies" occupies almost sixty. It very much resembles the earlier lexicons we encountered in the two parts of *The Lost Tales*. It should be noted, however, that the list itself is much more extensive than the version published under Christopher Tolkien's editorship even though the list was left incomplete by Tolkien. It was the son's decision only to offer a "small selection from the material" as the "Annals of Beleriand" (the major source for the list) defines many of the names in the list. The list itself dates from the 1930s. It runs from *Aldaron* to *Tulkas*.

The contribution of *Sauron Defeated* to our understanding of Tolkien's invented languages consists of something quite rare: a sustained and reasonably straightforward discussion of a language, in this case Adunaic. It occupies the final section of

Part III: "The Drowning of Anadûnê" and is titled "Lowdham's Report on the Adunaic Language" (413–40).[3] "The Drowning of Anadûnê" is a reworking of the Second Age material called "The Fall of Númenor" and bears a complex relation to "The Notion Club Papers" (an incomplete futuristic story created by Tolkien in a sort of writing competition with C. S. Lewis in the mid 1940s) and to *The Lost Road*. "Lowdham's Report" is quite remarkable, for although the typescript was abandoned by Tolkien after just seventeen pages, those seventeen pages present a succinct discussion (sometimes in the jargon of philologists) of Adunaic. It is as if since Tolkien needed a language for his Númenóreans, he decided to create one quickly.

It begins by laying out Adunaic's historical relation to two other languages: Avallonian and Khazadian. It continues by sketching the structure and grammar of the language even though Tolkien (through Lowdham) cannot resist the temptation to point out that the sketch is only a snapshot and, so, the reality of language was much more complex than the sketch can allow for. The language of Adunaic is largely triconsonantal but with some biconsonantal elements. As proof of such an arrangement, Lowdham provides two six-row-by-four-column tables of the principal consonant sounds (on pps. 416 and 418) of Adunaic and Later Adunaic. Lowdham also discusses word formations and assimilations in Adunaic in considerable detail. Lowdham's report then moves on to the language's vowels. Here, he points out that Adunaic used only three vowels (A, I, and U) and two diphthongs (AI and AU). Next, he discusses nouns. These he classes as "strong" or "weak" and as having four categories (masculine, feminine, common, and neuter), three numbers (singular, plural, and dual), and two cases (subjective and objective). Lowdham (that is, Tolkien) concludes with extensive examples of how nouns inflect according to their function in a sentence. This is wonderfully precise stuff, but his son as editor is surely right that had Tolkien returned to Adunaic instead of turning to the completion of *The Lord of the Rings* "Lowdham's Report" "would doubtless have been reduced to a wreck, as new conceptions caused shifts and upheavals in the structure" (Tolkien 1992: 439–40). Christopher Tolkien is also right, I think, in suggesting that throughout Tolkien's development of his many languages "'completion'" was not "the over-riding aim." The overriding aim was "[d]elight … in the creation itself, the creation of new linguistic form evolving within the compass of

an imagined time" (Tolkien 1992: 440). So, what we have with the
report is Tolkien's sense of what he wanted a language to look like
at one particular moment and in its entirety.

The War of the Jewels (the penultimate volume in Christopher
Tolkien's magisterial work The History of Middle-earth) contributes
significantly to the understanding of Tolkien's languages with
just one section: "Part Four: Quendi and Eldar" (Tolkien 1994d:
357–424). This section dates from 1959–60; it exists in just two
very similar versions, each about fifty pages in length; it has an
alternative title (Essekenta Eldarinwa); and it has a long and
informative subtitle:

> Enquiry into the origins of the Elvish names for Elves and their
> varieties clans and divisions: with Appendices on their names for
> the other Incarnates: Men, Dwarves, and Orcs; and on their [the
> Elves'] analysis of their own language, Quenya: with a note on
> the "Language of the Valar." (Tolkien 1994d: 359)

There is only one section proper in the essay and that concerns
itself with Elvish words for themselves. It occupies some twenty-five
pages in the published version (pp. 360–85), but it is followed by
four appendices (on "Elvish names for Men"; "Elvish names for the
Dwarves"; "Elvish names for the Orcs"; and on "*Kwen, Quenya,
and the Elvish [especially Ñoldorin] Words for 'Language'")
and one note ("Note on the 'Language of the Valar'"). In the
long section devoted to the Elvish names for themselves, Tolkien
discusses four principal linguistic elements as those elements appear
in Quenya, Telerin, and Sindarin (1994d: 360–72). This he follows
with a discussion (1994d: 372–80) of the "various terms applied
to the Elves and their varieties in Quenya, Telerin, and Sindarin"
(1994d: 372). He finishes with a discussion of the "Clan-names"
(1994d: 380–5). Some of this material (especially early on) is
quite technical even though Christopher Tolkien (probably wisely)
chose to omit from publication "a passage of extremely complex
phonology" (1994d: 359). Two characteristics dominate Tolkien's
discussion in the main section of the essay: first, he returns again
and again to history to explain linguistic differences; second, the
audience (if Tolkien imagined one) for the essay would have to
be those familiar with The Lord of the Rings and, in particular,
with its many appendices. One suspects, however, that Tolkien may

have created the essay for his own pleasure and with the possible publication of *The Silmarillion* in his own lifetime in mind. The appendices are less abstruse than the essay proper. From the first appendix, it should be noted that all the elves' words for men (*Atani, Apanónar,* and *Hildor*) stress the elves were the first born as these three words mean, respectively, "The Second Folk," "the After-born," and "The Followers." From the second, it should be noted that many of the elves' words for the dwarves are pejorative: *Naugrim,* or "The Stunted Folk"; and *Dornoth,* or "the Thrawn [stubborn] Folk." It is also noteworthy that Tolkien divides the dwarves into dwarves proper and "Petty-dwarves" with the latter termed (again pejoratively) *Nogotheg* (or "Dwarflet"). Again, Tolkien relies on history to make two points: the dwarves despised the petty-dwarves as "deformed or undersized" (388); and the elves had hunted the dwarves at one point in history (at least, so the dwarves alleged).

The third appendix, since its subject is the Elvish names for the orcs, goes in an expected direction with the word "orc" ultimately deriving from the Quenyan noun *urkō* (meaning "horror"). In Sindarin, the word of choice for the orcs was *Glamhoth* (or "Yelling-horde"). The fourth appendix spends quite some time arguing that the meaning of *Quendi* ultimately derives from a phrase or word meaning "those who form words with voices" (Tolkien 1994d: 391), while the word for "language" was *lambē* and the word *tengwa* meant "sign." At this point, Tolkien moves on to the relation between spoken word and gesture in order to point out that the elves were masters of using gesture to undermine or otherwise change the meaning of spoken words, and finishes with a return to the frame story of the Lost Tales (written many decades before) with a reference to Pengolodh the loremaster. Finally, in the note on the language of the Valar (Valarin), Tolkien continues the allusion to the frame story with extensive excerpts from the writings of Pengolodh, and suggests in a fascinating assertion that the Valar must have had a language when they became flesh since "the making of a *lambe* is the chief character of an Incarnate" (1994d: 397). The note continues with more than a dozen examples of Valarin words, just less than a dozen instances of Valarin names, a class of Valarin words whose authenticity is rejected by Pengolodh, and a few Valarin place names used to show that they were ultimately of Valarin origin. The note finishes with a historical explanation of why the Eldar did not preserve many Valarin words along with an assertion that the creation myth (the "Ainulindalë") must have been transmitted to us in Quenya since the Valar would have had to speak to the Eldar in a language they understood. Even toward the end of his life, then, Tolkien was always interpreting his own mythology in linguistic terms. *Doing so was simply essential to how he viewed his fantasy world.*

The Peoples of Middle-earth, the last volume in *The History of Middle-earth* series, contains three pieces of importance: a discussion (Tolkien 1996: 19–84) of "The Appendix on Languages" in *The Lord of the Rings*, and a printing with commentary of two of Tolkien's late writings: "The Shibboleth of Fëanor" (331–66) and "The Problem of *Ros*" (367–76). The first of these (which I will not dwell on but let the final version in *The Lord of the Rings* stand on its own merits) dates from about 1950 and consists of some manuscript versions of the appendix, which allow readers to compare earlier iterations of the appendix with the published version. The second piece (on Fëanor) and the third (on *Ros*) date from about 1968. Both of them offer important insights into the tremendous value Tolkien placed on language in his mythology.

In the second piece, whose title—"The Shibboleth of Fëanor with an Excursus on the Name of the Descendants of Finwë"— was added by Christopher Tolkien as the essay itself was untitled, Tolkien works through the ramifications (social, cultural, and political) of the scribal and phonic change in Quenya from þ to s. As Christopher Tolkien puts it in his headnote, the essay "records how the difference in pronunciation of a single consonantal element in Quenya played a significant part in the strife of the Noldorin princes in Valinor" (1996: 331). What of course fascinates here is that the consonant change was created by Tolkien for linguistic reasons, and he then had to play out its causes and effects at the level of narrative. The cause of the change, according to Tolkien, was that a majority of the Noldor agreed to it based on "phonetic 'taste' and theory" (1996: 332) with the change occurring after they had separated from the Vanyar (or light elves). The effect was to anger the Noldorian Fëanor (a loremaster) who insisted that þ not s was correct, but there were also personal reasons for his belief: his mother had been called "þerindë" (needlewoman) and his stepmother (Indis), whom he disliked intensely, had adopted the "s" when she joined the Noldor. Some may see in all this some sort of satire at the expense of philologists, but it doesn't seem to be that.

It just illustrates the precision of Tolkien's linguistic thinking as well as his understanding that some people are hot-headed and ignore the consequences of their choices. The Fëanor of *The Silmarillion* is definitely one of those, and his anger and resentment (one aspect of which is this "þ to s" argument) are central to the narrative of the Elder Days. As Tolkien puts it in the essay: "How this ill will grew and festered in the years that followed is the main matter of the first part of *The Silmarillion*: the Darkening of Valinor" (1996: 335).

With the third essay (which was called "The Problem of *Ros*" by Christopher Tolkien as the work was left untitled by his father), Tolkien felt the need to explain to his own satisfaction the derivation of names that he had created and which had appeared in print so that those names would be etymologically accurate. The most difficult of all of these was the name of *Elros*, which should logically and anthropologically have been of Bëorian origin. Tolkien's solution (after trying out several possibilities) was that the name was associated with the name of Elros's mother, Elwing. However, that solution doesn't work as *The Lord of the Rings* mentions Cair Andros, an island in the river Anduin north of Osgiliath, and Appendix A in that work defines it as Elvish in derivation and its meaning as "Ship of Long-foam." So, the name is necessarily Eldarin and not (as Tolkien would have liked) Bëorian. What is remarkable in all of this argument is that Tolkien felt the need to be internally consistent and didn't just, for example, declare the name *Elros* to be a linguistic anomaly or to have an unknown origin. He had, perhaps, an even higher standard of consistency in his invented languages than his readers would have expected—even of him. As Christopher Tolkien puts it in the headnote to the essay:

> In his last years my father attached the utmost importance to finding explanations, in historical linguistic terms, of names that went far back in the "legendarium" … and if such names had appeared in print he felt bound by them, and went to great pains to devise etymologies that were consonant with the now minutely refined historical development of Quenya and Sindarin. (1996: 367)

What is perhaps so remarkable in Tolkien's long work with language in his legendarium is not just that he cared so much about accuracy but that he also acted as if his invented languages were natural ones too—or needed to behave as if they were. It is also remarkable that his essays would be on one subject and yet touch on so much else in the legendarium. So, "Shibboleth" also touches on the division among Finwë's children and discusses at more length the early life of Galadriel in ways not looked at elsewhere by Tolkien. And so, "*Ros*" comments on the languages spoken by the houses of the Edain in the First Age, includes a conversation between Beren and Lúthien about her choice to speak her native tongue, and discusses some inconsistencies in Eärendil's having pleaded with Manwë in the languages of men and elves to aid both peoples in their fight against Morgoth. Yes, some of this discussion does get complex— even frustratingly so—but it illustrates one of the many reasons for the high regard in which Tolkien is held by millions: he cared so very deeply about the world he created. After all, it took him a lifetime.

Notes

1 The common distinction between "artificial" and "invented" is that all invented languages are artificial, but only artificial languages are invented—usually for the good of the humanity—to be adopted. It may also be said that invented languages are only meant for private use or to be understood by the cognoscenti alone. Tolkien's invented languages got rather out of hand in their appeal, but their major purpose was to make more convincing the social and cultural manifestations of his legendarium.

2 For those interested in tracing Tolkien's ideas by date of creation rather than publication, I have provided a table, below, of those dates as nearly as they can be established. I have included three citations from 1977, 1983, and 1984 because although the works referred to were created by Christopher Tolkien they rely heavily on the work of his father.

Table A: Chronology of Creation of Tolkien's Commentaries on Language Invention

Date	Title	Work
1915	Quenya Lexicon	*The Book of Lost Tales Part I*
1917	Goldogrin, or Gnomish, Lexicon	*The Book of Lost Tales Part I*
before 1920	Name List to *The Fall of Gondolin*	*The Book of Lost Tales Part II*

1930s	The List of Names	The Lost Road and Other Writings
1931, 1983	A Secret Vice	The Monsters and the Critics and Other Essays
mid 1930s	The Lhammas	The Lost Road and Other Writings
mid 1930s	Trees of Tongues	The Lost Road and Other Writings
1937–8, 1954–5	The Etymologies	The Lost Road and Other Writings
mid 1940s	Lowdham's Report on the Adunaic Language	The Lost Road and Other Writings
1950	The Appendix on Languages	The Peoples of Middle-earth
1954–5	Appendices E and F	The Lord of the Rings
1955, 1983	English and Welsh	The Monsters and the Critics and Other Essays
1959; 1983	Valedictory Address	The Monsters and the Critics and Other Essays
1959–60	Quendi and Eldar	The War of the Jewels
1967	Notes and Commentaries	The Road Goes Ever On: A Song Cycle
1968	The Shibboleth of Fëanor	The Peoples of Middle-earth
1968	The Problem of Ros	The Peoples of Middle-earth
1977	Elements in Quenya and Sindarin Names	The Silmarillion
1977	Note on Pronunciation	The Silmarillion
1983	Names in the Lost Tales Part I	The Book of Lost Tales Part I
1984	Names in the Lost Tales Part II	The Book of Lost Tales Part II

3 Lowdham is Arundel Lowdham (or Loudham), an important character in "The Notion Club Papers." He undertakes research, primarily of a linguistic nature, into the fall of Númenor and the language most associated with the Númenóreans: Adunaic (also Adûnaic).

4

Tolkien on Time

For the general reader of Tolkien's work, the most accessible source for understanding his view of time is Appendix B of *The Return of the King*. It is titled "The Tale of Years (Chronology of the Westlands)" and begins with a four-paragraph summary of the Four Ages: The First Age (which ended with the overthrowing of Morgoth); the Second Age (which ended with the first overthrow of Sauron, Morgoth's servant, and the capture of the One Ring); the Third Age (which ended with the second overthrow of Sauron and the destruction of the One Ring); and the Fourth Age, the Age of the dominion of men. In fact, however, the Appendix looks in detail only at events in the Second, Third, and (for a span of 120 years) the Fourth Ages.

We can make several useful observations at this moment. First, if Tolkien's useful summary of his view of time were this simple, there would, perhaps, be no need for this chapter. But as with all things Tolkienian, the picture is vastly more complicated than it initially appears. Second, Tolkien's view of time is that it is cyclical with each age (except for the Fourth, which is implicitly the one that we are now in) ending with the defeat of evil (Morgoth once and Sauron twice). Third, Tolkien loves wordplay, so the title of the appendix ("The Tale of Years") is a pun with "tale" being both a tally and a story. It is as if Tolkien can only tell of the passage of time in story. Finally, when Tolkien refers to the *Elder Days* (by which he means the First Age and the ascendancy of the elves), he is referring obliquely to *The Silmarillion*, which was as yet unpublished.[1] As he enigmatically puts it at the end of his summary: "The histories of that time [the Elder Days] are not recorded here" (1994c: 1082).

TIME

The Silmarillion

It is with *The Silmarillion* that we should begin in our efforts to clarify the dazzling richness of time as Tolkien worked with the concept over nearly forty years, both because it contains his earliest work and because the tale of the ages starts from this point. From there, I will tell the story of Tolkien's vision of time and take in his principal and some of his lesser works before ending where we began this chapter—with *The Lord of the Rings*. Throughout this account, it should be borne in mind above all how subtle and wide-ranging Tolkien's account is. It cannot *usefully* be reduced merely to a set of dates although Tolkien himself was perpetually trying to. Having discussed his concept of time, I will then briefly move on to analyze one of the ways in which time, for Tolkien, was differentiated in the form of ages: place. It is one of the least-known aspects of Tolkien's legendarium for the general reader that Middle-earth in the First Age is not the same as Middle-earth in the Fourth Age. In essence, Tolkien uses geography to reinforce temporal distinctions.[2] In a way, he is offering his own version of Ovid's *Metamorphoses* where the gods remake the world more than once over time in an effort to improve human behavior.

The first section of *The Silmarillion* is called "Ainulindalë" (or Music of the Ainur). The account (which dates from 1936 to 1945) describes Tolkien's creation myth. It begins with a Genesis-like moment when Eru/the One/Ilúvatar first creates the Ainur or "Holy Ones" by thinking them into existence (Tolkien 1999a: 15). So, the moment of first creation but no idea of time as such. The first mention of time—in a fashion so characteristic of Tolkien's style—is actually an allusion to a time beyond the scope of the legendarium itself, a time which the narrator knows of by oral tale ("it has been said"): the time when there is no time. In the fourth paragraph of "Ainulindalë," Tolkien writes of some greater music that will be created "after the end of days" (1999a: 15). Three subsequent references are equally useful, but in a different way from this first. After having talked of Melkor's introduction of his own strain of music into those created by Ilúvatar, Tolkien incorporates something radically indeterminate into his outline of time. According to him, Ilúvatar does not ever reveal all that will happen in the world. As a consequence, "in every age there come forth things that are new and have no foretelling, for they do not proceed from the past" (1999a: 18). So, to a notion of Four Ages (as in Appendix B of *The Return of the King*) must now be added a rider about how much any chronology distorts how time truly unfolds: some of time is causal and some (it is unclear which part or parts) is outside the realm of cause and effect entirely. It is also important to see how the reader is now presented with two related terms: Age with an initial capital (as in the Four Ages) and age (lower case), which seems to reflect a more common sense of what "age" means for the general culture—a group of years set off from the continuity of time because the group is in some helpful way intrarelated. And to Tolkien's qualities as an allusive writer must be added his powers as a creator of metaphor. Shortly after problematizing time as including the related terms "Age" and "age," he first mentions the word "time," but he does so when he talks of Ilúvatar finding a place for elves and men to dwell. That place is both physical (among the numberless stars) and temporal ("in the Deeps of Time") (1999a: 18). As a powerful metaphor, the latter reference cannot of course be reduced to something singular and concrete although it can, perhaps, be argued that Tolkien is suggesting here that all creation is subject to decay (Time) albeit in an exceedingly complex way (Deeps). To this view of time needs quickly to be added the fact that Tolkien soon after talks again of the concept in figurative terms. Now, time is viewed not in terms of volume (Deeps) but in terms of circularity ("the circles of time"), and now time is viewed as comprising "Later Ages," and now time is regarded as being unfinished ("history was incomplete") because Ilúvatar withdrew the sight of the world's creation from the Ainur so as to allow them to appreciate "Darkness" (1999a: 20).

So far, then, I can offer this insight into Tolkien's sense of time: the simplicity of four ages is useful but illusory as it is bracketed by a creation myth, by a sophisticated idea of causality, by the indeterminate relation between "Age" and "age," and by the literary devices of allusion and figurative language. It is also important to recall that the creation of *The Silmarillion* is in large part the work not of Tolkien but of his son as editor, that the creation of that story predates the publication of *The Lord of the Rings* by many decades even though it postdates the latter work—as far as publication is concerned—by more than two decades. So, the solidity of a "four ages" model is a later effort by Tolkien to provide simplicity with the minimum of reductiveness to a broad potential readership. In a way, that model attractively combines Tolkien's wish for accuracy and Tolkien's complex view of history. And, as usual, Tolkien is self-reflexively very aware of this play of simplicity and complexity in his vision, for he talks—on the same page as the one on which he complicates the concept of time (as elucidated above)—of the Ainur working both on a vast scale and on the smallest of canvasses (1999a: 18).

The reader is five pages into Tolkien's creation myth ("Ainulindalë") before Tolkien, in a sense, sets the clock ticking by referring to the Valar as having "entered in[to the world] at the beginning of Time" (1999a: 20). To which Tolkien adds that time is dependent on the Valar realizing that they will be responsible for making the vision of Ilúvatar a reality through the act of creation where, before, the world existed as a set of ideas described in terms of music. So, time (to which obviously the Four Ages model relates) is not neutral or detached but a consequence of agency: no creation, no time. Tolkien then goes on to describe the prehistoric struggle between the Valar and Morgoth over how the Earth would develop during its creation. "Ainulindalë" ends with a near-repetition of a phrase which is crucial to the context in which the account of the Four Ages appears in the legendarium: "in the Deeps of Time and amidst the innumerable stars" Arda was created as "the habitation of the Children of Ilúvatar" (1999a: 22).[3]

The second section of The Silmarillion is titled "Valaquenta" (or History of the Valar). It dates from the early 1930s and is admirably simple in its coverage of the Valar, the Maiar, and the enemies of the Valar: Melkor and his Maiar servant Sauron (also known, quite memorably, as Gorthaur the Cruel). It helps the reader understand the background to the achieved clarity of the Four Ages in The Lord of the Rings in important but (based on the brevity of the references to time in the account) tangential ways. In the list of the Valar (male and female), Tolkien mentions Vairë, the wife of Námo (better known as Mandos and the guardian of the houses of the dead). Throughout the "Valaquenta," Tolkien distinguishes the individual Valar in terms of their capacities, and his description of Vairë follows this pattern. She is given a heroic epithet: "the Weaver," and it is she who weaves everything into "storied webs." These "storied webs" (which are, essentially, tapestries) deck the halls of Mandos, halls which have increased in size as time has elapsed (1999a: 28).

So, again we have Tolkien working off the same sheet music in creating his legendarium. First, he plays with words when he uses the word "storied" (which means both "famous" and "related to story"). In a way, he is inserting himself as author into his own account, for without his role as writer Vairë could not be "storied" at all. Second, he uses the common term "ages" to describe time rather than specific Ages (as he was to do later). Then in the list of the Valar's enemies (Morgoth and Sauron), he refers to the battle between the Valar and Morgoth as going on over "long years" and "ages forgotten." There is surely an irony here, for one cannot count years (even long ones) without a pre-existing concept of historical moments (which we do not yet have). It is equally the case that however much time has elapsed it must be an extraordinarily long period since the ages are "forgotten" because they were so numerous or so long ago (or both). What the "Valaquenta" adds to the concept of Four Ages is crucial background, however poetic and sophisticated Tolkien makes the legendarium. The Four Ages are embedded in a back story that illuminates them just as the setting of jewel heightens the beauty of the object itself (or is, at least, is intended to).

The Two Lamps

If the first two sections of *The Silmarillion* provide a valuable if difficult background for the Four Ages, it is really only with the first chapter of the "Quenta Silmarillion" (or History of the Silmarils) that Tolkien offers the reader an absolutely relevant account of time (even though it is one which deals more with the Valar than with elves and men). And it does matter that this first chapter in the quenta should be concerned directly and exclusively with chronology: it is titled "Of the Beginning of Days." And it does matter that it begins the most substantial separable part of *The Silmarillion*. The model deserves some attention as the days are dependent on two lamps created by Aulë: Illuin in the north of Middle-earth and Ormal in the south. It is their light that creates the day, but it is an odd day of perpetual light. These lamps are destroyed by Morgoth, and their destruction brings about the end of spring in Arda (1999a: 37). Now we have added to the account (or web of the legendarium), the idea that time in an annual sense depends on the seasons (spring, for example) just as day depends on light.

The Two Trees

After the lamps are destroyed, the Valar retreat, create an abode for themselves called Valinor, and replace the lost and constant light of the two lamps with something new created by Yavanna: the Two Trees of Valinor. They are named Telperion and Laurelin. These trees wax and wane and create differential light during the day: predictably stronger or softer. It is from the moment when Telperion first shone forth that the Valar developed the idea of time as we (the readers of Tolkien's legendarium) know it: "Thus began the Days of the Bliss of Valinor; and thus began also the Count of Time" (1999a: 39). The days of bliss are specifically Valinorian; the count of time directly illuminates the idea of the Four Ages as it is from that moment that one can reckon forward to the appearance of the firstborn of the children of Ilúvatar in Middle-earth although even the Valar do not know when precisely the elves will appear. And as if to draw a line under this account of time in *The Silmarillion*, Tolkien finished the penultimate informal section of the second chapter ("Of the Beginning of Days") with this magisterial statement: "Now all is said concerning the manner of the Earth and its rulers in the beginning of days, and ere the world became such as the Children of Ilúvatar [Elves and Men] have known it" (1999a: 41).

The Sun and the Moon

The days of the bliss of Valinor do, however, come to an end when Morgoth with the help of Ungoliant the spider (of whom Shelob— it is frightening to think—is merely a lesser descendant) destroys the two trees (Telperion and Laurelin). Now another source of light must be found, and it is found when several Valar (Yavanna, Manwë, Aulë, and Varda) combine to preserve the fruit and flowers of the two trees, to enshrine them in vessels, and to make of them two lights sailing in the heavens (or Ilmen): the moon or Isil (from the tree called Telperion) and the sun or Anar (from the tree called Laurelin). It is from these new sources of light (each with the characteristics of constancy and waning that any contemporary reader would attribute to the sun and the moon in astronomy) that "the Valar reckoned the days thereafter until the Change of the World" (1999a: 101).

So, there is time as the days of the bliss of Valinor; time as the count of time; and time as experienced as four ages by the children of Ilúvatar. These are manifestly related concepts, but the first two are separable from the last. The last (the Four Ages) includes two principal elements: the First and Second Age material in the remainder of *The Silmarillion* and the Second and Third Ages in *The Lord of the Rings*, but *not* (oddly but explicably) in *The Hobbit*. However, before I come to look at those two very well-known and much-loved works, I must spend some paragraphs examining and explaining the concept of time in several lesser-known works of Tolkien's: "The Earliest Annals of Valinor," "The Later Annals of Valinor," "The Earliest Annals of Beleriand," "The Later Annals of Beleriand," and "The Tale of Years." Rather confusingly, Tolkien's son Christopher did not group the annals early and late along with "The Tale of Years" together in one volume of *The History of Middle-earth* (as he perhaps could have) but dispersed them in four volumes: *The Shaping of Middle-earth* (vol. IV in the series); *The Lost Road and Other Writings* (vol. V); *Morgoth's Ring* (vol. X; 1993); and *The War of the Jewels* (vol. XI). For the sake of clarity I will group my discussion across volumes: Valinor first, Beleriand second, the "Tale of Years" third. In essence, all of them together develop the story as I have already laid it out in my discussion of *The Silmarillion*. In essence, they offer the account of First Age and pre-First Age history that was deliberately omitted from Appendix B of *The Return of the King* because at the time that three-volume epic was published the material remained inchoate.

"The Annals of Valinor"

"The Annals of Valinor" (dispersed across *The Shaping of Middle-earth*, *The Lost Road and Other Writings*, and *Morgoth's Ring*) date in three versions from the early 1930s to 1951–2: labeled AV1, AV2, and AAm. The first version (AV1) runs from Valian year 0 (the creation by Ilúvatar) to 2998 (the chaining of Maidros by Morgoth). The second version (AV2) runs from Valian year 500 to year of the sun 1. The third version (called by Tolkien "The Annals of Aman"

(AAm), with Aman being an alternative name for the land where the Valar dwelt) runs from Valar year 1 to 3500. These versions give the reader four insights into Tolkien's sense of time. First, the Valar year is ten times the length of the solar year, so the period of time covered by these annals is 35,000 years as we calculate them now. Second, the precision of the annals' dates shows Tolkien struggling to provide the sort of clarity with a developing model of the universe that he achieved on a smaller canvas with Appendix B of *The Return of the King*. Third, the chronology is very much tied to the light of creation: stars, the two lamps, the two trees, the sun and the moon.

"The Annals of Beleriand"

"The Annals of Beleriand" date from the same eras as the three versions of the Annals of Valinor, and exist in four versions: AB1, AB2, GA1, and GA2. They are spread across *The Shaping of Middle-earth, The Lost Road and Other Writings*, and *The War of the Jewels* with the third and fourth versions of the Beleriand annals being called "The Grey Annals," a work that Tolkien abandoned before it was finished. As Beleriand is the name for a part of Middle-earth before the remaking of the lands of Middle-earth at the end of the First Age, the reader knows which period these annals deal with: history between the work of the Valar being largely completed and the expulsion of Morgoth from the world—essentially the First Age. The first version runs from year 1 to year 250. The second runs from year 1 to year 397. The third and fourth run from Valar year 1 to year of the sun 499. These versions give the reader several insights. First, at a narrative level, the annals focus on the theft of the Silmarils by Morgoth and his eventual defeat by the combined forces of the Valar, elves, and men. Second, as with the Annals of Valinor they show Tolkien's near obsession with chronological accuracy. For him, time is both mythic and alarmingly concrete: broad strokes and tiny touches. It is as if this world of his creation truly exists for him. Third, the last two versions of the Beleriand annals (GA1 and GA2) show substantial textual development. The earlier versions (AB1 and AB2) occupy less than twenty pages each; GA1 and GA2 occupy together almost 100 pages. Since GA1 and GA2 postdate the completion (but not the publication) of *The Lord of the Rings*, the reader may legitimately surmise that Tolkien was trying to give the First Age story of the Silmarils (creation, theft, recovery, loss) the same coherence and substance as *The Lord of the Rings*. In essence, he was returning to his earliest ideas (creation and the First Age) now that his later ideas (the Third Age) had reached fruition.

"The Tale of Years"

"The Tale of Years" (which appears as the fifth section of the third part of *The War of the Jewels*) is brief (at less than fifteen pages: 1999a: 342–56), but it is important because its second version (there were only two versions) dates from the early 1950s when Tolkien was trying to make the story of the Silmarils coherent and compelling—and for that to happen Tolkien needed to construct a calendar of events that would pass muster with him. Christopher Tolkien does not, unfortunately, in this case reprint the text and add a commentary. He simply has a commentary which refers to particular parts of the "Tale of Years" for illustrative purposes. What can be gleaned from the editor's treatment of the material is as follows. First, it is very much in agreement with the "Annals of Aman" and the "Grey Annals" until the latter was abandoned by Tolkien. Then (when it picks up the narrative where the "Grey Annals" left off), the "Tale" comes into its own as a "major source for the end of the Elder Days, and indeed in almost all respects the only source deriving from the completion of *The Lord of the Rings*, woefully inadequate as it is" (1994d: 344–5). Second, in his discussion, Christopher Tolkien focuses on the First Age years 500–600 to show how much time Tolkien spent polishing the details of the story—because he was a perfectionist and because the story (even if he may have doubted the narrative would ever be published in his lifetime) mattered to him. It had reality because it was his private universe given substance through an act of sub-creation. Third, verisimilitude mattered to Tolkien even in fantasy (or, perhaps, *especially* in fantasy). For example, Tolkien had some difficulties in his chronology deciding whether Morgoth's fortress of Angband was or was not built upon the ruins of his earlier fortress of Utumno. Tolkien simply wrote on the manuscript that two years (1495 to 1497) was "[t]oo small a time for Morgoth to

build Angband" and, later, "Time too small, should be 10 at least
or 20 Valian Years" (quoted on 1994d: 344). Fourth, Tolkien took
seriously the issue of labeling as it relates to time. So, when his
account deals with the moment the Elder Days ended he ascribes
that end to two possible narrative moments. As he puts it:

> Here end the Elder Days with the new reckoning of time,
> according to some. But most lore-masters give that name also
> to the years of the war with Morgoth until his overthrow and
> casting forth. (1994d: 343)

Some, then, use the term to cover only the days before the sun and
moon were created—the work of the Valar. Some, however, use the
term to cover all the events of the First Age (which would include
both elves and men). Why does this matter? Because Tolkien, in
describing the reach of time, could have chosen to be definitive but
pretended he couldn't be. Yet he wants it both ways for he lines up
"some" against "most": there is, then, a minority and a majority
opinion with Tolkien an absent judge. Finally, with time—just as
with my earlier discussion (in Chapter 2) of the legendarium—
Tolkien works within a complex frame story in the "Tale of Years"
as well as in the annals. To various authors are these texts or parts
of these texts attributed: Quennar Onótimo; Pengoloð, and Rúmil
(or some combination of these three). The effect of this narrative
envelope is to render the details contingent upon the authority of
the teller as well as distancing the real author (Tolkien) from the
creation of the text. In a sense (and this was probably Tolkien's
intent) the story becomes more real, and in his development of the
idea of time in a fantasy world that verisimilitude matters more
than in, say, a novel embodying realism.

The Hobbit

When it comes to the treatment of Time, *The Hobbit* is (as so often
in Tolkien) a very different sort of work. Published in 1937, it was
written by someone who had spent years creating a mythology
around the story of the Silmarils, and explicit in that story is an
emphasis on the idea of ages: First and Second and, by implication
at least, Third. *The Hobbit* makes only four mentions of this
concept of ages as outlined in *The Silmarillion*. Each shows how

little Tolkien is concerned with the broader legendarium as, after all, he is just engaged in writing a one-off children's story meant to explain who or what hobbits are. The first mention comes early in the story (Chapter 3), the second and third midway (Chapter 8), and the last one very late (Chapter 19). The first talks of Elrond in this way:

> The master of the house was an elf-friend—one of those people whose fathers came into the strange stories before the beginning of History, the wars of the evil goblins and the elves and the first men in the north. (2007a: 48)

So, we have in crude terms: First Age material (elves and orcs) and Second Age material (Númenor). The second mention occurs when Tolkien as narrator becomes preoccupied with defining the various types of elves. He opines that most of the wood elves "were descended from the ancient tribes that never went to Faerie in the West" (2007a: 154). Here, Tolkien merely touches on the long and painful history of the ways in which in *The Silmarillion* the elves are sundered from each other by dint of having different attitudes, broadly speaking, to Valinor. The third talks of the wood elves as having "lingered in the twilight of our Sun and Moon" (2007a: 154). As before, Tolkien is merely alluding to the complicated story of how light came to Eru's creation of Middle-earth. The last mention concerns a conversation between the wise at the end of the story. Gandalf and Elrond talk about the Necromancer (Tolkien's alternative term for Sauron). Gandalf and the rest of the white wizards had succeeded in driving the Necromancer out of Mirkwood. As a result, Gandalf says, Mirkwood "will grow somewhat more wholesome" (2007a: 271) and "The North will be freed from that horror [the Necromancer] for many long years, I hope." He finishes almost wistfully: "Yet I wish he were banished from the world!" (2007a: 271). To which Elrond replies, "It would be well indeed, but I fear that will not come about in this age of the world, or for many after" (2007a: 271). So, here is the age concept, but presented in a way that both acknowledges it and denies it, for in place of the three or four ages of the world the infinitely wise Elrond talks of "many." It is as if Tolkien subverts his mythology even as he pays attention to it. If this is the case, it is hardly surprising as *The Hobbit* is Tolkien's only sustained children's story, and it is a story focused on explaining at length who the hobbits are and why what they can accomplish (in the form of Bilbo Baggins' exploits) matters. Now, the hobbits are connected with Tolkien's legendarium through characters such as Gandalf and Elrond, but it is crucial to remember that the hobbits only become vital once Tolkien made the decision to have the One Ring be the means of joining one part of the mythology (*The Hobbit*, a children's story) with another (*The Lord of the Rings*, an epic). And that decision came after Tolkien published *The Hobbit* and had *The Silmarillion* rejected by George Allen & Unwin as its sequel.

The Hobbit does have numerous references to time, but these are colloquial and not ones specifically related to Tolkien's mythology. So, we have talk of "long ago" (2007a: 4) and "long ago in the quiet of the world" (5) and "a hundred years ago last Thursday" (24) and "ages ago" (89). There are more than a dozen references to time in this commonplace way. These references cumulatively emphasize the degree to which *The Hobbit* exists outside the developed and sophisticated chronology that was crystallized in Appendix B of *The Lord of the Rings*. It was only and ever conceived of as a children's story. That is its origin (an oral tale told to his three sons). It is not (as Tolkien's earliest biographer, Daniel Grotta, claimed in *The Biography of J. R. R. Tolkien: Architect of Middle-earth*), a work in which *The Silmarillion* and the legend of Númenor are "synthesized" (1992: 45). Far from it.

Appendix B of *The Lord of the Rings*

In essence, Appendix B (with a mention of which this chapter began) was Tolkien's last chance to explain his concept of time.[4] As I mentioned earlier, the appendix begins with a few simple statements about the First, Second, Third, and Fourth Ages. As the appendix only covers the Second and Third Ages in detail (one gets the sense that Tolkien in the early 1950s was feeling the winged chariot of time steered by his publisher more keenly than ever), the chronology as outlined omits the First and much of the Fourth Ages. However, each of the two ages that are covered in detail begins with a paragraph or two by way of summary, and each summary is fascinating for what it reveals of Tolkien's preoccupations with time. The Second Age shows how much Tolkien elided the reality of what he had been able to create by 1955 and the publication of *The Lord of the Rings*. The first paragraph about the Second Age reads:

These were the dark years for Men of Middle-earth, but the years of the glory of Númenor. Of events in Middle-earth the records are few and brief, and their dates are often uncertain. (1994c: 1057)

What matters here is Tolkien's sensitivity to audience: his readers are human, so it would matter to them what the status of humans would be ("Men of Middle-earth") more than that of the demigod Númenóreans. What matters also is how Tolkien elides the reality of authorship with the constraints of myth. Yes, the records of the Second Age are few and that can be put down to the cataclysmic way in which it ended, but they are few too because Tolkien wrote very little about this age—in part, I think, because conceptually that age was always too tightly bound up with the Atlantis story. So, just as many had written about King Arthur (and, so, that myth only appears in one work by Tolkien) so many had written about Atlantis. And, yes, there is no such thing as originality in creation, but some stories are more hackneyed than others. So, Tolkien understandably expended his energies on work that bore his own stamp (*The Silmarillion, The Hobbit, The Lord of the Rings*) rather than on something derivative ("Akallabêth"). In the best traditions of *Beowulf* (a work which Tolkien knew better than any philologist of his era), the remaining two paragraphs of the headnote to the Second Age are an exercise in extended name-dropping: Thranduil, Gil-galad, Celeborn, Thingol, Galadriel, Finrod Felagund, Beren, Barahir, Durin, Celebrimbor, and last (and greatest) Fëanor. To this list is added a third strategy on Tolkien's part: to use an opportunity to stress the camaraderie among peoples (in this case elves and dwarves: the "Elven-smiths of Eregion" and "the people of Durin").

The Third Age, perhaps in keeping with Tolkien's emphasis on that age in his epic *The Lord of the Rings*, begins with a five-paragraph headnote in contrast to the three paragraphs given over to the Second Age. Again, there is the epic name-dropping: Sauron, Saruman, Gandalf, Gil-galad, Galadriel, Círdan, and Elrond. And now there are a several new strategies. One is to point out that while the One Ring is always and only Sauron's, the three elvish rings of power do not always belong to the same individuals. Gil-galad, Círdan, and Galadriel were the original owners, but Gil-galad passed his to Elrond and Círdan his to Gandalf. So only Galadriel was sole possessor of her ring since its creation, and, as *The Lord of the Rings* points out, Galadriel passes the test of false or evil power: when she could have taken the One Ring from Frodo she resists the temptation. In the same way, her own ring is always used to protect living things—especially the trees in Lothlórien.

Another Tolkien strategy is to stress the amount of time that passes in Middle-earth ("When maybe a thousand years had passed" begins the second paragraph (1994c: 1059)). A third is to emphasize how important were the elves to Tolkien. In truth, they mattered even more to him than did the hobbits. The hobbits were the direct cause of his first mass-market success as a writer. The elves were the darlings of his early manhood, for they even predate the horrors of the Somme and came into full flower by the time he was thirty. So, the headnote does not begin with some statement about the Third Age being the age of men. No. Tolkien starts out with this stark comment: "These were the fading years of the Eldar." Men come to prominence because the Eldar fade and the Númenóreans' blood is adulterated with that of "lesser Men" and because the Istari (or Wizards) were dispatched to Middle-earth to deal with Sauron not in their true shape but "in the shape of Men" (1994c: 1059).

The Important Dates in Appendix B

There are some fifteen pages of chronology in the appendix (1994c: 1058–1072), so I will only highlight the dates that matter because they reveal something important about Tolkien's complex creation of Middle-earth. Before I do that, it is important to point out that the Third Age is subdivided (perhaps of necessity as it was the age on which Tolkien focused in *The Lord of the Rings*). An undifferentiated chronology in Appendix B is followed by sections given over to "The Great Years" (3018 and 3019), "The Chief Days" (3019–3021), and "Later Events Concerning the Members of the Fellowship of the Ring" (Shire Reckoning 1422 to 1541) (Tolkien 1994c: 1065, 1070, 1071). What this subdivision usefully tells us is how much Tolkien himself made value judgments in his attitude to time ("Great" and "Chief") and how much his focus turned from elves to hobbits (with the temporal calculation turning at the end to "Shire Reckoning" and away from the more magisterial and accepted annals of years). It is also worthwhile in understanding the sophistication of Tolkien's legendarium that he uses a simple device of approximation as a means of distancing himself as author from his creation while at the same time heightening the apparently separate and real existence of the world he has created. Seven times in the appendix he uses *c*. (that is, *circa* or "about") to indicate that a particular date is only approximate. So, for example, when it comes to the most important single creation in his entire legendarium, the One Ring, he can only say that it was created "*c*. 1600" of the Second Age. Indeed, he is equally vague about when the rings of power in general were created. In part, that is for a narrative reason: they were created in secret. In part, it is for the purpose of diminishing the power of Tolkien as sub-creator. He could be as specific as he likes with any and all dates. The fact that he isn't suggests the events have a reality beyond his ability to control them. It is an important, subtle device.

The Second Age

Year 1	The Grey Havens are founded. So, the Second Age begins at the place where the Ring Bearers' story ends, for it is in S. R. (Shire Reckoning) 1482 of the Fourth Age that, legend has it, Sam (Master Samwise) went to the Grey Havens "and passed over Sea, last of the Ring-bearers" (1994c: 1097).
Year 442	Elros dies. As the mortal brother of the immortal Elrond, Elros's death draws attention to the permanent and consequential nature of the choices we all make.
c. Year 1000	Sauron begins constructing Barad-dûr. The site of this fortress is indeed ancient by the end of the epic, and the building of it takes an extraordinarily long time as it is not until "*c*. 1600" that the fortress is completed.
Year 1693	The Three Rings of the Elves are "hidden."
Year 1697	Rivendell (Imladris) is founded by Elrond. It is, then, a much newer place than Barad-dûr. Is Tolkien making some point here about the nature of evil and good?

Years 1700–1701	Sauron is "defeated" and "driven out of Eriador." So it is important to note this early on that Sauron can be beaten. He is a lesser tyrant than Morgoth/Melkor. Yet the peace that comes from his defeat lasts only for about 100 years. Evil cannot be finally vanquished.
Year 2251	The Nazgûl first appear. So, they postdate Barad-dûr in Sauron's designs by 1,500 years.
Year 3262	Sauron is captured by the Númenóreans, but within forty-eight years (by 3310) Sauron has corrupted the Númenóreans. It may take Sauron 600 years to build a fortress, but corrupting men is an altogether quicker and easier act.
Year 3319	Downfall of Númenor. It has lasted less than 3,000 years.
Year 3430	The Last Alliance of Elves and Men.
Year 3441	Sauron is overthrown and Isildur takes the One Ring. Tolkien once again points out that evil can be defeated if its enemies combine. At the same time, power is corrupting. Had Isildur destroyed the One Ring in the Cracks of Doom when he had the chance, how different would the Third Age have been? It is also notable that once war happens it happens fast. The First War of the Ring lasts just eleven years—close to the combined total of World War I and World War II.

The Third Age

Year 2	If the Second Age began with a burst of creation (the founding of the Grey Havens), so does the Third Age, for it is in this year that Isildur "plants a seedling of the White Tree in Minas Anor" (1994c: 1060). So, good is in some ways a deliberate veneration of continuity and tradition. One can say many harsh things about Isildur, in particular about his foolish

possessiveness with regard to the One Ring, but this is a worthy and loving act toward nature. As if to emphasize its poignance, it is in this same year that Isildur and his three sons are slain by orcs. Isildur possessed the One Ring for less than two years.

Year 3   The shards of Narsil (the sword broken in the battle against Sauron that concluded the Second Age) are taken to Rivendell for protection. So, by the time Narsil is reforged as Anduril (an event not mentioned in the appendix), it has been in existence in broken form for more than 3,000 years.

Year 241   Arwen Evenstar (Undómiel) is born. When Aragorn dies, she is 2,896 years old. The elves' lifespan is extraordinary, just as their fading is a cause for sorrow. By contrast, Aragorn lives for only 210 years even though he is of the Númenórean race.

Year 1050   Evil returns to Greenwood. It is now called Mirkwood. So, it has taken only a little more than 1,000 years for Sauron to return.

c. Year 1300   The hobbits make their westward migration. By 1601, they have been granted rights to land in what becomes known as the Shire. So, by the time the Third Age comes to an end in 3021 they have occupied that land for over 1,400 years. That is ancient history to them; it would not be to the elves. Time, for Tolkien, is relative.

Year 1409   Amon Sûl (Weathertop) is destroyed by the Witch-king of Angmar. So, by the time Gandalf is attacked there as well as Aragorn, Frodo, Merry, and Pippin in October 3018, the tower has been ruined for more than 1,600 years. Amon Sûl itself was built around 3320 in the Second Age, so it existed in full or ruined state for nearly 3,200 years. The reputation *The Lord of the Rings* has for taking the long historical view is earned.

Year 1636   The White Tree dies in Minas Anor. By the time
                    Aragorn finds a sapling of the tree in 3019, it
                    has been almost 1,400 years since it died.
Year 1980   A balrog in Moria slays Durin VI. So when
                    Gandalf defends the fellowship against another
                    (or the same?) balrog in Moria in 3019 they
                    have been foes to dwarves, men, elves, and
                    Istari for more than 1,200 years. Evil lasts long
                    in Tolkien's world.
Year 2050   The rule of the stewards in Gondor begins after
                    King Eärnur is killed by the Witch-king. As the
                    reign of the stewards had lasted for almost a
                    thousand years by the end of the Third Age,
                    Denethor's belief that he is the rightful ruler
                    of the city of Minas Tirith and the kingdom
                    of Gondor is understandable but tragically
                    mistaken.
Year 2463   The White Council is formed. It is an ancient
                    council by the time it is dissolved in 2953. One
                    cannot help but think of the Inklings and how
                    long that group lasted.
Year 2470   Sméagol (Gollum) takes possession of the One
                    Ring. When he dies in the Cracks of Doom in
                    3019, he is nearly 550 years old. The power
                    of the Ring to bring long life to its owner is
                    remarkable.
Year 2747   Bandobras Took defeats a band of orcs in
                    the Shire. So, hobbits' knowledge of Sauron's
                    creatures is deep even if they forget that fact.
Year 2759   Saruman takes up residence in Orthanc. By the
                    time he is evicted by Gandalf and the ents, he
                    has been its tenant for more than 250 years.
Year 2933   Aragorn meets Arwen Undómiel for the first
                    time in Rivendell. By the time they marry in
                    3019 they have essentially been pledged to each
                    other for more than eighty years. Tolkien is a
                    romantic when it comes to love.
Years 2941–2942   The events recounted in *The Hobbit* occur in
                    these years, so there is a gap of some eighty
                    years between the time Bilbo finds the Ring

	and its destruction by Gollum. Again, Tolkien condenses history in the name of dramatic tension.
Year 2951	Sauron begins to rebuild Barad-dûr. It lasts for less than seventy years in its new iteration.
Year 2956	Aragorn and Gandalf meet for the first time (in Rivendell). Their friendship is one of more than sixty years when the Ring is destroyed.
Year 2980	Gollum meets Shelob for the first time, so they have known each other for almost forty years when Shelob almost succeeds in killing Frodo in Cirith Ungol.
Year 2994	Balin is killed in Moria by Orcs, so when the fellowship comes upon his grave he has been dead for twenty-five years.
Year 3001	Bilbo's farewell feast and the beginning of *The Lord of the Rings*. That narrative, then, recounts twenty years of events.
Year 3008	Gandalf pays his last visit to Frodo before the fateful years of the War of the Ring, so there is a ten-year hiatus in the narrative, a hiatus that Tolkien glosses over in the interests of narrative pacing.
Years 3018–3021	The years that form the principal action of *The Lord of the Rings*. In the appendix, Tolkien calls them "The Great Years." It is hard not to see this as a conscious echo of World War I being called the Great War.
Year 3021	The Third Age ends with the departure over the sea of Frodo and Bilbo and the "Three Keepers" of the elven rings: Gandalf, Elrond, and Galadriel. As before, an age ends with the defeat of evil.

Between the account of the Great Years and the last two sections of the appendix, "The Chief Days" and "Later Events," Tolkien inserts four paragraphs of summary that cover events not directly described in *The Lord of the Rings*. The two most interesting points to glean from this section are, first, that Galadriel left Middle-earth, but for a period of time her husband, Celeborn, stayed until he grew weary of Lothlórien and went to Rivendell to stay with Elrond. Galadriel, however, achieved one remarkable thing before she left for the Undying Lands. She defeated the remnants of Sauron's northern armies and destroyed Sauron's northern stronghold of Dol Guldur. She did so in a way reminiscent of the defeat of Morgoth at the end of the First Age (1994c: 1094). The second point worthy of note is that even after Sauron is defeated remnants of his followers continued to fight on. In addition to the northern army defeated by Galadriel and others, the Easterlings besiege the Lonely Mountain and slay King Brand and King Daín Ironfoot. Ultimately, the dwarves and the men of Dale are victorious, but this section of Tolkien's narrative summary shows that the historical arc of *The Hobbit* is a long one. He seems intent on connecting his earlier children's story with his later epic as if to prove once and for all that they are connected—precisely because they were *not* when he wrote *The Hobbit*.

The Fourth Age

Tolkien offers less than two pages of key dates in the early history of this age. These dates cover only 120 years, and they are in Shire Reckoning as if to stress how vital was the hobbits' contribution to the saving of the West.

These dates focus on the later civic life of Sam Gamgee. He becomes mayor of the Shire no less than seven times over a fifty-year period. They also point out that Merry becomes mayor of Buckland and Pippin the Took and Thain. The Shire grows in size with the acquisition by the king's gift of the Westmarch. The accounting of these years is sad too, however, with Sam's beloved wife, Rosie, dying in SR 1482. In that same year, Sam goes to the Grey Havens and passes over sea. In SR 1484, Merry and Pippin travel to see King Éomer and are never seen again in the Shire. In that year, too, Éomer himself dies. The final date in the appendix is SR 1541, and it comes after a gap of nearly sixty years in the accounting. In that year, there is death too: Aragorn dies, and Gimli and his great friend Legolas sail down the Anduin and pass over sea. At that point the story is truly over with all the members of the fellowship being accounted for. It is as if, in the end, Tolkien's accounting of time is less about the broad strokes of history and much more about the ways in which friendship lasts even until the inevitable end.

Tolkien writes history from the perspective of fantasy, but it is ultimately a movingly personal tale: *The Silmarillion, The Hobbit, The Lord of the Rings* and all the many ancillary works Tolkien's son, Christopher, has so faithfully brought to light and edited.

GEOGRAPHY

The Creation of the World

In the "Ainulindalë" (Tolkien's creation story), Eru (also called Ilúvatar) creates elves and men and then creates a world in which they may live. That world is called Arda (an Elvish word) and is a part of the wider universe that Tolkien terms "Eä, the World That Is" (1999a: 20), and the one part in which his creations live is dubbed Middle-earth.[5] The Ainur (or angels) are the ones responsible for giving Ilúvatar's ideas form. Quite remarkably, Tolkien comments that the world is one which "still the Ainur are shaping" (1999a: 18). That is, the sorts of physical changes to the world that occur in Tolkien's legendarium are still continuing in the world in which we (Tolkien's readers) live. This creation of Arda occurs long before the First Age even begins, and it is not an easy creation because of the interference of Melkor (later called Morgoth by the Elves). Nevertheless, Arda comes into being by the end of the "Ainulindalë" even though it is not the world as the Ainur meant it to be. On the contrary, Arda in no way wholly reflects the intentions of the Valar (1999a: 22). It is utterly fascinating (and disarmingly realistic) that Tolkien saw creation as a messy thing.

The First Age

During the First Age, that age in which elves, men, and later the Valar too battle with Melkor/Morgoth, Arda consists of an encircling sea (called Ekkaia), a land where the Valar dwell (Aman), and the Sundering Seas (Belegaer) separating Valinor from Middle-

earth (where the children of Ilúvatar and the dwarves dwell).
Middle-earth (also called Endor) consists of a northern region of
extreme cold (Dor Daidelos), a midsection (Palissor), the Hither
Lands, and the Dark Land in the south. The northwest of Middle-
earth was termed Beleriand.[6] In the first battle between the Valar
and Melkor when the Valar successfully overthrow Melkor in his
fortress of Utumno, the world is remade—as Tolkien describes
in some detail and with considerable specificity. The Great Sea
that separates Middle-earth from Aman (where the Valar dwell)
deepens and grows wider. The sea also creates many new bays,
in particular the Bay of Balar. And the countryside in the north
becomes "desolate" (Tolkien 1999a: 51). Then, in the final battle
of the First Age (called the Great Battle or the War of Wrath), the
conflict between the Valar and Morgoth was so colossal that the
world is remade once again as a result of immense destruction,
a process that creates new rivers and destroys old ones—among
them Sirion (Tolkien 1999a: 252).

The Second Age

In addition to the reshaping of Middle-earth as a consequence of
the War of Wrath, the Valar also reshaped the world by creating an
island for the Edain (men of the people of Haleth and the houses of
Bëor and Hador) who fought with the Valar against Morgoth. They
created an island (Andor or Númenor) separate from Middle-earth
and from Valinor. For almost all of the Second Age, much of Middle-
earth looked markedly different from the Middle-earth with which
the general reader of Tolkien's work is familiar from *The Lord of
the Rings* and, to a lesser extent, from *The Hobbit*. However, at the
end of the Second Age disaster strikes the Númenóreans, as a result
of their pride. Númenorë sinks below the waves, and the coasts of
Middle-earth are ravaged. Toward the end of the "Akallabêth" and
in describing the flight of Elendil and Isildur and Anárion from the
wrath of the Valar, Tolkien talks of how some islands disappear
and new ones are formed, hills are leveled, and rivers take a new
direction (1999a: 280). In addition, the world that was flat was
made round, and the ability of men to sail to Valinor was lost.

And, so, the map of the world in the Third Age came into being.

The Third Age

Much less needs to be said of the geography of this age, for there are well-known maps in *The Hobbit* and *The Lord of the Rings*. It is worth pointing out two things, however. First, the geography of Middle-earth in *The Hobbit* and *The Lord of the Rings* is not wholly in agreement. That is hardly surprising as the former was a children's story written without any idea of the latter creation. Second, at the end of the Third Age (which occurs when Bilbo, Frodo, Gandalf, Elrond, and Galadriel leave Middle-earth), there is no remaking of the world as there was at the end of the First and Second Ages. However, Tolkien leaves open the real possibility that such a reshaping may occur in the future as the Valar "watch the unfolding of the story of the world" (1999a: 282).

Notes

1 *The Return of the King* was published in 1955; *The Silmarillion* in 1977 (although the material contained therein dates back to early World War I).

2 For a detailed study of geographical change in Arda and Middle-earth, the best place to start is with Karen Wynn Fonstad's *The Atlas of Middle Earth* (1981; rev. edn, 1991).

3 On page 18, Tolkien had written "a place for their [Elves and Men's] habitation in the Deeps of Time and in the midst of the innumerable stars."

4 It is important to note here that the twelfth volume of Christopher Tolkien's *The History of Middle-earth*, which is titled *The Peoples of Middle-earth*, looks extensively in Chapters 6 and 8 at Tolkien's earlier versions and alternative versions of Appendix B in the published *Lord of the Rings*. I have decided in the interests of clarity not to discuss these alternative versions of the published material, but interested readers are encouraged to look there for a detailed sense of what Tolkien's thinking was about the important events in the Second, Third, and Fourth Ages of Middle-earth.

5 The word "Middle-earth" first appears in *The Silmarillion* in the section of the "Valaquenta" called "Of the Valar" (Tolkien 1999a: 25). There it is used to distinguish between two Elvish languages: that which was spoken in Valinor, and that which was spoken in Middle-

earth. The term is used almost offhandedly by Tolkien. That may be because of his deep knowledge of Anglo-Saxon, a language in which Middle-earth is used to describe the world in which all living things exist. It is not until the "Quenta Silmarillion" itself that Middle-earth is seen geographically as a location needing to be lit and as a location with a north through which Melkor invades and tries to overthrow the Valar (Tolkien 1999a: 35, 36).

6 That land, in which so many of the crucial events in *The Silmarillion* occur is fully described in the fourteenth chapter of the "Quenta Silmarillion": "Of Beleriand and Its Realms" (Tolkien 1999a: 118–24).

5

Tolkien on Peoples

The focus of this chapter is on the peoples or, better, species with which Tolkien filled his created world of Middle-earth. One can usefully compare, as far as creation myths are concerned, Tolkien's legendarium with Milton's *Paradise Lost*. Tolkien's story is markedly more complex, for Milton talked only of God and angels and humans. Tolkien talks of the Valar and elves and men and dwarves and orcs and, most famously, hobbits. And those are only the principal categories, for each category is further subdivided historically or geographically or linguistically or politically into different and distinct groups. There are also singletons to be considered, such as Tom Bombadil and Beorn as well as people and creatures who play crucial roles in the legendarium. So, there are wizards and ents and eagles and spiders. It is not my intent to be exhaustive; it is my intent to provide enough information to make engaging with Tolkien's world as rich an experience as I can for the enthusiast. It is, finally, also true that Tolkien's task was rendered much harder by a task he set himself. When he talks of elves he is determined to reinvent the concept of faerie. In a polemical way, he wished to overturn the nineteenth-century view of fairies as gossamer-winged, fragile creatures. In Tolkien's view, fantasy writers such as George MacDonald and mystery writers such as Sir Arthur Conan Doyle had much to answer for in popularizing this mistaken view of fairies, and he was determined to set the record straight.

What I will offer in this chapter is a synthetic, general view of Tolkien's depiction of peoples. I will focus on the major works (*The Silmarillion, The Hobbit, The Lord of the Rings*), but my portrait will be fleshed out by my understanding of other, less-well-known

Tolkien works.[1] My discussion will begin with Tolkien's portrayal of elves, for they are the "firstborn" children of Ilúvatar and, arguably, the people whom Tolkien cared for most and wrote about most. It will then move on to men (the "Followers" or "Aftercomers"), dwarves (who were created not by Ilúvatar but by Aulë), hobbits (beloved by Tolkien but troublesome latecomers to the legendarium), and orcs. It will then move on to groups of peoples worthy of study because they are important to the development of the legendarium's narrative: Valar, Maiar, wizards, and Nazgûl. It will conclude with the curious case of singletons in the legendarium: Beorn and Tom Bombadil.

Elves

The elves show up for the first time early in *The Silmarillion*: within four pages of the beginning of the creation story, "Ainulindalë."[2] Here Tolkien talks of the children of Ilúvatar (elves and men) and makes some crucial comments about them. First, elves (and men) were Ilúvatar's creation alone. That is, the Ainur had no role in their coming into being. Second, elves (and men) were part of Ilúvatar's third musical theme; they were not part of his original music. They were, then, a late idea of the creator's. Third, elves (and men) are particularly beloved by the Ainur because they are utterly different from them and possess strangeness and freedom. Fourth, elves (and men) are a reflection of Ilúvatar's wisdom and, so, show a part of Ilúvatar's mind that would be otherwise unknown to the Ainur (Tolkien 1999a: 18).

By the end of the "Ainulindalë," the picture of what elves are has become more complicated as Tolkien refers to "Eldalië" and "Eldar" as particular types (apparently) of elves. Yet a reader—even one reasonably well versed in the legendarium as a result of reading *The Hobbit* and *The Lord of the Rings*—might not remember what these labels refer to in the taxonomy of the elves. After all, *The Hobbit* first mentions elves of a particular kind when Elrond talks of "High Elves of the West" (Tolkien 2007a: 49). *The Lord of the Rings* first mentions elves as "Fair Folk" (Tolkien 1994a: 44) and subsequently talks of social hierarchy ("Elf-lords" (50) and "High Elves" (78)) and, most puzzling perhaps, of elves as "Exiles" (79).

Even the Appendices to *The Lord of the Rings* offer only a little help as Tolkien is more interested, there, in languages and hobbits and men and dwarves. Especially hobbits.

The best way to understand Tolkien's view of elves is to look at them historically, linguistically, and geographically while at the same time realizing that Tolkien used many labels for divisions and subdivisions among them. That is, he could sometimes be referring to the same group of elves and yet use a different terminology. When the elves were created by Ilúvatar they were one people.[3] The first major division between them (referred to as the "first sundering") occurred when the Valar become afraid for the safety of the elves and, wishing to have the elves' companionship, instruct them to leave Cuiviénen in Middle-earth and journey to Aman, specifically to Valinor (1999a: 52). Nearby, the Valar create for the elves a place called Eldamar (or Elvenholme). Those who obeyed the instruction are known as the Eldar or Edalië (which was the name the Vala Oromë first gave them and means "the people of the stars"). Those who did not obey are known as the Avari (which means "the Unwilling"). Tolkien makes it clear that the Eldar are superior to the Avari because they saw Aman. Indeed, they are superior to the Avari in the same way that the Avari are superior to men. There is that much difference between them (Tolkien 1999a: 104).

The Eldar were further subdivided into three groups: the Vanyar (also known as the "Fair Elves") led by Ingwë; the Noldor or Noldoli (also known as the "deep elves") led by Finwë and renowned for courage and wisdom; and the Teleri (also known as the "sea elves" or Falmari) led by Elwë Singollo and his brother, Olwë. Collectively, these three groups are called the Calaquendi ("elves of the light") because they have seen the light of the Two Trees that illuminate Aman. Then there are those (mainly of the Teleri) who never made it to Valinor even though they tried to. This group is called the Úmanyar (or "Those not of Aman") by the Calaquendi, and the Úmanyar and the Avari collectively are known, again by the Calaquendi, as the Moriquendi ("elves of the darkness").

Finally, there are four more groups of elves who need to be mentioned. The first is a group which fell into oblivion because they gave up the journey as a result of fear (Tolkien 1999a: 53). The second is a large group of the Teleri, led by Lenwë, who decide to go southwards down the river Anduin the Great. They were known as the Nandor ("Those who Turn Back") or wood elves and became deeply knowledgeable about all living things. Some of them eventually returned and settled in Ossiriand and became known as the Laiquendi or green elves. The third is a group of the Teleri led by Elwë Singollo. He falls in love with and marries a Maia, Melian. They settle in Beleriand, and their people become known as the Sindar (the "grey elves") and the elves of the twilight. The last is a group of Teleri, led by Círdan the Shipwright, who are persuaded by the Vala Ossë to settle on the west coast of Beleriand in an area called Falas. They became known as the Falathrim.

The second major division among the elves occurs specifically among one group of the Eldar: the Noldor. Fëanor creates the three Silmarils, beautiful beyond description. Melkor, now named Morgoth by the Eldar ("the Black Enemy"), steals them and flees Aman for Middle-earth. Fëanor and his seven sons swear a terrible oath to pursue until the end of time any creature who steals a Silmaril (Tolkien 1999a: 83). That oath causes 90 percent of the Noldor (among them Galadriel) to leave Elvenholme in Aman and make the perilous journey back to Middle-earth. However, even that group of the Noldor is riven by internal conflict. Fëanor and those loyal to him fight the Teleri for their ships and kill many of them in an act called "The Kinslaying." Fëanor then takes the ships, makes it to Middle-earth, and burns the ships so that the remaining Noldor (again including Galadriel) have to make the appallingly difficult journey to Middle-earth through the "bitterest North" and the "terror of the Helcaraxë and the cruel hills of ice" (Tolkien 1999a: 90). So, in essence, there are three principal groupings of elves by the end of the First Age: those who never journeyed to Aman; those who journeyed there and stayed; and those who journeyed there only to return to Middle-earth, in part because of Fëanor's oath and in part because they missed Middle-earth. The last group became the exiles. By the time of *The Lord of the Rings*, it will be remembered, we have two important elves in the narrative: Legolas, who is Sindarin and a wood elf, and Galadriel, who is Noldorin and one of those whom Mandos calls "The Dispossessed." All of these labels and names can be bewildering, but the most important thing to remember is not the labels themselves but what they represent: Tolkien's fascination with anthropological development. His insight is that over time one people will divide in predictable ways: geographically, historically, politically. His insight, too, is the academic one: that taxonomy is always a useful strategy for explaining a topic.

Another way to look at the various groups of elves is a way dear to Tolkien's heart: linguistically. As he was a philologist, Tolkien constructed his mythology in large part to allow him to construct convincing, detailed languages. It was on Elvish, however, that he spent the great majority of his time and considerable energy. If you think of how different English and American have become and why, or if you think of how different French and French-Canadian have become and why, then you can see the accuracy of Tolkien's depiction of linguistic variation among elves. Tolkien developed two principal Elvish languages: Quenya and Sindarin. Quenya is the language of those elves who journeyed to Elevenhome: the Vanyar and the Noldor and some of the Teleri. Sindarin is the language of those elves, the Avari, who stayed in Middle-earth and, so, never saw the light of the Two Trees. Within these two broad categories are various dialects, so one can speak, for example, of Noldorin Quenya (which has the same elevated status as Latin) and Nandorin (the language of those elves who stayed in Middle-earth and specifically journeyed south).

Much can also be written about the physical characteristics and customs of elves, but that topic lies outside the limits of this book as most of these can be gleaned by anyone prepared to read *The Hobbit* and *The Lord of the Rings* thoroughly.[4] It is important to note, however, that the elves are different in one vital respect from men and dwarves and orcs: they are immortal. They can only die from wounds in battle or from grief. They can literally fade away from sorrow. *The Silmarillion* emphasizes this difference by having Ilúvatar himself (in the form of reported speech) be the one to outline the distinction (Tolkien 1999a: 42).

Men

Before I launch into the same sort of categorization as I just undertook with the elves, I should begin with the mortality of men, for it is the single biggest distinction between men and elves. In the same section of *The Silmarillion* as that in which Ilúvatar talks of elvish immortality as a sorrow, Tolkien contrasts that quality with the brevity of human life and considers this brevity to be akin to a sort of freedom "to shape their life, amid the powers and chances of the world" (Tolkien 1999a: 41). For Tolkien, the fact that humans die is a "gift" that even the Ainur shall come to envy, and he concludes by arguing that the reason we see death as a thing to be feared and not as a gift is because of Melkor, who has made of it something dark and evil—something to be afraid of (1999a: 42). In truth, death is a gift and a light and a good and a hope. Indeed, it is very much the sort of *Eucatastrophe* or "Consolation of the Happy Ending" (Tolkien 1997c: 153) that Tolkien talks about in his essay "On Fairy-Stories."[5]

Men are not coeval with elves. The elves date from before the First Age begins, but men do not awaken until the First Age begins with the rising of the sun. Interestingly, this detail is the first one that the chapter titled "Of Men" mentions (Tolkien 1999a: 103–5). It is also interesting how little space Tolkien gives to men at this point in the narrative (one and a half pages) in comparison to the space devoted to the first appearance of the elves: eight pages (1999a: 47–54). Men are born in the East of Middle-earth but travel west because that is where the sun first arose (1999a: 103). They are called the Atani by the Eldar (which means the second people) and the Hildor (the followers) and the Apanónar (the after-born) and the children of the sun as well as many other less flattering soubriquets: the sickly, the mortals, the usurpers, the strangers, the inscrutable, the self-cursed, the heavy-handed, and the night-fearers (Tolkien 1999a: 103). Only one group of men plays an important role in the early history of Middle-earth, the Atanatári or Edain, and they do so only because of an accident of geography, they "wandered into the North of the world" at that time (Tolkien 1999a: 103). Yet, and perhaps most remarkably, Tolkien finishes the short chapter "Of Men" by pointing out that the defeat of Morgoth was very much the result of elves *and* men, for Beren was a Man who fell in love with an Elf (Lúthien) and wrested one of the Silmarils from Morgoth, and Eärendil was half-Elven (the son of a Man (Tuor) and an Elf (Idril)). It was he who persuaded the Valar to unite with elves and men in defeating Morgoth forever, and the children of Eärendil and Idril were Elros (first king of Númenor) and Elrond, one of the wisest beings in Middle-earth.

The Edain (who do not play a role in the narrative of the First Age for more than 300 years after the Noldor return to Middle-earth from Elvenhome) are divided into three houses in very much the same way that the elves formed three clans: the house of Bëor (he who was first named Balan); the house of Hádor the Goldenhaired (led by Marach); and the house of Haleth the Hunter (led by Haldad). Bëor's people settle in Estolad ("The Encampment") in Beleriand; the group led by Haldad settle in the forest of Brethil near the elven kingdom of Doriath; and the group led by Marach settle southeast of Estolad. All three houses play an important role in the history of Middle-earth and become elf-friends although it is the men of the house of Hádor the Goldenhaired that outshine the others because of their strength and their might (Tolkien 1999a: 148). All three houses of the Edain speak a language which is a version of Sindarin derived from their contact with the dark elves (those who had never journeyed to Valinor). However, as they now come into contact with the Eldar, the Eldar's language (Quenya) influences them too. Tolkien makes clear, also, that there are other groups of men who do not encounter the Eldar. The Edain, however, greatly benefit from such contact, not the least in that their lifespan increases beyond that afforded other men. Tolkien makes it equally clear that the Easterlings (or Eastrons), a race of swarthy men who came into Beleriand from the east in the First Age, are not to be trusted. One chief in particular, Uldor, being called "The Accursed." On the contrary, they betray the Edain and the elves more than once and are secretly in alliance with Morgoth, an alliance for which Morgoth rewards them with land. Tolkien also looks unfavorably on the Southrons (or black men) in the legendarium, for they are in league with Sauron in the Second and Third Ages. In appearance, they have swarthy skin and black hair.

At the end of the First Age, the Edain who have survived the previous battles with Morgoth combine with the Valar and the elves to defeat Morgoth for all time in the Great Battle or War of Wrath. They are the only group of humans to do so; all the rest side with Morgoth. For their loyalty and courage, the Valar give the Edain many gifts: wisdom, power, a long life, and their own island close to Valinor on which to live. That island is called Númenor or Andor ("the Land of Gift" in Valarin) (Tolkien 1999a: 260). Having received a paradise from the Valar, the Edain proceed over the course of the Second Age to lose it through pride and arrogance and foolishness, for they listen to the blandishments and flattery and honeyed words of Sauron. The event that leads to this loss is called "the Drowning

of Númenor" ("Akallabêth" (Tolkien 1999a: 281)).[6] Few of the
Númenóreans (or Dúnedain) escape: just nine ships (four captained
by Elendil; three by Isildur, his elder son; and two by Anárion, his
younger son). In Middle-earth, they found kingdoms, and Aragorn
claims descent from this royal line. However, that is the matter of
The Lord of the Rings and well known to many readers. Rather
than trace the history of men in that direction, I will instead look
briefly at only one culture of men because it was dear to Tolkien
and because it shows how he developed his narrative into such a
convincing representation of an entire fictive world.

The Rohirrim

Tolkien's presentation of the culture of the Rohirrim (also known as
the men of Éothéod, or the men of the mark, or the house of Eorl)
occupies a pivotal part of the narrative of *The Lord of the Rings*. The
culture is also mentioned in "Of the Rings of Power and the Third
Age" (Tolkien 1999a: 285–309) and is discussed at some length in
Appendix A of *The Lord of the Rings* ("The House of Eorl" (Tolkien
1994c: 1038–45)) as well as in *The Peoples of Middle-earth* ("The
House of Eorl" (Tolkien 1996: 270–4)).[7] The Rohirrim originally
lived in lands beyond Mirkwood and were related to the kings of
Rhovanion. From this relation, they claimed kinship with the kings
of Gondor. Before the Third Age, they moved to the vales of Anduin
between the Carrock and the Gladden, and then they moved to land
near the source of the Anduin to the south of the Misty Mountains
and north of Mirkwood. That land became known as the Gap of
Rohan (with *Rohan* meaning "Land of Horses"), and they moved
there because the kings of Gondor ceded them land in the interest
of protecting the Gondorian flank. The history of the kingdom is
divided by Tolkien into three hereditary lines: The first line runs
from Eorl the Young to Helm Hammerhand (2485–759); the
second line runs from Fréaláf Hildeson to Théoden (2726–3019);
and the third line begins with Éomer Éadig (2991–FA 63). The
Rohirrim were known for their horsemanship and for their loyalty
to Gondor in the war against Sauron and Saruman. In creating this
culture, Tolkien was intentionally paying tribute to the historical
Anglo-Saxon culture. Like the Anglo-Saxons, the Rohirrim were
fair-skinned and blond-haired. The Rohirrim also used armor and

employed battle tactics similar to the Anglo-Saxons. Finally, names among the Rohirrim echo Anglo-Saxon names. It is also interesting to see how few changes the Rohirrim underwent as the legendarium developed. It is as if Tolkien knew almost from the beginning of his work on *The Lord of the Rings* what that culture should look like. In part, that may simply be because Tolkien himself was for most of his academic career a professor of Anglo-Saxon.

Dwarves

Commonly known as Durin's folk after their first recorded leader, Durin the Deathless (in the First Age), the dwarves are remarkable in two ways.[8] First, they were not among the children of Ilúvatar. They were the creation of the Vala Aulë, who grew impatient to have students to whom he could teach his stonecraft. Had Ilúvatar not instructed Aulë to have the dwarves sleep until the elves should awaken they would have been the first beings to live in Arda. Second, one of the dwarves, Gimli, was the only dwarf ever to be allowed to sail to the Undying Lands (a privilege previously accorded only the elves and the ringbearers). Legend has it that he wished to go to see again the beauty of Galadriel and that Galadriel persuaded the Valar to permit it.[9] The dwarves were by character rather like the stone they quarried: "Therefore they are stone-hard, stubborn, fast in friendship and in enmity, and they suffer toil and hunger and hurt of body more hardily than all other speaking peoples; and they live long, far beyond the span of Men, yet not for ever" (Tolkien 1999a: 44). As well as being superb miners, the dwarves were unmatched in their work with metal and especially chainmail, greater even in this regard than the Sindarin elves. They helped greatly in the building of two elven cities: Menegroth and Nargothrond. They prized three pieces of jewelry above all others: the Arkenstone (so important to the narrative of *The Hobbit*); a pearl they called Nimphelos; and a carcinet of gold they called Nauglamír. They loved mithril above all other metals. In the First Age, the dwarves aided the elves in their battles against Morgoth, but only one dwarf (a petty dwarf, or exiled dwarf) named Mim plays a crucial role in the stories of that age when he betrays Túrin to the orcs. In the Second Age, the dwarves participated in the Last Alliance against Sauron and the battle in which the One Ring is cut from Sauron's finger by Isildur. In the Third Age, the dwarves achieve narrative prominence, of course, through the dwarves who take part in the quest in *The Hobbit* and through Gimli and his friendship with Legolas in *The Lord of the Rings*.

Tolkien says little about female dwarves except this teasing paragraph in "The Later Quenta Silmarillion" (1994d: 201–15):

> For the Naugrim [dwarves] have beards from the beginning of their lives, male and female alike; nor indeed can their womenkind be discerned by those of other race, be it in feature or in gait or in voice, nor in any wise save this: that they go not to war, and seldom save at direst need issue from their deep bowers and halls. It is said, also, that their womenkind are few, and that save their kings and chieftains few Dwarves ever wed; wherefore their race multiplied slowly, and now is dwindling. (Tolkien 1994d: 205)

Hobbits

Perhaps I need say little of these creatures, who were so dear to Tolkien and so very much his own invention. They are central to *The Hobbit* and *The Lord of the Rings* and well known to every reader of Tolkien's legendarium. What I will focus on in a brief discussion is to point out those parts of their story that are not obvious from the main arc of the narrative of Middle-earth. First, there is the oddity that they came late to Tolkien's legendarium and adjustments of that legendarium had to be made. In essence, once he had created them he needed to give them a convincing backstory without having to rewrite major parts of the legendarium. He gives them some tribal structure, whereby the hobbits were from the beginning a race comprised of three distinct subgroups: the Harfoots, the Stoors, and the Fallohides. He seems to have chosen to give less information rather than more about their early history and more rather than less of their history once they reached the Shire. It is clear, however, that they originally settled near the Anduin river between Mirkwood and the Misty Mountains. In the Third Age, they moved as a people to settlements near Bree and in Dunland. Then, they moved to what became known as the Shire. Finally, as if to compensate for the brevity of the backstory, Tolkien spends a great deal of time on hobbit culture in the part of the Third Age covered by *The Lord of the Rings*. Appendices C and D (Family Trees, and Calendars) are solely devoted to the hobbits. These provide a great deal of information, but it is the sort of information that deliberately doesn't interfere with the logical coherence of the wider story.[10]

Orcs

A casual reading of *The Hobbit* and *The Lord of the Rings* would tell a reader two things: first, that the goblins of *The Hobbit* are the orcs of *The Lord of the Rings*; second, that in *The Lord of the Rings* there are two basic breeds of orc. One is the breed devised by Sauron, which is relatively small and hates the sight of the sun. The other is the breed of super-orc called the Uruk-hai devised by Saruman. It is larger, more bloodthirsty, and does not fear the sun. What is less obvious is precisely what their origins are and how much difficulty Tolkien had in deciding the matter. *The Silmarillion* (as edited by Christopher Tolkien) offers one clear answer to origins.[11] Orcs were bred, according to one line of elven thinking, by Melkor from elves whom he had cruelly imprisoned and enslaved and corrupted in his first fortress, Utumno (Tolkien 1999a: 50). Another line of thinking is offered a few chapters later: Sindarin elves thought the orcs were "Avari [those elves who stayed in Middle-earth] who had become evil and savage in the wild; in which they guessed all too near, it is said" (Tolkien 1999a: 94). These two ideas with some effort can be seen as both being possible, but it is fascinating that Tolkien hints that neither is necessarily true: "in which they guessed all too near." Some of that hesitancy may be due to Tolkien actually considering the orcs as consisting of more than two breeds: the two I have already mentioned and "lesser breeds" which were referred to by those deliberately bred by Sauron and Saruman as *snaga* or "slave" (1994d: 390). It is perhaps not surprising that Tolkien was so ambivalent about how orcs came into being, for as a man of faith the orcs presented to him a narrative condundrum: how is one to account for evil in a world that was created by a beneficent being, Ilúvatar. Tolkien's ambivalence, however, did not stop him from examining the question of origins in several places. One is rather well known (Appendix F of *The Lord of the Rings*: "Orcs and the Black Speech" (Tolkien 1994c: 1131–2)); the rest are fairly obscure: *The Annals of Aman* ((Tolkien 1993: 72–4, 78, 109–10, 123–4)); "Notes on Motives in the Silmarillion" (1993: 406); and three separate brief essays on "Orcs" in "Myths Transformed" (1993: 408–24). The first dates from 1955; the notes on motives in *The Silmarillion* from 1937 with revisions in 1958; the brief essays on orcs apparently from 1959 to 1960. What we have then is the well-known 1955 version of things and then over the next few years some reconsiderations.

Appendix F categorically says: "The Orcs were first bred by the Dark Power of the North [Morgoth] in the Elder Days" (Tolkien 1994c: 1131). Very straightforward and admirably designed for a mass audience. *The Annals of Aman* (where orc is spelled as *ork* and orcs *orkor*) gives a longer version of what is in *The Silmarillion*. It adds in Section 2, for example, that "the Orkor had life and multiplied after the manner of the Children of Ilúvatar" and, since no one but Ilúvatar can grant life, then Melkor must have corrupted already living beings: elves (Tolkien 1993: 74). *The Annals of Aman* also makes two strong statements: one is psychological; one a value judgment. The first is about the psyche of orcs: "And deep in their dark hearts the Orkor loathed the Master [Melkor] whom they served in fear, the maker only of their misery" (Tolkien 1993: 74). The second is about the relation between Melkor and Eru/Ilúvatar: "This [the corruption of the orc] maybe was the vilest deed of Melkor and the most hateful to Eru" (Tolkien 1993: 74). In the same *Annals*, Tolkien seems to have reconsidered this explanation, for in Section 5 of the work he declares "These creatures Morgoth bred in envy and mockery of the Eldar" (Tolkien 1993: 109). By the late 1950s, Tolkien seems to have changed his mind again: "The progeniture of things was corrupted. Hence *Orcs*? Part of the Elf-Man idea gone wrong" (1993: 406). Within a year Tolkien offers another idea: "It remains therefore terribly possible that there was an Elvish strain in the Orcs. These may even have been mated with beasts (sterile!)—and later Men" (1993: 411). Perhaps it is fairest to say that Tolkien never made up his mind, so he was absolutely right in saying that "The origin of the Orcs is a matter of debate"

(1993: 416) just as he is disarmingly honest when he says: "Their [Orcs'] nature and origin require more thought. They are not easy to work into the theory and system" (1993: 409).

At this point, the chapter has dealt with all of the major peoples in Middle-earth. I shall now turn to several groups of people and spirits in the legendarium upon which Tolkien expended a great deal of energy and effort: the Valar and the Maiar; the wizards (or Istari); and the Nazgûl. Whenever I teach Tolkien's works, these groups get a great many questions asked about them.

Valar and Maiar

These two groups belong together as part of Tolkien's creation myth. The principal work in which they appear is the "Valaquenta: Account of the Valar and Maiar according to the Lore of the Eldar" (Tolkien 1999a: 25–32). Earlier, related accounts do, however, exist: "The Coming of the Valar and the Building of Valinor" (Tolkien 1983: 64–93); "Of the Valar" (Tolkien 1993: 143–52); and "The Valaquenta" (1993: 199–205). It is, however, with *The Silmarillion* account that I mainly concern myself for the sake of clarity. According to Tolkien, the Valar consist of those Ainur (essentially angels) who were sufficiently interested in Ilúvatar's creation to wish to take part in its embodiment in this world (1999a: 25). In fact, however, the Valar are actually a subset of a subset, for only those who are considered "The Great" among the Ainur who became involved in creating Arda (the Earth) are actually Valar. There are seven Valar (male gods) and seven Valier (female gods). The seven Valar are (in order of importance): Manwë, Ulmo, Aulë, Oromë, Mandos, Lórien, and Tulkas. The seven Valier are: Varda, Yavanna, Nienna, Estë, Vairë, Vána, and Nessa. Once Melkor was considered a Vala but no longer because he became indubitably evil (Tolkien 1999a: 26). He was replaced among the Valar by Tulkas Astaldo, who fought against Melkor early in the history of the creation of the world. Many of the Valar are paired with the Valier. So, Manwë's spouse is Varda; Aulë's spouse is Yavanna; Oromë's spouse is Vána; Mandos's spouse is Vairë; Lórien's spouse is Estë; Tulkas's spouse is Nessa. One of the Valar is unmarried, Ulmo; one of the Valier is unmarried, Nienna.

Each of the Valar and Valier has particular interests or foci; some are related to each other; some of them have alternative names; some form a coterie within the Valar and Valier. The Valar first. Manwë, who is considered by Ilúvatar the king of the Valar and Valier, has a focus: the air. Ulmo is "Lord of Waters" and second in power to Manwë (Tolkien 1999a: 26). Aulë's focus is the Earth. Oromë is a hunter and a lover of trees. Mandos is "keeper of the Houses of the Dead" (28). Lórien is "master of visions and dreams" (28). Tulkas is master of "contests of strength" (28–9). The Valier next. Varda is beautiful because "the light of Ilúvatar lives still in her face" (26); she is the one Melkor fears most of all the Valar and Valier. Yavanna is "the Giver of Fruits" (27). Vairë is the "Weaver" (28). Estë is the healer. Nienna represents pity and "endurance beyond hope" (28). Nessa loves running and dancing. Vána is the "Ever-Young." Then the relationships. Mandos and Lórien are brothers and known as the Fëanturi "master of spirits." Nienna is the sister of Mandos and Lórien. Then the alternative names. Mandos's real name is Námo; Lórien's real name is Irmo; Oromë is known as Aldaron or Tauron by the elves, with both epithets meaning "Lord of Forests." Finally the coterie: Manwë, Varda, Ulmo, Yavanna, Aulë, Mandos, Nienna, and Oromë form the "Aratar, the High Ones of Arda" (29). Once Melkor was one of them and they were nine. Now, he is banished and the Aratar are eight.

The Maiar are lesser spirits than the Valar; they are "their servants and helpers" (Tolkien 1999a: 30). Their number is unknown, and few can be named. Those whose names are known include Ilmarë, the handmaiden of Varda; Eonwë, the herald of Manwë; Ossë, the vassal of Ulmo; Uinen (Ossë's spouse and beloved by the Númenóreans), who successfully persuaded Ossë not to take sides with Melkor early in the creation of Arda; Melian, servant of both Vána and Estë; and Olórin (also known as Gandalf and Mithrandir), who learned pity and patience from Nienna. It is Olórin who befriends elves and men and takes pity on them. It is Olórin who gives hope in the face of despair to those who will be guided by him (Tolkien 1999a: 31). Gandalf has come far from his first appearance in *The Hobbit* where he is described merely as a wizard and belittled by Bilbo as "the wandering wizard that gave Old Took a pair of magic diamond studs that fastened themselves and never came undone till ordered" (Tolkien 2007a: 7).[12] As has been said before, one of the difficulties with Tolkien's legendarium is that it is not static but a lifetime's achievement and inherently dynamic and changing.

The Wizards

Also known in Quenyan as the Istari (singular "Istar") and in Sindarin as Ithryn (singular "Ithron"), these are a group over whom Tolkien toiled more than many other aspects of his legendarium. Beyond the major role of Gandalf in *The Hobbit* and *The Lord of the Rings*, the major role of Saruman in *The Lord of the Rings*, and the minor role of Radagast, there are four principal sources for our understanding of the wizards. One is an essay called "Of the Rings of Power and the Third Age" (Tolkien 1999a: 285–304). One consists of four paragraphs from the headnote to the Third Age section of Appendix B: "The Tale of Years" (Tolkien 1994c: 1059–60). One is an essay called "The Istari" (Tolkien 1980: 388–402). One is a brief note on "The Five Wizards" (Tolkien 1996: 384–5). All except the first date from about the same time: 1954–5. The first was completed in about 1948.

The outline of Tolkien's thinking from Appendix B is as follows. The Istari mysteriously appear in Middle-earth in about the year 1000 of the Third Age. They come from the "Far West." There are said to be five of them. They have the status of "messengers." Their purpose is "to contest the power of Sauron." However, those who sent them limited their authority: "they were forbidden to match his [Sauron's] power with power, or to seek to dominate Elves or Men by force or fear." They take the shape of men, but that is not their true form. The appendix mentions only two of them and considers them "the two highest of this order": Curunír ("the Man of Skill"), also known as Saruman and as Curumo in Quenyan; and Mithrandir ("the Grey Pilgrim"), also known as Gandalf and Olórin and Incánus.[13] Curunír journeys often to the east and, at last, dwells in Isengard. Mithrandir journeys mainly in the west and is nomadic. He is a particular friend of the elves. To Mithrandir, Círdan the Shipwright gives one of the three elven rings: Narya, "the Ring of Fire." He does so because he knows where Mithrandir comes from and where he will return to, and he knows how hard his task will be (Tolkien 1994c: 1060).[14] That is what Appendix B offers the reader.

The longer essay in *Unfinished Tales* fleshes out this picture. Now, Elrond and Galadriel (as well as Círdan) may know something about Mithrandir's role, but it is by no means certain that they actually do, for Tolkien precedes his mention of the pair with the phrase "none save maybe" and adds that if they do know then they had to "discover" what the role was.[15] Now it is also made clear that it was the Valar ("the Lords of the West"; Tolkien 1980: 389) who sent the wizards. Now there are five members of the group but they are called "chiefs," so there may be others. The first to arrive in Middle-earth is Curunír; he is raven-haired, has a "fair voice," is skilled with his hands, and is considered the head of the order (Tolkien 1980: 389). He is followed by two clad in sea-blue, and one clad in earthen brown. The last of the five to appear is Mithrandir, erroneously called by some men "the Elf of the Wand" (Tolkien 1980: 391): shorter than the others, older in appearance, grey haired, wearing clothes of grey, and leaning on a staff. He "seemed the least," but Círdan saw that he is actually "the greatest spirit and the wisest" (Tolkien 1980: 389). As we know from the narrative of *The Lord of the Rings*, there is considerable ill will between Saruman and Gandalf; it dates from Saruman's discovery that Círdan gave the Ring of Fire to Gandalf and not to him.

The two wizards in blue are not named but are called collectively "Ithryn Luin" (blue wizards). They go into the east with Saruman and also to the south but never return. Tolkien suspects they failed in their mission although he is not clear what that mission was. In a letter written in 1958, he suggests that in addition to failing they become "founders or beginners of secret cults and 'magic' traditions that outlasted the fall of Sauron" (quoted in note 3 of "The Istari" (Tolkien 1980: 401)). The Istar clad in brown is named Radagast, and he "became enamoured of the many beasts and birds that dwelt in Middle-earth, and forsook elves and men, and spent his days among the wild creatures" (Tolkien 1980: 390). Of the five Istari, only Gandalf succeeds in his mission. Tolkien ascribes this high rate of failure to the Istari being "embodied": that meant that they "had need to learn much anew by slow experience" (1980: 390).

In the brief note titled "The Five Wizards," Tolkien names the two wizards clad in blue; they are Morinehtar ("Darkness-slayer") and Rómenstámo or Rómenstar ("East-helper"). Now Tolkien suggests they may *not* have failed but that in fact "They must have had great influence on the history of the Second Age and Third Age in weakening and disarraying the forces of the East" (1996: 385). In the same note, Tolkien also wonders aloud if Glorfindel was an Istar but doesn't take that speculation any further.

So, this was Tolkien's considered position at the time *The Lord of the Rings* was published. There were subtle differences in Tolkien's depiction of the Istari in "Of the Rings of Power and the Third Age" (an essay which predates the other material by about six years), but rather than focus on those more subtle differences I will merely point out that Tolkien adds to the picture some details about a council of the wise (also known as the White Council), which was created when in the Third Age it appeared that Sauron was growing in power again. Galadriel wanted Gandalf to head the group, but Gandalf refused, and Saruman, always hungry for power, took on the role.[16]

With the remainder of this chapter, I only have time to look briefly at those few beings about whom students of Tolkien's work have most questions: the Nazgûl, Beorn, and Tom Bombadil.

The Nazgûl

These are nine in number and are also known as the Black Riders, the Ringwraiths, and the Úlairi. They play no part in the narrative of the First Age and are not mentioned in *The Hobbit*. According to the "Akallabêth," three of the nine were Númenoréan lords (Tolkien 1999a: 267). They are led by the Witch-king of Angmar. According to "Of the Rings of Power and the Third Age," the Ringwraiths were enslaved with the Nine Rings and were "kings, sorcerers, and warriors of old." They were Sauron's "most terrible servants; darkness went with them, and they cried with the voices of death" (Tolkien 1999a: 289). Their abode is Minas Morgul, the Tower of Sorcery, the fortress that was named Minas Ithil before they captured it. *The Lord of the Rings* shows how the Witch-king is finally killed. It also shows how the ringwraiths disappear once Sauron is defeated. It is clear that the Nazgûl were an idea that Tolkien came up with around the time he began writing *The Lord of the Rings*. In a letter dated February 2, 1939, he comments that in the sequel to *The Hobbit* "the new (and very alarming) Ringwraiths are a feature" (2000: 42). He also commented that the Nazgûl were the only ones of Sauron's servants to use the Black Speech consistently (Appendix F, *The Lord of the Rings*; Tolkien 1994c: 1105). In their creation, he adapted material from his work on *The Lost Road*.

Beorn

Beorn only appears in two places in *The Hobbit* (Chapter 7, "Queer Lodgings" and Chapter 18, "The Return Journey"). He is known to Gandalf but to no one else of those going to the Misty Mountains. Gandalf is quite mysterious about who Beorn is. He calls him "Somebody" and makes clear that he is dangerous unless approached carefully. Bilbo finally gets Gandalf to tell him this much:

> He is a skin-changer. He changes his skin: sometimes he is a huge black bear, sometimes he is a great strong black-haired man with huge arms and a great beard. I cannot tell you much more, though that ought to be enough. Some say that he is a bear descended from the great and ancient bears of the mountains that lived there before the giants came. Others say that he is a man descended from the first men who lived before Smaug or the other dragons came into this part of the world, and before the goblins came into the hills out of the North. I cannot say, though I fancy the last is the true tale. He is not the sort of person to ask questions of. (Tolkien 2007a: 108)

In addition to giving the company bed, board, and advice, Beorn plays a crucial role in the battle of Five Armies. Just when it appears that all is lost even after the intervention of the eagles, Beorn appears, and his contribution is enough:

> In that last hour Beorn himself had appeared—no one knew how or from where. He came alone, and in bear's shape; and he seemed to have grown almost to giant-size in his wrath.
>   The roar of his voice was like drums and guns; and he tossed wolves and goblins from his path like straws and feathers. (Tolkien 2007a: 263–4)

He saves the mortally wounded Thorin and carries him back to his fellow dwarves. Then he returns to the battle, kills Borg (the orc chieftain), and disappears. As if to round out his character, Tolkien says that after the battle of Five Armies Beorn becomes an important chieftain in the Anduin Vale. He leads his followers (called Beornings). He has a son called Grimbeorn the Old, who becomes the Beornings' chieftain after Beorn's death. Tolkien also provides some information about who he was in a 1954 letter to Naomi Mitchison: "Though a skin-changer and no doubt a bit of a magician, Beorn was a Man" (2000: 178).

Tom Bombadil

Tom Bombadil, even more than Beorn, is limited in his role to one particular part of the broader narrative of *The Lord of the Rings*. It is interesting that the whole Tom Bombadil episode in the epic (Chapter 7, "In the House of Tom Bombadil") is the only part that Peter Jackson did not film in his three-part version of the story. He may have felt, as many do, that Bombadil strayed from a children's story and does not truly belong in an epic. And yet, Tom Bombadil was popular enough to spawn a sequel as it were: *The Adventures of Tom Bombadil and Other Verses from the Red Book*, published seven years after *The Lord of the Rings*. In a letter to Naomi Mitchison written in 1954, Tolkien remarks that Bombadil is not important to the narrative, but he is somewhat important as a "comment" (2000: 178). He dates, as Tolkien points out, from about 1933 (that is, before even *The Hobbit* was published) and was based on a doll that Tolkien's son, Michael, had. The question then arises as to his status as a "comment." One view is that he represents a pacifist point of view in a time of war. Another is that he represents the rapidly disappearing countryside (Tolkien 2000: 26). Yet another that he is an intentional enigma (174). A fourth is that he is exemplar of natural science (192). Regardless, Tolkien himself acknowledged that many find him incongruous but then shut down further speculation by remarking that it was his editorial decision to keep him (192).

Notes

1   These lesser-known works include "The Coming of the Elves and the Making of Kôr" (Tolkien 1983: 113–39); "The Earliest Annals of Beleriand" (Tolkien 1986: 294–341); "Of the Valar," "Laws and Customs among the Eldar," and "Myths Transformed" (Tolkien 1993: 143–52; 207–53; and 367–431); "The Grey Annals," "Of Men," "Concerning the Dwarves," "Of the Coming of Men into the West," and "Quendi and Eldar" (Tolkien 1994d: 3–170; 173–5; 201–15; 215–38; and 357–424); "The House of Eorl," "Durin's Folk," and "Of Dwarves and Men" (Tolkien 1996: 270–4; 274–89; and 295–330); "A Description of the Island of Númenor," "The Northmen and the Wainriders," and "Of the Journey of the Black Riders according to the Account That Gandalf gave to Frodo" (1980: 165–72; 288–95; and 337–41). There are also numerous comments on the peoples of Middle-earth in Tolkien's letters, first published in 1981.

2   Early on in the creation of his legendarium, Tolkien used the term "gnomes" rather than "elves." The latter became the correct form by the early 1930s.

3   The elves' name for themselves is Quendi. It means "those who speak with voices."

4   For those who want a challenge, then there is the extraordinarily dense essay by Tolkien titled "Quendi and Eldar" (Tolkien 1994d: 359–424), an essay that dates from 1959 to 1960 and includes this fascinating detail about the origins of the elves:

> According to the legend, preserved in almost identical form among both the Elves of Aman and the Sindar, the Three Clans were in the beginning derived from the three Elf-fathers: *Imin; Tata;* and *Enel* (sc. One, Two, Three), and those whom each chose to join his following. So they had at first simply the names *Minyar* "Firsts," *Tatyar* "Seconds," and *Nelyar* "Thirds." These numbered, out of the original 144 Elves that first awoke, 14, 56, and 74; and these proportions were approximately maintained until the Separation. (Tolkien 1994d: 380)

> For those who want to know about the marriage customs of the elves, Tolkien discusses them in detail in an essay titled "Laws and Customs among the Eldar" (1993: 207–33). The essay is dated by Christopher Tolkien as having being written in the late 1950s.

5   However, Tolkien is not always so optimistic about men's mortality being a gift, for in the chapter titled "Of Men" in *The Silmarillion* he emphasizes the less pleasant aspects of human life: frailty, sickness,

and ageing (1999a: 104), and he admits he is uncertain about what happens to humans after death (105). In a little-known work of Tolkien's titled "Athrabeth Finrod ah Andreth" (1993: 303–66), Tolkien introduces the idea that the Edain did not think human mortality was an idea conceived of by Ilúvatar; rather, human mortality was created "by the malice of Melkor" (304). The Eldar reject the idea quite convincingly, but Tolkien has deliberately (and unnecessarily) raised the possibility in the first place.

6   Tolkien provides many versions of this Atlantean story in his legendarium. There are no fewer than three other versions as edited by Christopher Tolkien: two he calls "The Fall of Númenor"; one he calls "The Drowning of Anadûnê." See *The Lost Road and Other Writings* (Tolkien 1987: 11–35, and 1992: 331–440).

7   My description of this people tries to take account of the various versions of their culture as developed by Tolkien.

8   Durin was the first of the legendary Seven Fathers of the Dwarves. (See Appendix A, *The Lord of the Rings* (Tolkien 1994c: 1045)). Other names for the dwarves included Khazad, the Naugrim, and Gonhirrim.

9   This is, at least, what "*one of the last notes in the Red Book*" indicates (Appendix A, *The Lord of the Rings* (Tolkien 1994c: 1055)).

10   For those interested in following the development of the hobbits as a people, *The Peoples of Middle-earth* (Tolkien 1996: 85–139) provides a rich vein of material on the Shire.

11   I present this issue of origins in some depth because it mattered a great deal to Tolkien and, also, to show readers how complicated the world Tolkien created is. I could perhaps have gone as deep in my discussions of most of the peoples and individuals who are the subject of this chapter, but that would have run counter to my intent: brevity and clarity.

12   Whether Gandalf's being a Maia means that all the five wizards named by Tolkien are also Maiar is unclear, but it seems likely.

13   Tolkien points out that we do not know their true names, so the ones we are given are accurate but assumed.

14   Círdan's speech in Appendix B of *The Lord of the Rings* when he gives Narya to Mithrandir exists elsewhere in two slightly different versions. See "The Istari" essay (Tolkien 1980: 389) and "Of the Rings of Power and the Third Age" (Tolkien 1999a: 304).

15   "Of the Rings of Power and the Third Age" comments that actually Círdan told Elrond and Galadriel that the Istari "came over the Sea" (Tolkien 1999a: 299).

16   In notes to "The Istari" provided by Christopher Tolkien, there is
     some material written by Tolkien that relates to the reasoning behind
     the Valar sending these particular Maiar to Middle-earth (1980:
     392–4). This part of the story appears nowhere else. It is fascinating,
     but its discussion lies beyond the compass of this chapter.

6

Tolkien's Themes

The focus of this chapter is on answering the one question most frequently asked by those studying Tolkien: What are the themes in his legendarium? I will focus on those themes I find to be important in Tolkien's legendarium along with those found by other scholars and students that are also important in my view. The list is not exhaustive, and the examples I provide in support of my view that these themes are significant are likewise limited. Any discussion of themes is just a means to an end: to stimulate discussion of the meaning and relevance of Tolkien's legendarium. In this respect, I am aware that some of the following discussion is tendentious. The list is alphabetical in order to avoid an unhelpful argument about which theme or themes dominate in the legendarium.

Blood Will Out

Blood (or family or tribe) is a fundamental way in which beings organize their lives. The clearest example is, of course, the identity and mission of Aragorn in *The Lord of the Rings*. There are many proofs that he is, indeed, Isildur's legitimate heir, but one of the most powerful is the Paths of the Dead episode. Had Aragorn not been Aragorn, he would have been unable to pass that way and live. Another example would be the power of King Théoden as legitimate king of the Mark. Once he is freed from Wormtongue's insidious hold, he becomes the true leader who dies so bravely at the battle of the Pelennor Fields.

The Contributions of the Poor and Powerless Matter More Than Those of the Great

In his well-known synoptic letter to Milton Waldman (probably written in 1951), Tolkien writes that the roles of the hobbits show that even the unknown and the weak play an important part in the history of the world, and that only "the One" knows the true arc and meaning of life (2000: 149). And there are examples from the narrative of the legendarium. Beren (a mere mortal) wins the hand of Lúthien by taking one of the Silmarils from Morgoth's iron crown. Frodo (a mere hobbit) along with Gollum (a mere stoor) destroys the One Ring in the Cracks of Doom despite Sauron's desperate and sustained efforts to stop him.

Courage Consists of Accepting the Nature of Things

Two moments in the legendarium come to mind among many to illustrate this theme. The first (in *The Fellowship of the Ring*) is Frodo's decision to take the One Ring and destroy it in the Cracks of Doom. He does so because he sees that he is the logical choice as ringbearer, and does so even though he is afraid (Tolkien 1994a: 263). The second (again in *The Fellowship of the Ring*) is Gandalf's decision on Caradhras the Cruel to turn back and take the road south through the Mines of Moria. It is a courageous decision that has two pieces to it. One is to retreat from the Redhorn Gate, and Gandalf makes that decision because he is wise enough to know that the fellowship must get off the mountain before night comes on (Tolkien 1994a: 286). The other is to decide to go through the Mines of Moria to get into the Dimrill Dale east of the Misty Mountains. Despite Moria's sinister reputation, it is the logical choice, and, so, Gandalf argues to the company that it is the route that should be taken. He avers also (only in part correctly) that they will make it through safely (Tolkien 1994a: 289). So, courage is, perhaps, the wise acceptance of best choices as inevitable even when they are dangerous and even though foresight has its limits.

Death Is a Gift Not a Curse

This theme is the closest Tolkien ever got in his legendarium to the expression of a religious point of view. Tolkien knows that all humanity fears death. So he rehearses an argument and uses two examples: elves and men. Elves are immortal. It would seem, then, that they are to be envied. In fact, they are not, for as they age they simply fade. Men are to be envied for they die, and in death find a particular kind of freedom. Tolkien expresses this idea clearly in the first chapter of the "Quenta Silmarillion," titled "The End of Days" (1999a: 42). It is a supreme example of what Tolkien in "On Fairy-Stories" terms "Eucatastrophe" (the good catastrophe) and the "Consolation of the Happy Ending" (1997c: 153).

Despair Is a Terrible Error

In *The Lord of the Rings*, Denethor despairs because he has looked in a palantír and been persuaded by Sauron that there is no hope for the west. He commits suicide. Saruman despairs. He has looked in a palantír and been persuaded by Sauron that the way to power can only be through him. He is murdered. By contrast, Galadriel, when she hears of Gandalf's apparent death, does not despair. Instead, she avers that hope is powerful and that its power needs to be understood and appreciated. For Galadriel, hope depends upon the assembled company remaining true to the quest (*The Fellowship of the Ring*; Tolkien 1994a: 348).

Later in the epic, Legolas does not despair even though Merry and Pippin have been captured by orcs and Sam and Frodo have gone off on so difficult a quest alone. Rather, he gives this advice to Aragorn and Gimli: "[D]o not cast all hope away. Tomorrow is unknown. Rede oft is found at the rising of the Sun" (*The Two Towers*; Tolkien 1994b: 419). And Gandalf does not despair. Instead he says to Aragorn and Legolas and Gimli in Fangorn Forest: "We meet again. At the turn of the tide. The great storm is coming, but the tide has turned" (*The Two Towers*; Tolkien 1994b: 484). And Sam does not, ultimately, despair when Frodo is apparently killed by Shelob. He gives in to that feeling initially ("black despair came down on him"), but then he reasons that he himself must take up the quest to destroy the One Ring. As he puts it to Frodo, who lies before him apparently dead: "I have something to do before the end. I must see it through, sir, if you understand" (*The Two Towers*; Tolkien 1994b: 714).

And Théoden does not despair but reasons accurately that action is the better choice in the coming conflict. He says to Éomer: "If the war is lost, what good will be my hiding in the hills? And if it is won, what grief will it be, even if I fall, spending my last strength?" (*The Return of the King*; Tolkien 1994c: 775). And Aragorn does not despair at the Black Gate when everything appears lost. He seems to be transformed into a force of nature: "Aragorn stood beneath his banner, silent and stern, as one lost in thought of things long past or far away; but his eyes gleamed like stars that shine the brighter as the night deepens" (*The Return of the King*; Tolkien 1994c: 927). The antonym to despair is hope, but it is also resolution and a sense of duty. Gandalf puts it best at the "last debate" after the battle of the Pelennor Fields when he says to Legolas and Gimli and Aragorn and the sons of Elrond (Elladan and Elrohir):

[I]t is not our part to master all the tides of the world, but to do what is in us for the succour of those years wherein we are set, uprooting the evil in the fields that we know, so that those who live after may have clean earth to till. What weather they shall have is not ours to rule. (*The Return of the King*; Tolkien 1994c: 861)

Evil Is Recursive Not Singular

Much of the First Age is given over to the defeat of Melkor/Morgoth. Finally, he is defeated by the alliance of the Valar, the elves, and men and cast out for ever (Tolkien 1999a: 254–5). Yet Sauron, his servant, takes his place to the ruination of so much in the Second and Third Ages. For, in Tolkien's view, evil can never be finally defeated. It is recursive. It takes many forms. It has to be defeated again and again. In the last chapter of the "Quenta Silmarillion" ("Of the Voyage of Eärendil"), Tolkien offers this adage: Evil is "a seed that does not die and cannot be destroyed; and ever and anon it sprouts anew, and will bear dark fruit even unto the latest days" (1999a: 255).

Fate and Freewill Are Connected in a Complicated Way

Just as with Tolkien's beloved *Beowulf*, so in his legendarium the relation between fate and freewill is complicated. However, Tolkien does seem to suggest that there is a role for providence in life and that it is an important and neglected one. When Gandalf is explaining to Frodo, early in the narrative of *The Lord of the Rings*, the history of the One Ring up to the present time, he emphasizes that events appear to have happened for a reason. He begins by pointing out the oddity that it was Bilbo who found the Ring, and he continues:

> Behind that there was something else at work, beyond any design of the Ring-maker. I can put it no plainer than by saying that Bilbo was *meant* to find the Ring, and *not* by its maker. In which case you also were *meant* to have it. And that may be an encouraging thought. (*The Fellowship of the Ring*; Tolkien 1994a: 54–5)

And then there is Éowyn. Of her free own will, she dresses as a male warrior and assumes the name Dernhelm in order to contribute to the cause of the Rohirrim's fight against Sauron and Saruman. It is her presence on the battlefield of her own free will that leads to the death of the Witch-king of Angmar, and it is a presence that was predicted in lore. As Gandalf remarks to Pippin during the siege of Gondor, the Witch-king will be killed by something other than "the hand of man," but even Gandalf does not know precisely what his fate will be (*The Return of the King*; Tolkien 1994c: 801). And the Witch-king has apparently heard the same lore, for when Éowyn disguised as Dernhelm challenges him to battle, the Witch-king replies incredulously, "Hinder me? Thou fool. No living man may hinder me!" (823). To which Éowyn responds, "But no living man am I! You look upon a woman. Éowyn I am, Éomund's daughter" (823). Of course, providence is more complex than this response suggests, for the Witch-king is actually killed by two people, neither of whom is a man: Éowyn (a woman) and Merry (a hobbit). Merry stabs the Witch-king behind the knee, and that blow causes the king to stumble forward and *that* allows Éowyn to stab him in the neck between crown and mantle.

That Tolkien believed in providence (a sort of free will blended with fate) is clearest, because most simply stated, at the end of *The Hobbit*. Almost the last words Gandalf speaks in that story are to Bilbo, who has returned triumphantly from his adventure. Bilbo has just declared to Balin and Gandalf that "the prophecies of the old songs have turned out to be true, after a fashion!" To which Gandalf replies:

> Of course! ... And why should they not prove true? Surely you don't disbelieve the prophecies, because you had a hand in bringing them about yourself? You don't really suppose, do you, that all your adventures and escapes were managed by mere luck, just for your sole benefit? (Tolkien 2007a: 276)

Heroism Requires the Acceptance of Death

Boromir tries to take the One Ring from Frodo as the fellowship breaks up at the end of *The Fellowship of the Ring*, and he pays for it with his life, but he does die honorably—and that matters to Tolkien. In his last moments, Boromir accepts his error and acknowledges it to Aragorn: "I tried to take the Ring from Frodo. I am sorry. I have paid" (*The Two Towers*; Tolkien 1994b: 404). He never thinks about running away but, instead, defends himself and the hobbits to the end. And his death cost the lives of many orcs. He is given a formal burial on a makeshift bier of branches despite the need for haste on the part of his companions. Aragorn and Legolas sing a lament for him, and Anduin takes him and protects him as the "elven-boat" in which his body lies navigates the rapids, passes through Osgiliath, and carries him out even into the "Great Sea" (407).

Boromir dies a hero despite having fallen morally, seduced as he was by the power of the Ring. He represents very much the Anglo-Saxon idea of heroism as expressed in "The Battle of Maldon" fragment. There, against hopeless odds Beorhtwold rallies those who remain faithful to their slain leader, Beorhtnoth:

Courage shall grow keener, clearer the will,
The heart fiercer, as our force faileth. (Alexander 1991: 104)
(Hige sceal þe heardra, heorte þe cenre,
mod sceal þe mare, þe ure mægen lytlað). (2009: 313–4)

Tolkien himself found this concept of "Northern courage" "the great contribution of early Northern literature" (1997a: 20) even as he makes clear in "The Homecoming of Beorthelm, Beorhtnoth's Son" that the concept is deeply problematic: its expression in "The Battle of Maldon" came about as a direct result of *ofermod* (or pride) on the part of Beorhtnoth. And one could say, of course, that Boromir's heroism is a direct result of a moral failing. As always, Tolkien—ever the academic—makes his presentation of this theme subtle and complex. He does not, however, make the picture so ambivalent that we cannot see its antithesis for what it is. If we focus on Saruman for a moment, we can see that he is not in any way a hero and at the end of his life he is doing everything he can to stay alive. After having been spared by Merry, Sam, and Frodo, he curses them and is murdered by Wormtongue who has finally had enough of being his slave. Wormtongue murders him bestially by cutting his throat. No one mourns him; no one gives him a burial. Tolkien instead focuses on how repellent his death is (*The Return of the King*; Tolkien 1994c: 997).

Immortality Is Always Desired; Death Is Always Feared

On several occasions in the late 1950s, shortly after, that is, the publication of *The Lord of the Rings*, Tolkien argued in his letters that this theme was the one about which the legendarium (and, more specifically, *The Lord of the Rings*) is most concerned (2000: 246, 262, 284). This theme is expressed in several ways: by the contrast between the immortal elves, the long-lived dwarves, the long-lived humans (the Númenóreans), and ordinary mortals; by the desire for perpetuity through family (Sam Gamgee and Rosie Cotton's thirteen children come to mind); and by the desire to perform deeds of renown (Théoden at the battle of the Pelennor

Fields, for example). It is, however, in the "Akallabêth" and associated stories of the fall of Númenor and the Second Age that this theme is most persistently expressed. Because the Edain helped the Valar defeat Morgoth at the end of the First Age, they are rewarded with a lifespan much longer than that accorded ordinary humans. That is, however, not enough for them, for the driving force behind the hubristic efforts of the Númenóreans to sail to the Undying Lands against the proscriptions of the Valar is the desire for immortality and that desire alone (1999a: 263). Manwë, through his messengers, makes clear, however, that such a wish is ill advised as it is based upon a misunderstanding: it is those who live in the Undying Lands that make it deathless and not the other way around. Were the Númenóreans to reach these lands, they would be consumed as moths are consumed by a bright flame (Tolkien 1999a: 264). Furthermore, the messengers from Manwë suggest that the Númenóreans are guilty of wanting things both ways: to live in Middle-earth when they want (and accept mortality) and to come to Valinor when they desire (and embrace immortality) (1999a: 264). Tolkien's genius lies in inverting expectation, for from his point of view the human wish for immortality is actually a trap (one would fade and not be eternally young) and death is actually to be desired as a sort of eucatastrophe. The messengers to the Númenóreans make this point in a subtle way: the elves' immortality is simply a part of who they are; men's mortality is similarly integral to their being. It is not clear whether either group should envy the other. Elves are bound to the world though sometimes they weary of it; men escape it through death (1999a: 264–5). Tolkien is suggesting that immortality may not be desirable as that state binds you to the world forever, and death is not to be feared as it allows you to be free.

Loss Persists in Life

This theme is everywhere in the legendarium. The loss of the Silmarils to the sky (Eärendil) and the earth (Maedhros) and the water (Maeglin). The loss of the One Ring to Orodruin. The loss of Thorin Oakenshield to the hunger for the Arkenstone. And there are less dramatic losses. The death of Aragorn while his elven wife,

Arwen, lives on to mourn him. The death of Théoden with his two adopted children (Éowyn and Éomer) to mourn him. The loss of every ringbearer to Middle-earth in a long and painful sequence. It is not hard to understand why this theme is so powerfully presented by Tolkien. He lost two of his best friends in World War I: Rob Gilson and Geoffrey Bache Smith were killed at the battle of the Somme, a battle in which Tolkien himself also saw action. So powerful is the theme that Tolkien has Aragon deliver an "ubi sunt?" lament on the way to Edoras and to a battle everyone knows is coming:

> Where now the horse and the rider? Where is the horn that was blowing?
> Where is the helm and the hauberk, and the bright hair flowing?
> Where is the hand on the harpstring, and the red fire glowing?
> Where is the spring and the harvest and the tall corn growing?
> They have passed like rain on the mountain, like a wind in the meadow;
> The days have gone down in the West behind the hills into shadow.
> Who shall gather the smoke of the dead wood burning,
> Or behold the flowing years from the Sea returning?
>
> (*The Two Towers*; Tolkien 1994b: 497)

It's a beautiful and haunting lament and—from the point of view of plot and action—absolutely unnecessary, which in itself shows how important it was to Tolkien.

Memory Is Both a Blessing and a Curse

Two examples may be used to illustrate the way in which memory is a curse. Frodo is wounded on October 6, 3018, on Weathertop (that is, Amon Sûl) by the Witch-king of Angmar. One year later to the day, he is listless and distracted and in pain. Gandalf asks him if he is all right, and Frodo replies that the memory of his being wounded lies heavy on him. To which Gandalf responds with a maxim (as one might expect of him): "[T]here are some wounds that cannot be wholly cured." In turn, Frodo replies: "Where shall I find rest?" (*The Return of the King*; Tolkien 1994c: 967). In the Undying Lands, Gandalf knows, but he does not reply.

Galadriel reveals that her memories are equally sad (or even sadder): of the long exile from Valinor and of what will happen even if Sauron is defeated—or, rather, *because* of Sauron's being defeated. The first memory she talks of to the assembled guests in Lothlórien. She does so in the context of her marriage to Celeborn. Together, they have "fought the long defeat" (*The Fellowship of the Ring*; Tolkien 1994a: 348). Surely, there can be few more sorrowful memories. The second (the result of Sauron's being defeated) she acknowledges in a dialogue with Frodo as they stand before her mirror. As she puts it, the choice is simple: either the elves will depart into the west or become merely the stuff of folklore (1994a: 356). And that choice—that is really no choice at all—is deeply bound up with all she recalls of the elves' sustained battle against evil: first in the form of Melkor/Morgoth and then in the guise of his servant, Sauron.

So, in what ways is memory a blessing? The answer lies in the narrative of the entire legendarium but most spectacularly in Appendices A–C of *The Lord of the Rings*. Without memory— without a veneration for the past—you will have no sense of your own history or the history of your people or the history of your culture. In his own way, Tolkien is arguing for the truth of George Santayana's aphorism: "Those who cannot remember the past are condemned to repeat it" (1953: 82). Memory is also a blessing in a less straightforward way. Had Gollum not constantly recalled the loss of his "Precious" (the One Ring), he would not have pursued Frodo to the death. Had he not done so, the One Ring would not have been destroyed and Sauron would not have been defeated.

And memory may not be quite as sad a faculty as the discussion above suggests. In the same dialogue between Galadriel and Frodo before her mirror to which I just referred, she does indeed begin by outlining the choice that is no choice, but she ends by saying that if the elves become the stuff of folklore they will slowly forget their once-exalted status and will, in turn, slowly be forgotten (*The Fellowship of the Ring*; Tolkien 1994a: 356). Memory is not perfect. Memories fade. That may be a crucial element in Tolkien's expression of this theme, for even his memories of World War I— horrific as they were—must have begun to fade as he aged.

Men and Women Have Particular Roles in Life

It is frequently observed that there are no female characters in *The Hobbit* and very few female characters with agency in *The Lord of the Rings* and *The Silmarillion*. There are two reasons for this. The first is that Tolkien's grew up in a world markedly more phallocentric than it is now. The second is that he believed men and women had particular roles in life. If we look at the Tom Bombadil episode in *The Fellowship of the Ring*, we can see what those roles are. Bombadil's lady is Goldberry, and she is the daughter of the River. Bombadil is called simply "master." When Bombadil greets Goldberry, he comments possessively that she is pretty, comments on what she is wearing, and asks her if the meal is ready according to his specifications (*The Fellowship of the Ring*; 1994a: 122).

If we look at another female character, Rosie Cotton, we see the same assignment of a domestic role. Rosie is a second Goldberry. While Sam is gone for a year, Rosie waits for him at her parents' house. When he finally comes back from the successful quest to destroy the One Ring, she chides him for being gone so long, comments on how handsomely he's dressed, supports him in his need to scour the Shire, and then tells him to be careful and to hurry back once his tasks are done. Traditional, even stereotypical, roles: male performing action; female solicitously waiting. These roles are repeated at the very end of the epic. The last paragraph records Sam's return from the Grey Havens, where he said goodbye to Elrond, Galadriel, Gandalf, Bilbo, and Frodo. He returns to a house that is lit by candlelight and warmed by a fire. His meal is ready, and Ros[i]e is waiting for him. She welcomes him, sits him down in his chair, and puts their baby daughter, Elanor, on his lap (*The Return of the King*; Tolkien 1994c: 1008). Together, Sam and Rosie have thirteen children (most of whom are named after *Sam's* friends), and she plays the role of a traditional wife while Sam achieves agency within the Shire as the seven-time mayor of the Shire. The closest Rosie comes to adventure is to spend a year in Gondor as the guest of King Aragorn Elessar II. Sam lives with her faithfully, and after she has died he is able to fulfill his part in the larger quest as a ringbearer by passing over sea to the Undying Lands.

There are, however, very definitely some exceptions to Tolkien's traditional view of the female role in life. Three in particular deserve mention: Éowyn, Galadriel, and Lúthien. The first bridles at having to play a traditional helpmeet role. She assumes a male disguise as Dernhelm, fights at the battle of the Pelennor Fields, and is largely responsible for slaying the leader of the Ringwraiths, the Witch-king of Angmar. The second (Galadriel) is one of the most powerful and significant elves in Middle-earth. She it is who calls the White Council into being; she it is (and not her husband, Celeborn), who wears Nenya, one of the three elven rings of power; she it is who interacts so much with the company as they travel on their quest and arrive in Lothlórien; she it is who has a biography (outlined in various works by Tolkien) dating back to before the First Age had even begun. Lúthien is described as the most beautiful of the children of Ilúvatar. Together, she and her future husband, Beren, successfully fulfill the nearly impossible task of bringing back one of the Silmarils to her father, Elu Thingol. They do so because Morgoth is charmed into blindness and sleep by her beauty and her surpassingly lovely song (Tolkien 1999a: 180). She has agency even if that agency relies upon stereotypical female attributes. She has agency even though she stereotypically sacrifices so much for love when she chooses to become mortal in order to stay with Beren.

And then there is the very important role the entwives play in the narrative although they are never seen. Treebeard says plaintively to Merry and Pippin that the ents have lost the entwives, and this comment leads to a two-page interlude that is among the most interesting parts of the entire legendarium. Treebeard says that once the ents and the entwives lived together, but that they had ceased to do so because their "hearts did not go on growing in the same way" (*The Two Towers*; Tolkien 1994b: 464). The entwives "desired order, and plenty, and peace" while the ents desired to be out in the world and to wander (464, 465). The entwives age, so when Treebeard last sees them they are "bent and browned by their labor; their hair parched by the sun to the hue of ripe corn and their cheeks like red apples" (465). Once Treebeard erotically desired Fimbrethil; now she would be old. And then Treebeard recites an Elvish song of seven verses about the ents and the entwives. It is a duet between an ent (verses 1, 3 and 5) and an entwife (verses 2, 4, and 6) with a two-line seventh verse sung together. The entwife says that she will not return to the ent in springtime "because my land is fair," and she

will not return in summer "because my land is best!" but she will
wait for him in wintertime so that "Together we will take the road
beneath the bitter rain!" (466). What the entwife is saying is that she
will not compromise unless the ent also compromises so that they
may both be happy. What Tolkien is saying is that in relationships
men and women grow apart because they have different interests
and different needs. It is a fascinating moment in which the reality
of life outside of an achieved fantasy is dwelt on.

The male role is more easily examined because there are no
exceptions to male agency being valorized. A list of names is itself
sufficient: Aragorn, Gandalf, Saruman, Théoden, Bilbo, Frodo,
Beren, Túrin, and so on. What is interesting is that women do not
seem important in the lives of men with the exception of Aragorn
(who has Arwen), Beren (who has Lúthien Tinúviel), and Túrin
(who has Níniel/Nienor). Indeed, women are largely absent from
male experience. Desire is absent too so that although Sam and
Rosie produce thirteen children together desire is not something
that forms a significant part of their relationship. Love, yes, but not
desire. And when men and women are brought together it is seen
as a sacrifice or taboo. So Arwen and Lúthien give up their elvish
immortality to be with the ones they love: Aragorn and Beren. So
Túrin weds Níniel only to discover later that she is his sister. That
discovery leads to their suicide—with Níniel throwing herself into
a ravine (Cabed-en-Aras) and Túrin throwing himself on his own
sword, Gurthang.

Music Is the Staff of Life

Two examples of this theme should suffice. The first comes from
the creation myth ("Ainulindalë"; Tolkien 1999a: 15–22). In that
myth, Ilúvatar first makes the Ainur (or Holy Ones). Then he speaks
to them, but he does so only in "themes of music" (15). The Ainur
sing to him and after a while achieve greater "unison and harmony"
(15). This is the "Great Music" of creation. There is at first one
theme, but Morgoth selfishly adds another out of pride, but it is
discordant. Then Ilúvatar shows the Ainur a vision of a newly
created world that has come about solely through music. "Behold
your Music!" he says (17). As far as Tolkien is concerned: no music,
no creation.

The second example involves the legendarium as a whole, and it is simply this: Song and music are ubiquitous, so it is hardly surprising that Tolkien toward the end of his life should have collaborated with the musician Donald Swann on a collection of a few of his legendarium poems set to music: *The Road Goes Ever On* (1967). *The Hobbit* gets not quite ten pages into the story before we have an impromptu song: "Chip the glasses and crack the plates!"(Tolkien 2007a: 13), which the dozen assembled dwarves apparently sing to make the task of cleaning up the kitchen easier. One page later the dwarves get into some after-dinner relaxation at Thorin Oakenshield's request: "Now for some music! ... Bring out the instruments!" (14). And he gets some music in the form of a ten-quatrain song about Smaug's treasure ("Far over the misty mountains cold"; 14–16). We have to wait all of thirty pages for another song, but this one is special because it is the first time Bilbo meets elves, and their presence is preceded with the sound of their singing a four-verse nonsense song, "O! What are you doing / And where are you going?" (46). *The Lord of the Rings* is similarly filled with music and song. It is prefaced with the "Ring Verse" ("Three Rings for the Elven-kings under the sky" [*The Fellowship of the Ring*; 1994a:v]). Bilbo's farewell party includes "songs, dances, music, games, and, of course, food and drink" (27). As the four hobbits (Frodo, Sam, Merry, and Pippin) travel through the Shire, Frodo responds to Sam's question: "Do Elves live in those woods?" with an answer in the form of an eight-line song: "The Road goes ever on and on" (72), and none of the assembled hobbits think this behavior odd because song and music is so fundamental a form of communication for them. Soon after, the hobbits sing a "walking-song" as opposed to a "supper-song" or a "bed-song" (76) to make the journey easier. It is a song composed by Bilbo and taught to Frodo as the two of them walked in the Shire and talked of "Adventure." It is titled "Upon the hearth the fire is red" (76).

The question of why song and music are thematically so important has more than one answer. There is the biographical one: Tolkien's family was musical; Tolkien's wife, Edith, was a musician. There is the universal emotional one: music and song express joy and happiness, sorrow and regret. There is the narrative one: the songs break up the quest narrative. There is the artistic one: music and song are aesthetic and lovely. And there is the speculative one. Tolkien's daughter, Priscilla, suggested (in a 1977-talk at Church

House Westminster) that "the power and beauty of music may ... represent the feeling of unsatisfied longing in my father" (quoted in Scull and Hammond 2005: 2, 615). She does not, unfortunately, go on to explain the nature and cause(s) of this "unsatisfied longing."

Oaths Are Not to Be Taken Lightly

There are three important oaths in the legendarium. The first is Fëanor's oath. The second is the oath of Eorl. The third is the oath sworn to by the people of the White Mountains to support Isildur in his struggle against Sauron. A useful context for studying this theme of the significance of oaths is the description of Hrothgar, the ruler of Denmark, in *Beowulf* (the text which Tolkien knew above all others). Hrothgar, the poem says, was a mighty king in part because "[h]is vow he belied not: the rings he dealt and treasure at the feast" (Tolkien 2014: 15, ll. 64–5). Taking an oath is a serious matter; breaking an oath has serious consequences.

Fëanor's oath is the single most dramatic moment in the "Quenta Silmarillion." It is also the moment with the greatest narrative consequences. The oath is Fëanor's, and it is sworn to by Fëanor and his seven sons. The oath reads:

Be he foe or friend, be he foul or clean,
brood of Morgoth or bright Vala,
Elda or Maia or Aftercomer,
Man yet unborn upon Middle-earth,
neither law, nor love, nor league of swords,
dread nor danger, not Doom itself,
shall defend him from Fëanor, and Fëanor's kin,
whoso hideth or hoardeth, or in hand taketh,
finding keepeth or afar casteth
a Silmaril. This swear we all:
death we will deal him ere Day's ending,
woe unto world's end! Our word hear thou,
Eru Allfather! To the everlasting
Darkness doom us if our deed faileth.
On the holy mountain hear in witness
and our vow remember, Manwë and Varda!

("The Annals of Aman"; Tolkien 1993: 112)

And in case the reader doesn't understand the seriousness of the moment, the paragraph in which the oath is quoted in full ends ominously: "For so sworn, good or evil, an oath may not be broken, and it shall pursue oathkeeper or oathbreaker to the world's end" (Tolkien 1993: 112). The reason for the oath is that Morgoth had stolen the Silmarils from Fëanor's stronghold in Formenos. Morgoth now has the jewels in his possession, and Fëanor, their creator, wants them back at any price. And the price is high. The majority of the Noldor journey to Middle-earth from Aman in hopeless pursuit of the jewels. Then the sons of Fëanor fight the elves of Beleriand since Lúthien comes to possess one of the jewels. Then they destroy the kingdom of Doriath. In the end, Fëanor and six of his sons die; the seventh (Maglor) is left a broken wanderer.

The second oath is a simpler one with a happier outcome. Eorl, the first king of Rohan, and Cirion, the twelfth steward of Gondor, swear to support each other in any struggle against Sauron. As did the oath of Fëanor, Eorl's oath has consequences attached to it. If it were broken, the shadow would fall upon the oathbreaker, and he would be accursed. It is this oath that binds Rohan to Gondor in Gondor's hour of need in 3018; it is this oath to which Théoden remains true when he fights at the battle of the Pelennor Fields outside the walls of Minas Tirith.

The third oath is again simpler in its narrative consequences than Fëanor's oath, but like that oath it is broken with terrible consequences. The oath is sworn to by the people who live by the White Mountains. They swear to support Isildur against Sauron, but they break that oath and remain neutral in the battles at the end of the Second Age, the battles that defeat Sauron. The consequence? Exactly what they swore would happen if they broke their oath. The oathbreakers dwindle and die out and become ghosts ready to be called upon by Isildur's heir in any future battle with Sauron. They follow Aragorn and Gimli and Legolas from the Stone of Erech to Pelagir and defeat the corsairs of Umbar in southern Gondor. With that accomplished they finally die forever. Only then.

And why does Tolkien argue that oaths matter so much? This may seem odd in these days when truth is endangered in so many ways in our postmodern culture, but Tolkien lived through two world wars, both of which happened because countries swore oaths to each other, oaths of mutual defense. World War I was a family squabble in which more than eleven million soldiers and six million civilians died. Tolkien would have classified that as an example of taking oaths lightly in the sense that the world powers at that time did not think enough about the possible consequences of the promises they made. World War II was a necessity. Hitler had to be defeated, but it cost the lives of about twenty-five million soldiers and thirty million civilians. Tolkien would have classified that as horrible but necessary, and it began with the fulfillment of a pact (a sort of modern-day written oath). Germany invaded Poland; Britain declared war against Germany because it had a pact to defend Poland if it was invaded: the British–Polish Common Defence Pact. World War II began on September 1, 1939.

Looked at from another perspective, Tolkien was also a devout Catholic and a believer in the Ten Commandments, one of which reads "Thou shall not bear false witness." Tolkien was also a world-renowned philologist of Anglo-Saxon, Middle-English, and Scandinavian languages. The literature in those languages repeatedly emphasizes the importance of loyalty and truth-bearing. The legendarium does precisely the same thing.

Peace Needs to Be Preserved in Order to Stay Peace

The long history of Middle-earth in *The Silmarillion* is a battle between the Valar and the elves (and some men) to subdue Morgoth and achieve the peace that was initially part of Ilúvatar's creation. The history of the First Age is one of pocket utopias (Doriath and Gondolin among them) being protected against the wrath of Morgoth and, to a lesser degree, Sauron. Again and again there are wars to protect peace until the Great Battle or the War of Wrath finally destroys Morgoth and he is banished for ever from this world and peace returns. The history of the Second Age is one in which the Edain are handed a pocket utopia (the island of Númenor) by the Valar as a reward only to destroy that utopia through their pride. That land (which is also called Andor or the Land of Gift) is a "country fair and fruitful" at the beginning of the "Akallabêth" (or the account of Númenor's downfall). It disappears forever beneath the waves at the end. Tolkien appears to be suggesting that the protection of peace against external enemies is not enough; it has to be protected against internal enemies (such as pride) and evil which has the appearance of good (Sauron).

The Third Age also focuses on the preservation of peace but not peace at all costs. The Shire is Tolkien's idealized vision of an agrarian England. Hobbits are free and happy and well-fed and prosperous, but they are so because the Rangers (such as Aragorn) protect its borders ceaselessly (*The Fellowship of the Ring*; Tolkien 1994a: 59). Rivendell and Lothlórien are utopias of another kind: of learning and high culture. They are protected by the vigilance of the elves and by the power of Elrond, Celeborn, and Galadriel. Tom Bombadil's kingdom near the Barrow Downs is a perfect world preserved by a sort of natural magic, but that is not a model that can be broadened to include a wider geography. There is only one Tom Bombadil. And the narrative of *The Lord of the Rings* is one in which the forces of the west defeat Sauron and destroy the One Ring in the Cracks of Doom. They do so because they realize that they must make war to create a meaningful peace. The members of the Council of Elrond consider other strategies: keeping the One Ring secret in Rivendell or giving it to Tom Bombadil for safe keeping. However, both of those strategies they realize quickly are examples of peace at any cost through the apparent avoidance of war. Nor does anyone consider suing for peace with Sauron or with his underling, Saruman. Neither can be trusted, so any peace would not last long.

And why would Tolkien consider the theme of peace having to be preserved through war so important as to enshrine it in his legendarium? Here his biography is important again. He lived through two world wars and fought at the battle of the Somme. Two of his sons fought in World War II. He knew under what conditions peace had to be preserved. He spent the early years of his life as a poor orphan, a boy who knew a great deal about the struggle for life. He spent much of his adult life as a very successful academic. Before he died, he was a world-renowned author of fantasy. From a state of doubt and struggle to a state of peace and that was achieved by something as simple as sustained and tireless industry. It is hard not to read the legendarium through the life.

Pity Is One of the Greatest Virtues

Pity is so powerful a virtue in Tolkien's view that without it the quest to destroy the One Ring would have failed. Frodo would simply have become another Gollum and would have been quickly defeated by Sauron. Pity plays a central role both in *The Hobbit* and its sequel, *The Lord of the Rings*, but it is fair to say that this role evolved as Tolkien developed the legendarium. If one looks at the original (1937) published version of *The Hobbit*, it is not pity that characterizes Bilbo's behavior. The interaction between him and Gollum is noticeably different from that in the revised (1951) version. In the 1937 version, he simply says goodbye to Gollum, who has agreed to show him the way out of the tunnels because he is not able to give Bilbo his ring for winning the riddle contest as it has gone missing. In the 1951 version (revised to make the story align with *The Lord of the Rings*), Bilbo is tempted to kill Gollum ("He must stab the foul thing, put its eyes out, kill it"; Tolkien 2007a: 81) but refrains because he has pity for it. He comprehends how terrible a life Gollum has been leading: "A sudden understanding, a pity mixed with horror, welled up in Bilbo's heart: a glimpse of endless unmarked days without light or hope of betterment, hard stone, cold fish, sneaking and whispering" (81).

In the Prologue to *The Lord of the Rings*—the section titled "4. *Of the Finding of the Ring*"—Tolkien reiterates the role of pity but increases its agency: Bilbo thought of killing Gollum, but pity makes him refrain from committing the act, in part because Gollum is so wretched and in part because Bilbo's invisibility gives him an unfair advantage (*The Fellowship of the Ring*; Tolkien 1994a: 12). In the second chapter of *The Fellowship of the Ring*, "The Shadow of the Past," Gandalf rehearses the riddle game between Gollum and Bilbo once more, and in response to Frodo's assertion that Bilbo should have stabbed Gollum, Gandalf sternly replies that Bilbo rightly showed pity toward him and that doing so made it possible for him to avoid much of the evil influence of the Ring (58).

Pity is clearly a crucial virtue for Tolkien. Early on in *The Fellowship of the Ring*, he has chosen to repeat the story of Bilbo's finding of the ring and the role of pity in that story, and Gandalf's stern reply to Frodo (referred to above) is emphasized rhetorically through a combination of capitalization (Pity not pity), irony and paronomasia (two meanings of the word "pity"), and repetition combined with periodicity ("Pity" is repeated three times in the passage from "The Shadow of the Past" and the word both begins and ends Gandalf's admonition). And just in case the reader does not get the point—that pity is a transcendent virtue—Gandalf speculates that Bilbo's pity for Gollum may yet yield benefits: "My heart tells me that he [Gollum] has some part to play yet, for good or ill, before the end; and when that comes, the pity of Bilbo may rule the fate of many—yours not least" (Tolkien 1994a: 58).

There are other examples of the value of pity in the legendarium but those cited above are sufficient to prove its importance. The question now is: Why does pity matter so much to Tolkien? Pity is not a specifically Christian or Catholic virtue. It is, however, clearly related to ideas of piety—they share the same etymology—and compassion, and the latter was the driving force behind Christ's crucifixion. That is, Christ's compassion for humanity led to his passion in order to produce compassion in humanity. And Christ's crucifixion is the central event in Christian history.

The explanation for Tolkien's emphasis on pity as a virtue may be both more personal and more utilitarian, however. From the utilitarian perspective, pity often retards a narrative by postponing action and sustaining agency. (In simple terms, Gollum may have been spared because his presence would lead to a more complex, morally nuanced and developed plot.) It is also the case that pity in a biblical context is associated with friendship. So, we have Job 6.14: "To him that is afflicted, pity should be shewed from his friend," and we have Job 19.21: "Have pity upon me, have pity upon me, O ye my friends, for the hand of God hath touched me." Indeed, pity is enough of a Christian virtue that God repays its expression, as in Proverbs 19.117: "He that hath pity upon the poor lendeth unto the Lord; and that which he hath given will he pay again." From the personal perspective, Tolkien was an orphan from a young age, so close friendship was essential to him in a way it would not have been for someone with the social benefit of a family. His history is replete with groups to which he belonged, and from which he drew lifelong friends: the TCBS and the Inklings are just the best known two among many. In a way, then, pity fulfilled both a personal need for others and represented an expression of Tolkien's devout Catholicism.

I suspect, however, that Tolkien's fondness for pity as a concept derives from his own expression of his faith mixed in with a little bit of Shakespeare perhaps (even though many think—wrongly—that Tolkien routinely disparaged that dramatist's work). In a draft letter to Eileen Elgar written in 1963 (long after his legendarium was essentially finished), he offers a philosophical reflection on pity, which he equates with mercy (Tolkien 2000: 326). According to Tolkien, we should hold *ourselves* to the highest moral standards because we are flawed beings, so if we do not do so we will surely fail to achieve what we could otherwise manage. However, we should show mercy when judging the actions of *others*—because we should show good will, because we naturally tend to think well of ourselves, because there may be reasons for others' behavior of which we are unaware, and because everyone has limits to their strength of character. And Shakespeare? Well, Tolkien in this letter to Elgar sounds a lot like Portia in *The Merchant of Venice* and her famous "quality of mercy" speech (4.1.184–205).

Power Corrupts

It is common for scholars to assert that power is the most important topic in the legendarium and that Tolkien sees power almost always as intensely negative. In his correspondence, Tolkien argues that *The Lord of the Rings* is an allegory of power used with the intent to dominate. However, he does not consider the theme to be the most significant one in the epic. Power, according to Tolkien, is more a setting and a means to introduce the subject of war (letter to Joanna de Bortadano, April 1956; Tolkien 2000: 246). In other letters, Tolkien states that Morgoth is only concerned with power as domination (2000: 146) and that in the real world it seems that those in authority who do not abuse power are very rare indeed (Letter to Christopher Tolkien, November 29, 1943; 2000: 64). So, he will doubtless have agreed with Baron Acton's bon mot "power tends to corrupt and absolute power corrupts absolutely" (quoted in Scull and Hammond 2006: 2.779).

So the theme of the corrupting nature of power is expressed in the legendarium, but what is not sometimes observed is how carefully Tolkien makes of it a narrative device in *The Lord of the Rings*. The symbol of power in that part of the legendarium is, of course, the One Ring, and in the broad arc of the narrative Tolkien organizes events so that nearly every important figure in the story has the opportunity to take possession of the Ring and all but two refuse. It is as if he wanted to reinforce the theme by having it double as a structural device—almost a motif.

We first have Gandalf. Frodo directly offers him the ring in the simple way typical of hobbits. Gandalf's response is quick, long, and typically forthright. He will not accept the ring. Were he to do so, he would become another Sauron even though he would begin by using the ring to do good in the world, to show pity, and to help the weak. He knows enough about the limits of his own strength to realize, too, that he could not just hold on to the ring and not use it, for he would be too tempted to wield it (*The Fellowship of the Ring*; Tolkien 1994a: 60). Gandalf is wise enough to know his limitations—even as an Istari.

Next we have Tom Bombadil. Tolkien plays with the reader a little at first by having Bombadil sound menacing when he first orders Frodo to show him the ring, which he ominously calls "precious" (*The Fellowship of the Ring*; Tolkien 1994a: 130). Frodo does as he is told, but the ring has no effect on Bombadil. In truth, it becomes for Bombadil an unexpected means to a humorous end. Before he returns it to Frodo, smiling as he does so, he spins the ring in the air and makes *it* rather than its wearer suddenly vanish. In a sense, Tolkien is suggesting that Tom Bombadil has unlimited beneficent power in his own small kingdom, so why would he exchange that for maleficent power in the wider world?

And then there's Aragorn who is tested. At *The Prancing Pony*, Frodo, Sam, Merry, and Pippin meet Strider/Aragorn. Aragorn knows very well what they possess, and he rejects it with something of a thespian flourish: "If I was after the Ring, I could have it— NOW!" (*The Fellowship of the Ring*; Tolkien 1994a: 168). And his rejection of the corrupted power it represents becomes an opportunity for Tolkien to show Aragorn's ancestry and the purity of his motivations in seeking out the ringbearer and his companions, and to emphasize them with a little alliteration of the "h," "s," "k," and "a" sounds too (which I have highlighted through underlining):

<u>H</u>e [Aragorn] <u>s</u>tood up, and <u>s</u>eemed <u>s</u>uddenly to grow taller. In <u>h</u>is eyes gleamed a light, <u>k</u>een and <u>c</u>ommanding. Throwing back

his cloak, he laid his hand on the hilt of a sword that had hung concealed by his side. They [the hobbits] did not dare to move. Sam sat wide-mouthed staring at him dumbly.

"But I *am* the real Strider, fortunately," he said, looking down at them with his face softened by a sudden smile. "I am Aragorn son of Arathorn; and if by life or death I can save you, I will." (Tolkien 1994a: 171)

On the journey south from Rivendell, Boromir is also tempted by the ring. He has been for some time—ostensibly because he wants it as an invaluable aid in the defense of Gondor; in fact because he is tempted by the power that it would offer him were he to possess it. As the company nears Gondor and Boromir finds himself alone with Frodo near the falls of Rauros, he sees his opportunity. On the one hand, Boromir is bent on doing good, for he would use the ring to defeat Mordor. On the other, he is attracted to the ring because it would give him the ability to command anyone to do his bidding (*The Fellowship of the Ring*; Tolkien 1994a: 389). Quickly his desire to take the ring gains control as he moves, seemingly effortlessly, from the idea that he *could* possess the ring to the idea that he *should* do so: Thus, he moves from rumination to directly commanding Frodo to give him the ring (390). Looked at from one perspective, Boromir has fallen into the trap that Gandalf wisely avoided at the beginning of the trilogy: Power corrupts by tempting the individual to do good—at least initially. When Boromir realizes his error (he considers it a temporary fit of madness), he slays as many orcs as he can in order to give the hobbits a chance to escape. However, he knows the ring did corrupt him and accepts that he must pay for his failure (*The Two Towers*; Tolkien 1994b: 404). As if to emphasize the enormity of Boromir's fall and the very real but very human error he committed, Tolkien frames Boromir's dying words with Aragorn's kind acts as the latter kneels beside him, takes his hand, and kisses him on the forehead.

On the journey south, the company sojourns in Lothlórien to try to come to terms with their grief at the loss of Gandalf. There, arguably the most powerful and learned of all the elves, Galadriel, finds herself tempted to take the One Ring. She gives Frodo the chance to look in the mirror of Galadriel, and in the ensuing dialogue Frodo offers her the ring in almost the same simple way he did with Gandalf ten months before. Yet there are some subtle differences.

When Frodo offered Gandalf the ring, he did so because he knew him to be wise and already powerful (perhaps powerful enough, he seems to think, to master it). Now, he offers Galadriel the ring because she is wise (like Gandalf) and courageous and beautiful and because he has come to know the ring well as it has traveled south with him and is daunted by it (*The Fellowship of the Ring*; Tolkien 1994a: 356). However, she recognizes the corrupting power of the ring, and says so very clearly in a sustained description of what would happen were she to accept Frodo's offer. She would become powerful beyond imagining, and those she ruled would love her, be terrified of her, and they would despair (356). Galadriel's sustained description is just part of a rhetorical debate with herself, however, one where she knows the right answer even as she debates. She concludes by refusing the ring as she proudly remains Galadriel and predicts, correctly, that she will leave Middle-earth with the rest of the Eldar (357).

There are two more demonstrations of the power of the ring to corrupt—at least, to corrupt those whose hearts are not true. The first involves Sam at Cirith Ungol. With Frodo apparently killed by Shelob, Sam has to decide whether to take the ring in order to continue the quest. Initially, he considers suicide as a way of avoiding the decision. Then he decides he is unworthy of the ring. Then he realizes that he has to take the ring and continue the quest, and in typical Sam fashion he expresses it with great simplicity: "'No, it's sit here till they [orcs] come and kill me over master's body, and gets It; or take It and go.' He drew a deep breath. 'Then take It, it is!'" (*The Two Towers*; Tolkien 1994b: 715). The second is Gollum at the Cracks of Doom. He is tempted to take the ring, and he does so. And that is only to be expected as Gollum/Sméagol had killed his friend Déagol more than 500 years before in order to possess his "Precious." As if to emphasize how much power may corrupt, Gollum takes the ring by bestially gnawing off Frodo's ring finger before falling backward into the Cracks of Doom.

As to the question of why Tolkien should be so aware of the subtle corrupting nature of power, there are two short answers: the bloody history of the twentieth century (with Hitler and Stalin being merely the most notorious of a long list of brutal leaders), and academic politics. Tolkien was a professor for almost forty years: first at the University of Leeds and then at Oxford University. He fought a long and successful battle while at Oxford fundamentally to change the English curriculum. That would have taught him much about power and the abuse of power. In a letter to his son Christopher in 1943, he delivers the heartfelt judgment that fewer than one in a million can remain uncorrupted by power. Only those who do not wish for power have even a chance of using it well (Tolkien 2000: 64).

The Quest Is an Essential Part of Life

There are numerous examples from all the three Ages of the importance of this theme to Tolkien, and at least one example of what happens to someone when he doesn't have a quest. It is, of course, a theme that Tolkien encountered frequently in Anglo-Saxon and Middle-English literature. In *Beowulf*, the eponymous hero has his quest: to destroy Grendel and his mother and (much later) an unnamed dragon. In *Sir Gawain and the Green Knight*, Sir Gawain has to fulfill his "Christmas game." In the *Canterbury Tales*, all of the pilgrims are on an identical quest: to travel to the shrine of St. Thomas à Becket at Canterbury and return to London. And it is a theme that Tolkien himself enshrined in the arc of his life. It was a remarkably successful quest to go from being an impoverished orphan to a much-admired professor at one of the major universities in the world. Along the way he had a family and a long and successful marriage to Edith Tolkien (neé Bratt). And his quest for success in life mirrored his legendarium when he chose to have the names "Beren" and "Lúthien" inscribed on the tombstone of the grave he shares with his wife.

Let us start with the First Age to see how this theme of the essential nature of the quest in life plays out. I'll use three examples: Beren and Lúthien, Eärendil, and Túrin Turambar. The first of these is the classic Hercules' labors story. King Thingol of Doriath (an elf) requires Beren (a man) to bring back one of the Silmarils (currently possessed by Morgoth) in order to marry his daughter, Lúthien, the most beautiful being in the world (Tolkien 1999a: 165). After many adventures, he does so, and Thingol allows their marriage. However, Beren is mortally wounded in the quest. Lúthien travels to the halls of Mandos and sings of her sorrow at the death of her husband. Mandos is moved by her sorrow: He restores Beren to life and grants mortality to Lúthien. They live out their lives in

Ossiriand and after a long time both die a mortal death. Tolkien returned again and again to this story and over the course of the history of his creating the legendarium wrote several versions most notably "The Tale of Tinúviel" and "The Lay of Leithian." In 2017, his son Christopher edited a book-length version of the story titled simply *Beren and Lúthien.*

Eärendil's quest is a very different one from that on which Beren and Lúthien were engaged although his love for his wife, Elwing, is every bit as remarkable. Eärendil's quest is to get aid from the Valar in the struggle between Morgoth and elves and men. Eärendil is the first man to set foot in Valinor; his plea for aid to the Valar succeeds; and together the Valar and elves and men defeat Morgoth, with Morgoth being permanently removed from the world (Tolkien 1999a: 254). From one perspective, Eärendil's quest is the most important in the entire legendarium. Without it, Morgoth might not have been defeated and the history of Middle-earth would have been very different and even more tragic.

If Eärendil's life story is proof of the importance of the quest in life, Túrin Turambar's is proof of the opposite: what happens to someone who doesn't have a quest. It could be argued that he does have quests (finding Finduilas, slaying Glaurung), but these are really just moments in a life given over to being an outlaw. It could be argued, flippantly, that his quest is to gain as many epithets as he can: Neithan, Gorthol, Agarwaen, Thurin, Adanedhel, Mormegil, and Turambar among them. But really his lack of a quest comes from the sort of story he finds himself in. With Túrin, Tolkien created a figure like Oedipus, for Túrin suffers mightily during his life. During that life he accidentally marries his sister, Nienor/ Níniel. When they realize what has happened they each commit suicide. I have suggested that Túrin's story shows how wasted a life may be if it does not have a quest, but it may also be that the story of Túrin's tragic life illustrates in part the reach of Morgoth's power to do evil in the world, for so much that happens to Túrin happens because Morgoth is intent upon destroying Ilúvatar's creation.

Thus far, we have had examples of quests that were successful and of lives that were without a quest. In the Second Age and with the Númenórean king Ar-Pharazôn, we have an example of a quest that is unworthy. Beren's quest was for love; Eärendil's quest was for divine aid; Ar-Pharazôn's is for self-aggrandizement and immortality—and that quest is doomed to failure because mortality is an essential part of what it is to be human. At first, when Ar-Pharazôn claims Valinor for his own it seems as if he has been successful. After all, who could possibly stand against fleets so massive as to block the sunset? Yet it is almost as if Ar-Pharazôn knows he will be unsuccessful, for he nearly turns back at the sight of Taniquetil sitting so high and silent and immovable on the shores of Valinor (Tolkien 1999a: 278). And what does Ilúvatar do in response to Ar-Pharazôn's arrogant quest for immortality? He remakes the world and punishes Ar-Pharazôn and his troops more severely even than the oathbreakers at the Paths of the Dead in *The Lord of the Rings*. All of them are eternally imprisoned in the Caves of the Forgotten (1999a: 278–279). It is surely meant by Tolkien as a supreme irony that Ar-Pharazôn got what he had always wanted: immortality. Unfortunately, it is an immortality of imprisonment until the end of all things. *Sic semper tyrannis*.

The quests in the Third Age need less discussion here because they are so well known. Suffice it to say that without the quest for Smaug's treasure, *The Hobbit* would not exist. It would have been a very different and dull book in which Bilbo has *no* adventure but just stays in Bag End and in Hobbiton being a hobbit and indulging his passion for food and pipe tobacco and parties. Suffice it to say, too, that without the quest to destroy the One Ring there would have been no epic or a very different one in which Aragorn's allied quest for his rightful kingship would have been unsuccessful or successful only at the cost of his honor, for he might have been able to defeat Sauron by using the One Ring against him. However, that would have led to Aragorn becoming evil over time, and the moral purpose of this part of the legendarium would have been vitiated. It is important to note that the two quests in the Third Age—to acquire Smaug's treasure and to destroy the One Ring—are polar opposites as one is about possessing wealth and the other about destroying it. It is hard not to see Tolkien as a scholar of Anglo-Saxon recalling that beautiful passage in *Beowulf* where the poet talks of the pointlessness of acquiring treasure.

> In that [burial] mound they [Beowulf's followers] laid armlets and jewels and all such ornament as erewhile daring-hearted men had taken from the hoard, abandoning the treasure of mighty men to earth to keep, gold to the ground where yet it dwells as profitless to men as it proved of old. (Tolkien 2014: 105, ll.2650–4)

Sociability Is Central to Happiness

As with some of the earlier themes, it is important to consider Tolkien's biography for a moment. Tolkien was a very sociable person, especially with men and especially with academics. Over the course of his life he belonged to many clubs, the best known being the TCBS and the Inklings. Tolkien clearly valued the society of others, and one can see this in both *The Hobbit* and *The Lord of the Rings*. Both start with parties: one may be "unexpected" and the other "long-expected," but they are both parties which the assembled company (a wizard and dwarves in the one and a wizard and hobbits in the other) thoroughly enjoys. By contrast, it is singletons or loners who are dangerous: Sauron himself (alone in Barad-dûr); Denethor (alone in the White Tower); and Saruman (alone in Orthanc) come to mind. It is as if evil or madness grows without the restraining company of others.

Technology Is Corrosive and Disruptive

It is well known that Tolkien disliked technology. He associated it with industrialism and the loss of a quieter, more rural way of life that he deeply loved. In a letter to his son, Christopher, in 1944, Tolkien wrote that the tragedy of machinery is that it is used only to foster power. Machines which would save people time and effort lead, in fact, to worse sorts of labor. Too often and because we live in a lapsarian world, our creations are used for evil ends (Tolkien 2000: 87–8). In the legendarium itself, Morgoth creates fortresses (Utumno and Angband) with colossal damage done to nature. In the legendarium, Saruman uses technology to create the Uruk-hai, a sort of super-orc, and he destroys some of Fangorn—wantonly and because he has no love for nature. And in the legendarium, Sauron transforms Mordor into a dead land in pursuit of power through weaponry and force (*The Return of the King*; Tolkien 1994c: 902).

There is little actual technology in the legendarium as if to show how much Tolkien loathed it, but there are the palantíri, and these show how technology may be misused. Originally, the seven palantíri (or seeing stones) were an advanced form of communication created by the Noldor and used to keep in touch across great distances and, apparently, across time itself (*The Two Towers*; Tolkien 1994b: 583–4). However, Sauron and Saruman use the ones they possess for evil; Denethor uses his to try to discover Sauron's purposes; and Pippin uses the one he takes from Gandalf because he is an inquisitive fool. Saruman through the palantír decides wrongly that the only way to survive the coming war is to serve Sauron. Denethor decides all is lost and goes insane. Pippin suffers a seizure but is not permanently harmed. Gandalf makes clear, however, what he thinks of technology, for he sees Pippin's use of the seeing stone as mischievous and devilish—a view which is echoed later by Gimli calling the same palantír "that accursed stone of wizardry!" (*The Return of the King*; Tolkien 1994c: 763).

There is only one wise use of this technology, and that is when Aragorn uses the palantír of Orthanc to wrest the power of the stone away from Sauron and to cause Sauron to doubt the success of his designs. This is a crucial moment in the narrative from Tolkien's point of view, and, so, he has Aragorn recount at length his struggle with Sauron to Gimli and Legolas while they rest in the Burg (*The Return of the King*; Tolkien 1994c: 763). Aragorn's wise and brave use of the palantír causes Sauron to strike against Minas Tirith too early—before his plans are fully developed, that is. As Aragorn remarks to Gimli: "The hasty stroke goes oft astray" (763). Aragorn's use also enables him to see a threat to Gondor from the south which no one knew about, and that *alone* causes Aragorn to take the Paths of the Dead and to overthrow the corsairs of Umbar with the help of the oathbreakers. In a sense, then, Gondor would have fallen had not Aragorn used the palantír.

Tradition Is an Essential Element in Social Organization

There are several ways in which the importance of tradition manifests itself in the legendarium. One is through the power that lore and prophecy have. There is the lore that surrounds the healing properties of a herb called kingsfoil (or athelas). The herb saves Frodo, and it saves Faramir, and it saves Éowyn from death due to being poisoned by the enemy. Frodo is stabbed with a Morgul blade on Weathertop; Faramir is shot with a Nazgûl dart; Éowyn is hurt by having delivered the death blow to the leader of the Nazgûl: the Witch-king of Angmar. The lore is inscribed in a rhyme that begins "*When the black breath blows*" (*The Return of the King*; Tolkien 1994c: 847).

Another way in which tradition shows it matters to the legendarium occurs in the appendices to *The Lord of the Rings*. Appendix A is titled "Annals of the Kings and Rulers." It contains information on Númenor, the house of Eorl, and Durin's Folk. Appendix B is titled "The Tale of Years" and subtitled "(Chronology of the Westlands)." Appendix C is titled "Family Trees" and covers the family history of hobbits only. The one thing that unites these appendices, which are full of material Tolkien would have liked to have included in some form in the legendarium proper had he had time and energy, is tradition—whether that is national or cultural or familial. In essence, Tolkien is saying that tradition (or the sense of history) is essential to keeping a social organization healthy.

One can see this point most clearly, perhaps, in the history of governance in Gondor. The last king of Gondor before Aragorn returns as king was Eärnur. He had been crowned king in 2043 but was treacherously murdered by the Witch-king of Angmar. Since no successor could be found whose claim all could agree on, the stewards ruled in the place of the king and from the first (Mardil Voronwë) to the last (Denethor II) there were twenty-six stewards. Each of them took an oath: "to hold rod and rule in the place of the king, until he shall return" (*The Return of the King*; Tolkien 1994c: 1028). And that oath meant something, for part of Denethor's madness—as it is described in the legendarium—occurs because in his pride he would forget his oath and remain ruler of Gondor even if it was proved that Aragorn's claim to the throne is legitimate. Denethor makes this fallacious line of reasoning very clear as he spars verbally with Gandalf after the battle of the Pelennor Fields (*The Return of the King*; Tolkien 1994c: 835–6). Denethor forgets tradition. He forgets his oath. He kills himself in despair over the death of Boromir and (he thinks) Faramir. Indeed, part of the purpose of the way the epic ends is to restore tradition by having Faramir happily relinquish *his* stewardship only to have Aragorn show *his own* power by restoring to Faramir the Steward's ceremonial role: "That office is not ended, and it shall be thine and thy heirs' as long as my line shall last." "Do now thy office!" he declares (945). And Faramir does fulfill that office by publicly announcing the return of the king and by taking the ancient crown of Eärnur (the last king of Gondor) from its casket. And then Aragorn seals tradition by repeating the words that Elendil spoke in Quenya when he set foot on Middle-earth at the end of the Second Age: "Et Eärello Endorenna utúlien. Sinome maruvan ar Hildinyar tenn' Ambar-metta!" ("Out of the Great Sea to Middle-earth I am come. In this place will I abide, and my heirs, unto the ending of the world") (946). Yet, in Tolkien's view, tradition is in some ways a living thing and should not be treated as absolutely sacrosanct, so Aragorn departs slightly from the expected ritual by having Frodo give him (Aragorn) the crown and by having Gandalf place the crown on his head in honor of their vital roles in restoring his kingship. What we have is the veneration of tradition but not in some ossified way, veneration of the words and oaths of (as Faramir puts it) "our longfathers of old" (946).

True Love Involves Sacrifice

There are three classic examples in the legendarium of the truth of this theme: Beren and Lúthien, Aragorn and Arwen, and Eärendil and Elwing. Of the first two pairs of lovers this chapter has talked already, but of Eärendil and Elwing it has said little. Elwing possesses one of the three Silmarils. To stop Maedhros (one of the sons of Fëanor) from taking it, she throws herself into the sea. The Vala Ulmo rescues her from the sea and transforms her into a great white bird. In this form, she flies with the Silmaril upon her breast to her husband on board his ship, Vingilot. That night, she is miraculously transformed back into a woman and Eärendil's wife so that in the morning Eärendil finds her sleeping in his arms (Tolkien 1999a: 247). Eärendil knows the peril she has put herself in for love of him and tries to distance her from any anger the Valar may feel at his having sailed to Valinor to plead for their aid against Morgoth. It is a danger that Manwë acknowledges when he talks of Elwing having "entered into peril for love of" Eärendil (249). And the love of Eärendil and Elwing is perpetual, for when he guides his ship across the heavens shining like a star with the Silmaril at its prow Elwing flies to meet him from her white tower north of the Sundering Sea (250). And that happens as predictably and eternally as the sun rises and sets.

In an interesting twist on the idea of love requiring sacrifice, where Lúthien and Arwen both chose mortality in order to be with the husbands even in death, Elwing chooses immortality for herself, and Eärendil chooses the same even though he misses the world of men and Tuor's, his father's, people in particular. So, whether the wife sacrifices or the husband does so, love requires sacrifice in Tolkien's view.

Afterword

In August 2018, as this book was getting close to being finished, Houghton Mifflin Harcourt published Tolkien's *The Fall of Gondolin* as edited by his son, Christopher. *The Fall of Gondolin* is the third of the four great stories of the First Age: *The Children of Húrin*, *Beren and Lúthien*, and "The Tale of Eärendel" being the other three. Because there is likely not enough material for a separately published volume devoted to Eärendel, *The Fall of Gondolin* brings to a close the long and remarkable saga of Tolkien's legendarium and his son's devotion to his father's achievement.

The fall of the city of Gondolin is, of course, well known to many Tolkien enthusiasts from *The Silmarillion* and *The Book of Lost Tales*, and while the separately published volume which recently appeared adds much detail to the version in *The Silmarillion*, it is not that which matters to me here, for the simple reason that it adds nothing unexpected or unusual. It is, however, an important document in several respects, which I will outline in this Afterword.

The Personal Element

Christopher Tolkien is now in his ninety-fifth year. He had thought that *Beren and Lúthien* (published in 2017) would be his last book. Now *The Fall of Gondolin* will be for sure: "it is certain that the present book is the last," he writes (Tolkien 2018: 13). I find myself deeply moved by Christopher Tolkien's extraordinary, selfless achievement over more than forty years and by the tone of sorrow at time past in the Preface.

Editing

In *The Fall of Gondolin*, Christopher Tolkien foregrounds the question of how best to edit his father's work. With *The Silmarillion*, he opted for a heavily reconstructed work in which clarity won over accuracy. What mattered then (in 1977) was that his father's monumental work of the First Age should be presented coherently— even if that choice ran roughshod over the reality of textual confusion. After all, Tolkien had been dead for only four years at that point. (Christopher Tolkien now calls that strategy "'contrived'" (2018: 11).) With the twelve-volume *The History of Middle-earth* series (1983–96), he opted for a very different approach: to present "the whole narrative movement as it evolved through the years" in order to show the legendarium "longitudinally" (over his father's lifetime) and not "transversely" (as a series of finished projects) (2018: 13). With *The Children of Húrin*, Christopher Tolkien took one story, made it coherent in a way analogous to his work with *The Silmarillion* thirty years before, and discussed in an appendix the alterations to the narrative over time. With *Beren and Lúthien* and *The Fall of Gondolin* he adopted a fourth strategy: to present various versions of the story in full and sequentially.

This is, tacitly, an honest admission of his own developing attitude to editing and one which raises a marvelously resonant question: What is the best way to edit the legendarium?

Macrocosm and Microcosm

In reflecting on his own achievement in *The History of Middle-earth* series and his father's achievement in the legendarium, Christopher Tolkien usefully explains the unique quality of his father's work:

> My *History* of that age, so long and complex as it is, owes its length and complexity to this endless welling up [in the legendarium]: a new portrayal, a new motive, a new name, above all new associations. My father, as the Maker, ponders the large history, and as he writes he becomes aware of a new element that has entered the story. (Tolkien 2018: 10)

A beautiful expression of a complicated, lifelong evolution.

The Legendarium

The Fall of Gondolin is a memorable and satisfying story in its own regard. It is the equal of the other major tales in the legendarium. It is, however, also unique in a significant way that has been little noted. Tolkien's creative writing is full of heroes (large and small). The titles of his many books emphasize this very fact: *The Hobbit* (Bilbo); *Farmer Giles of Ham; The Lord of the Rings* (Aragorn—or is it Sauron?); "The Homecoming of Beorhtnoth, Beorthelm's Son"; *The Adventures of Tom Bombadil; Smith of Wootton Major; Roverandom; The Children of Húrin; The Legend of Sigurd and Gudrún; The Fall of Arthur; The Story of Kullervo; The Lay of Aotrou and Itroun*; and *Beren and Lúthien. The Fall of Gondolin* alone is concerned with something else: the sack of a city. Yes, Tuor (a man) is important to the action, but destruction is central to the meaning and purpose of the tale. Perhaps in *The Fall of Gondolin* Tolkien takes on warfare as a focus and exorcises his experiences in World War I. It was, after all, the first of his early stories to be fully committed to paper (in about 1916–18, during and shortly after his experiences at the battle of the Somme). It was the first of his stories to be presented to an audience: the Essay Club of Exeter College at Oxford University. The year was 1920 and Tolkien was just twenty-eight. It was and would always be, as he wrote to W. H. Auden in 1955, "the first real story of this imaginary world" (quoted in Tolkien 2018: 22). It will, fittingly, be the last of his books to be published.

APPENDIX A
TOLKIEN'S SOURCES

This appendix consists of six tables followed by some notes intended to contextualize the information presented.

Table A: Anglo-Saxon Sources

Work	Date	Description	Significance
The Battle of Maldon (fragment)	991–1075 CE	325 lines (*Cotton MS*)	The definitions of heroism and pride (*ofermod*) match those in the legendarium
Beowulf	500–700 CE	3,182 lines (*Nowell Codex*)	Tolkien devoted his academic life to studying the poem and its meaning. Its influence on the legendarium cannot be overstated
Exodus	Unknown	590 lines; a retelling of the Israelites' flight from captivity in Egypt (*Junius MS*)	Use of history, description of heroism, contrast between orthodoxy and paganism mirror those in the legendarium
The Finnesburg Fragment	Unknown	50 lines; a battle between Hnaef and the Frisians (original MS missing)	The dangers of oath-breaking

Maxims I and II	Unknown	A set of enigmatic statements (*Exeter Book*)	Connection to Treebeard's recondite lore and enigmatic utterances
"The Ruin"	700–800 CE	49 lines (*Exeter Book*)	The descriptions of Gondor in its prime (in contrast to the Third Age), Osgiliath, and Weathertop (Amon Sûl)
"The Seafarer"	700–800 CE	124 lines (*Exeter Book*)	Evocation of the power of the sea; the "ubi sunt?" theme
"Solomon and Saturn"	800–925 CE	*Corpus Christi College, Cambridge* MS 422	Riddle contest, cf. *The Hobbit*
"The Wanderer"	875–925 CE	115 lines (*Exeter Book*)	Elegiac tone and emphasis on the qualities of a good leader

Table B: Middle-English Sources

Work	Date; Language; Source	Description	Significance
"The Franklin's Tale"	1390–1400 CE; London dialect of Middle English; Geoffrey Chaucer's *The Canterbury Tales*	A tale of the difficulties of married life	The idea of impossible labors is reminiscent of the tale of Beren and Lúthien
Lais of Marie de France	1175–1200 CE; Anglo-Norman	Breton lais; twelve short narratives	Elevated language; distanced narrative; the concept of courtly love echoes the love of Aragorn and Arwen, cf. Tolkien's *The Lay of Aotrou and Itroun*

Layamon's Brut	*c.* 1190–1215 CE	16,095 lines long; a history of Britain with a section about King Arthur	Éowyn's word *dwimmerlaik* comes from this source
Le Morte d'Arthur by Sir Thomas Malory	1485 CE; London dialect of Middle English	Eight sections; tells the story of King Arthur's life	The topics of kingship, battle, and betrayal are central to the legendarium, cf. Tolkien's *The Fall of Arthur*
"The Nun's Priest's Tale"	1390–1400 CE; London dialect of Middle English; Geoffrey Chaucer's *The Canterbury Tales*	626-line beast fable	The idea of talking animals occurs in the legendarium
Pearl	1385–1400 CE; Northwest Midland dialect of Middle English; *Cotton Nero A*	A dream poem about the loss through death of a young girl	Idealization of the female, cf. Arwen and Galadriel and Lúthien
"The Reeve's Tale"	1390–1400 CE; London dialect of Middle English; Geoffrey Chaucer's *The Canterbury Tales*	A fabliau, sexually coarse in content	The connection is linguistic with Tolkien: fascination with dialects and language in general
Sir Gawain and the Green Knight	1385–1400 CE; Northwest Midland dialect of Middle English; *Cotton Nero A*	A quest romance involving one of the knights of the Round Table; 2,530 lines; 101 stanzas	Topics of temptation, wandering, and moral struggle are Tolkienian
Sir Orfeo	1330 CE; London dialect of Middle English; three separate MSS	A retelling of the tale of Orpheus	The Orpheus tale mixed with faerie lore is Tolkienian (specifically the Beren and Lúthien story)

The Travels of Sir John Mandeville	1357–1371 CE	A narrative of voyages to extraordinary places	Tolkien may have taken his Trees of Sun and Moon and the passage of the Dead Marshes from this work
"The Wars of Alexander"	*Alexander C* MS in two versions in the Bodleian Library and Trinity College Dublin	A romance telling the story of the life of Alexander the Great	The superhuman Alexander is reminiscent of Aragorn

Table C: Scandinavian Sources

Work	Language; Source	Date	Description	Significance
"Fáfnismál"	Old Norse; *Poetic Edda*	1200 CE	Poem	Bilbo/Smaug discussion in *The Hobbit*
Kalevala: "The Story of Kullervo"	Finnish	1835, 1849 CE	22,795 verses. Epic (compilation by Elias Lönnrot); the Kullervo story occupies runos 31–36 of the larger epic	Deeply influential on Tolkien through the 1907 W. F. Kirby translation, particularly the character of Kullervo, cf. Tolkien's *The Story of Kullervo*
Prose Edda	Old Icelandic	1225–1241 CE	Compiled by Snorri Sturluson	The creation myth in *The Silmarillion* was influenced by the *Prose Edda*

The Saga of King Heidrek the Wise	Old Norse	1325–1650 CE	Fornaldarsögur (Sagas of the Old Times)	Elegiac tone; riddle contest; sword naming
The Saga of King Hrolf Kraki	Old Norse	1400 CE	It exists in more than forty MSS	Beorn in The Hobbit owes much to the character Bödvar Bjarki
"Skirnísmál"	Old Norse; Poetic Edda	1200 CE	Poem	Orcs and Misty Mountains (in The Hobbit)
"Vafðrúðnismál"	Old Norse; Poetic Edda	1200 CE	Poem	Riddle contest
Völsunga Saga	Old Norse	1250–1300 CE	Fornaldarsögur translated by William Morris in 1870	Dragon slaying; combination of natural and supernatural; the ring, a cause of so much trouble, cf. Tolkien's The Legend of Sigurd and Gudrún
"Völuspá"	Old Norse; Poetic Edda	1200 CE	Poem	Names of dwarves and Gandalf in The Hobbit

Table D: Celtic and Germanic Sources

Work	Date; Language	Description	Significance
"Kilhwch and Olwen" in *The Mabinogion*	1100–1200 CE; Middle Welsh	A story that relates directly to the larger arc of the Arthurian tales	This particular story influenced the tale of Beren and Lúthien
The Mabinogion	1100–1200 CE; Middle Welsh	A compendium of eleven varied stories	The Celtic Otherworld and the idea of the Blessed Islands correlate with the legendarium
The Niebelungenlied	1180–1210 CE; Middle High German	2,400 stanzas; the story of Siegfried, who kills a dragon	Siegfried's vulnerability is reminiscent of Smaug's
The Red Book of Hergest	1382–1410 CE; Middle Welsh	An MS containing prose (The Mabinogion) and poetry	The obvious source for Tolkien's naming of *The Red Book of Westmarch*
"The Second Battle of Mag Tuired"	800–1100 CE; Irish	A story of oppression and the effort to overthrow that oppression	Features the Tuatha Dé Danaan, who were very elvish beings; the story itself is reminiscent of *The Silmarillion*
"The Voyage of Bran Son of Febail"	900 CE; Irish	A story which contains the constituent elements of the *imram* (or voyage)	Reminiscent of the voyages in *The Silmarillion*; Tolkien himself wrote a poem called "Imram"

Table E: Sources in Fantastic Literature

Author	Work(s) and Dates	Explanatory Notes
John Buchan	"The Far Islands," 1899	Sea's haunting power
S. R. Crockett	*The Black Douglas*, 1899	Wargs
Walter de la Mare	*The Three Mulla-Mulgars*, 1910	*The Hobbit* quest
Lord Dunsany	*The Gods of Pegāna*, 1905; *The Sword of Welleran and Other Stories*, 1908	Valar and creation myth
E. R. Eddison	*The Worm Ouroboros*, 1922; *Stybiorn the Strong*, 1926; *Egil's Saga*, 1930	General influence; Tolkien much admired Eddison's powers of invention
Kenneth Grahame	"The Reluctant Dragon" (in *Dream Days*, 1898)	Dragon lore
William Hope Hodgson	*The Night Land*, 1912	Depiction of Moria
Rudyard Kipling	*Puck of Pook's Hill*, 1906; *Rewards and Fairies*, 1910	Smithcraft; Englishness; dislike of Victorian image of fairies
E. H. Knatchbull-Hugessen	"Puss-Cat Mew" (in *Stories for My Children*, 1869)	Troll episode in *The Hobbit*
David Lindsay	*A Voyage to Arcturus*, 1920	Voyaging as spiritual experience
George MacDonald	*Phantastes*, 1858; "The Golden Key," 1867; *The Princess and the Goblin*, 1872; *The Princess and Curdie*, 1882; *Lilith*, 1895	General influence
A. Merritt	*The Ship of Ishtar*, 1924	Eärendil's voyage
William Morris	1. *The House of the Wolfings*, 1888; 2. *The Roots of the Mountains*, 1889; 3. *The Glittering Plain*; 4. *The Wood beyond the World*; 5. "The Folk of the Mountain Door"	1. Riddermark; 2. Gollum; 3. Quest for Undying Lands; 4. Fangorn Forest; 5. The Paths of the Dead

E. Nesbit	"The Dragon Tamers," 1889	Dragons; Chrysophylax Dives in *Farmer Giles of Ham*
Austin Tappan Wright	*Islandia*, 1942	Dislike of technology; fullness of created vision
Ludwig Tieck	"The Elves," 1812	Part of Tieck's three-volume *Phantasus*, 1860
E. A. Wyke-Smith	*The Marvellous Land of Snergs*, 1927	Creation of the hobbits

Table F: Other Important Sources

Work and date	Author	Significance
A Book of Danish Ballads, 1939	E. M. Smith-Dampier, translator	Tolkien's love of song in his legendarium
Der Ring des Nibelungen, 1848–1874	Richard Wagner	The content of this opera cycle parallels the legendarium: riddle contest; broken weapon as dynastic symbol; power of the ring
The English and Scottish Popular Ballads, 1882–1898	F. J. Child	Tolkien's love of song in his legendarium
Folklore in the English and Scottish Ballads, 1928	Lowry C. Wimberly	Tolkien's love of song in his legendarium
Folk-Songs from the Southern Appalachians, 1917	Olive D. Campbell and Cecil I. Sharp	Tolkien's love of song in his legendarium
The Last of the Mohicans, 1826	James Fenimore Cooper	The journey of the hero and his companions to Fort Henry is reminiscent of the fellowship's journey from Tol Brandir

Interpreting the Tables

Much of what I have provided is self-explanatory; however, it is important to bear in mind the following qualifiers.

1. Tolkien disapproved of source hunting as it drew attention away from the primary text and because it focused discussion on originality rather than on tradition.

2. Tolkien had a very definite attitude to the depiction of the fairy world as is clear from his essay "On Fairy-Stories."

3. I have only listed those sources that definitely fed his creative energies. It is hard to circumscribe the matter of influence as Tolkien was an academic and a voracious reader. So, his works are the product of a lifetime of reading, both academic and casual.

4. I disagree with and find rather unhelpful Tom Shippey's distinction between a "true" source and a "heretical" source. (See Appendix A: "Tolkien's Sources: The True Tradition" in his *The Road to Middle-Earth*, revised and expanded edition; 2003: 388–98.) Such a distinction allows Tolkien to control the terms of the discussion. Just because Tolkien, for example, said he disliked Shakespeare or George MacDonald doesn't mean that they weren't influential. That said, Shippey's discussion of sources in *The Road to Middle-Earth*—along with Scull and Hammond's *J. R. R. Tolkien: Companion and Guide*—were tremendously helpful in my creating this appendix.

5. With regard to Tolkien's use of mythology, it is important to remember that in recent years several of his imaginative re-creations of those myths have been published.

APPENDIX B
FILMS OF THE
LEGENDARIUM

The history of the effort to bring Tolkien's legendarium to the screen begins, rather ignominiously, with Morton Zimmerman and Forrest Ackerman's proposal for an animated version of *The Lord of the Rings* in 1957–8. Tolkien disliked it intensely—the scenario more than the idea itself. There is, next, in 1966, a one-reel, twelve-minute animated film of *The Hobbit* by Gene Deitsch, Jiri Trnka, and Adolf Born. It was shown publicly in New York City in 1969. For a mass audience, however, the screen history of Tolkien's legendarium really begins with three cartoons produced between 1977 and 1980. The first was *The Hobbit* in 1977. It was directed by Jules Bass and Arthur Rankin Jr. and was broadcast by NBC on November 27, 1977. The second was *The Lord of the Rings* in 1978. It was directed by Ralph Bakshi and was theatrically released on November 15, 1978. The third, *The Return of the King* (1980), was by Bass and Rankin again. It was broadcast by ABC on May 11, 1980. These three cartoons can be quite quickly dismissed. All three are dreadful. Poor character design, poor animation, annoying musical and incidental soundtrack, a plethora of errors to annoy purists. I thought that when they first came out; I think that still. They are inadequate as demonstrations of cartoon talent; they are inadequate as representations of key parts of the legendarium. The only thing going for the three is that if you watch them all you will have *some* sense of the plot of the most fully realized parts (by Tolkien) of the legendarium.

The Peter Jackson Films

Peter Jackson's cinematic version of *The Lord of the Rings* and *The Hobbit* consists of six individual films: three films of *The Lord of the Rings* and three films of *The Hobbit*. The three devoted to *The Lord of the Rings* were released as follows: *The Fellowship of the Ring* (2001), *The Two Towers* (2002), and *The Return of the King* (2003). There was then a nine-year gap before Jackson made his version of *The Hobbit: An Unexpected Journey* (2012), *The Hobbit: The Desolation of Smaug* (2013), and *The Hobbit: The Battle of the Five Armies* (2014). These two trilogies represent a significant, even remarkable, achievement. There are websites and sections of websites and blogs and fanzines and newspaper stories that have spent a great deal of time anatomizing in minute detail the differences between the film versions and Tolkien's originals. I am grateful for that as it allows me to do something rather different in this appendix: assess the overall value of what Jackson accomplished over a thirteen-year period. That will require me to talk in general terms about how Jackson altered Tolkien's work, but I won't be looking minutely at his changes.

The most important point to stress initially (and this is something that many of those who have looked at the changes Jackson made rarely acknowledge) is that film and novel are two utterly different art forms, so Jackson could have made a very faithful representation of Tolkien's world but as film it could have been dreadful. Similarly, Jackson could have paid scant regard for Tolkien's four books but have made films that deserve to be considered masterpieces.

Let's look at the two trilogies in sequence.

The Lord of the Rings

With *The Lord of the Rings*, Jackson made some choices that were clearly dictated by his sense of what his audience would want. So, he adds Gimli's dwarf-tossing jokes (two of them); he substitutes Arwen for Glorfindel in the sequence that gets the hobbits and Aragorn from the Ettenmoors to Rivendell; he expands the roles of Galadriel and Éowyn. These choices are shrewd and effective. The world of 1955 (when *The Lord of the Rings* was published in its entirety) is not the world of 2000. The needs of cinemagoers are not the same as the needs of those who read *The Lord of the Rings*. Yes, there is an overlap, but many of those who went to see Jackson's films had never read the books on which the films were based.

In addition to these changes that resulted from Jackson's sense of audience, there were deletions from the trilogy: the entire Tom Bombadil sequence was cut; the Scouring of the Shire was cut (except for a glimpse or two during the mirror of Galadriel sequence). These are the principal deletions. There were, I think, different reasons for these two deletions.

The Bombadil sequence just didn't fit in with the tone and content of the rest of the three-volume epic. The Scouring of the Shire would have lengthened a film series that was already very long (coming in at nine hours and eighteen minutes in the *un*extended versions). I think these were sensible choices by Jackson. The Bombadil chapters are very different from the rest of the epic—even cringingly so at times. Tolkien chose to dramatize the life of a doll that his son Michael had once owned. I am not at all sure that was a good idea, although the Barrow-downs sequence is important to the narrative. The Scouring of the Shire is very important thematically to Tolkien's narrative, but Jackson was right to be sensitive to length. As it is, the film version of the third part of the trilogy came in at 201 minutes and that *by any standard* is a long film. Ironically, had Jackson extended the film to include the scouring then it might have put paid to critics' rather silly but frequent complaint that the end of the third film consists of a series of goodbyes. Yes, and so what? The major unfortunate side effect of not filming the scouring episode is that Saruman has to be killed somehow, but in a different way from the end chosen by Tolkien in the epic. Here I think Jackson was seriously at fault. Having Saruman falling from Orthanc's balcony and being impaled on a water wheel at its base was a mistake. Overly theatrical and an echo of the worst excesses of the Hammer Dracula films of the 1950s. The fact that the late Christopher Lee played Dracula in those films *and* Saruman is no excuse although it is a tribute to Lee's longevity.

As well as appeals to audience and deletions of parts of the narrative, Jackson also reorganized the plot in several ways and added some scenes. As to reorganization, Jackson's films start and end at points different from the original narrative; *The Two Towers'* infrequent changes of narrative focus (book) are replaced with a much greater use of cutting from scene to scene (film); there are transpositions of scenes and speeches; there are alterations in the timeline. All of these were done for defensible (even laudable) cinematic reasons. The overall effect is to improve the films, even though purists, understandably, may object to Jackson being so free in his adaptation. As to additions, the warg-riders episode on the journey to Helm's Deep (with Aragorn falling over a cliff) is wholly invented. In a lesser way, Faramir deciding to have the One Ring go to Gondor before changing his mind (apparently because of Sam's persuasiveness) is invention. The first works brilliantly as cinema, but I don't think it fits well with Aragorn's ethos and talents as a warrior. The second is an unfortunate alteration to a narrative that works well in Tolkien's book.

Overall, the effect of the myriad changes Jackson makes to Tolkien's original is considerable: he emphasizes particular themes at the expense of others; he excises much of the philosophical speculation, probably because it would retard the films' narrative; he uses a great many helicopter shots to simulate the epic scale of Tolkien's work.

Several points need to be made about Jackson's *Lord of the Rings* trilogy before I move on to his interpretation of *The Hobbit*. First, Jackson's films are superb as films. Second, Jackson actually takes very few liberties with Tolkien's epic. Third, it is clear that Jackson is very familiar with *The Lord of the Rings* and he admires it. It is also clear that he is technically more than competent. Finally, all of us who enjoyed the films should be grateful that it was Jackson who made the films (an enthusiast and not a skeptic), and that the films were made when special effects had advanced to the point where cinematic reality is a sustained and successful trompe l'oeil. Had the trilogy been made in the 1980s, say, it might have been an earnest effort, but it would have been laughable.

The Hobbit

The Hobbit trilogy by Jackson is a spectacular disaster as an interpretation of Tolkien and unsuccessful as film. We do not have to go far to see the source of the problem, although the effects of the problem are widespread and varied. Where Jackson made *The*

Lord of the Rings an epic—and rightly so—he chose also to make *The Hobbit* an epic, but this is a serious category error. To give *The Hobbit* (a children's story) the epic treatment is to misunderstand genre alarmingly. Where the three films of *The Lord of the Rings* cover over a thousand pages in the original books, the three films of *The Hobbit* (nearly eight hours of runtime) cover a work that is only one quarter as long as *The Lord of the Rings*. It was as if, having been so successful with *The Lord of the Rings*, Jackson foolishly decided to try the same recipe, but where the directions for one recipe (say a soufflé) would produce a great soufflé in the hands of a talented chef, that same recipe would not—indeed could not—produce a great pot roast, no matter the chef's talents.

And it is as if having decided to make a generically different film from Tolkien's original book, Jackson was then inspired to go much further than he did with *The Lord of the Rings* to make changes—wholesale changes—to that original. So he adds characters to the plot in the hope, I assume, of drawing audience interest. Azog, Finbul, Frodo, Galadriel, Grinnah, Legolas, Radagast, Saruman, Tauriel are the major instances in a longer list. Some of these characters are in *The Lord of the Rings*, and he brings them back—but into *The Hobbit*—because they worked well once (so why not twice?); some are characters who are named in *The Hobbit* but play no role (so he gives them one); some are characters who are dead but he brings them back to life; some are wholly invented. It is hard to see how the films are improved by any of this. Then there are plot alterations. Jackson changes how Bilbo acquires Sting and the One Ring. He excises Thorin's funeral and Dáin's coronation. He invents a fight between the dwarves and Smaug. He changes the whole relation between Radagast and Gandalf and the Necromancer. These are the major instances in a much longer list. And again, it is hard to see how the films are improved by any of these alterations. The unintended consequence may well be that for the audience who had read *The Hobbit* before they saw Jackson's trilogy it made them appreciate Tolkien's wonderful and slight children's story all the more for its simplicity and its artistic unity.

It is hard not to convict Jackson of hubris (or, as the Anglo-Saxons termed it, *ofermod*). One may certainly accuse him of becoming too enamored of technology. How else may one explain his choice of forty-eight frames per second rather than twenty-four as the format for the three films? He did so to make the action sequences more realistic and less blurry. But the effect is to make the film hyper-real and so, ironically, more distanced from its audience. This view is, of course, subjective, but it is a view held by many who have seen the films. The effect is unexpected and visually disturbing. Had the Jackson trilogy worked as film then it is likely critics would have characterized the choice of a higher frame rate as idiosyncratic and unnecessary. As it is, the films were not particularly well received and, so, this choice is added to a long list of things Jackson should not have done. It is worth noting that *The Lord of the Rings* garnered seventeen Oscars and twenty-four nominations (with *The Return of the King* receiving eleven Oscars alone, which puts it in the elite company of *Titanic* and *Ben Hur* as the most decorated films of all time by the Motion Picture Association of America). *The Hobbit* trilogy won no Oscars but was nominated eight times. The film industry spoke loudly and fairly.

So, what does all this discussion of film versions of Tolkien's legendarium tell us? Perhaps it is best to go back to Tolkien's reaction in 1958 to a proposed film treatment by Morton Grady Zimmerman of *The Lord of the Rings*. What he says there applies well to *The Hobbit*'s flaws and to *The Lord of the Rings'* strengths as film. In a letter to Forrest J. Ackerman, he complains that Zimmerman's proposal treats his work cavalierly and without a clear understanding of its purpose. In essence, it garbles *The Lord of the Rings* (Tolkien 2000: 270, 277). The reason why Jackson's film version of *The Lord of the Rings* works so well is precisely because he understood the meaning of *The Lord of the Rings* on its own terms. The reason why Jackson's film version of *The Hobbit* spectacularly fails is that it is recklessly careless and has no understanding of what the book is all about. It exaggerates characteristics of the children's story to the point of caricature. It adds unnecessary material. It garbles the original. And in doing all of this, it creates a new story with very little to recommend it cinematically. It is better than the Bass and Rankin 1977 cartoon, but that is saying very little. Very little indeed.

APPENDIX C
THE SCHOLARSHIP
ON TOLKIEN

This list consists of those texts (books and articles) that I consider essential reading, along with useful websites and journals. I have followed it with some comments about what remains to be done in Tolkien studies.

Essential Books and Articles

Allan, Jim, ed. *An Introduction to Elvish*. Hayes: Bran's Head Books, 1978.

Anderson, Douglas A., ed. *The Annotated Hobbit*. Rev. and expanded edn. Boston, MA: Houghton Mifflin, 2002.

Birzer, Bradley. *J. R. R. Tolkien's Sanctifying Myth: Understanding Middle-earth*. Wilmington, DE: ISI Books, 2002.

Burns, Marjorie. *Perilous Realms: Celtic and Norse in Tolkien's Middle-earth*. Toronto: University of Toronto Press, 2005.

Carpenter, Humphrey. *The Inklings: C. S. Lewis, J. R. R. Tolkien, Charles Williams, and Their Friends*. London: George Allen & Unwin, 1978.

Carpenter, Humphrey. *J. R. R. Tolkien: A Biography*. London: George Allen & Unwin, 1977.

Crabbe, Katharyn W. *J. R. R. Tolkien*. Rev. and expanded edn. New York: Continuum, 1988.

Croft, Janet Brennan. *War and the Works of J. R. R. Tolkien*. Westport, CT: Praeger, 2004.

Drout, Michael D. C. *J. R. R. Tolkien Encyclopedia: Scholarship and Critical Assessment*. New York: Routledge, 2006.

Flieger, Verlyn. *Green Suns and Faërie: Essays on J. R. R. Tolkien*. Kent, OH: Kent State University Press, 2012.

Flieger, Verlyn. *Interrupted Music: Tolkien and the Making of a Mythology*. Kent, OH: Kent State University Press, 2005.

Flieger, Verlyn. *A Question of Time: J. R. R. Tolkien's Road to Faërie*. Kent, OH: Kent State University Press, 1997.

Flieger, Verlyn. *Splintered Light: Logos and Language in Tolkien's World*. 2nd edn. Kent, OH: Kent State University Press, 2002.

Flieger, Verlyn, and Carl F. Hostetter, eds. *Tolkien's Legendarium: Essays on the History of Middle-earth*. Westport, CT: Greenwood Press, 2000.

Fonstad, Karen Wynn. *The Atlas of Middle-earth*. Rev. edn. Boston, MA: Houghton Mifflin, 1991. First published 1981.

Foster, Robert. *The Complete Guide to Middle-earth: From The Hobbit to The Silmarillion*. London: George Allen & Unwin, 1978.

Gilliver, Peter M., Jeremy Marshall, and Edmund Weiner. *The Ring of Words: Tolkien and the Oxford English Dictionary*. Oxford: Oxford University Press, 2006.

Hammond, Wayne, with the assistance of Douglas A. Anderson. *J. R. R. Tolkien: A Descriptive Bibliography*. New Castle, DE: Oak Knoll Books, 1993.

Hammond, Wayne, and Christina Scull. *J. R. R. Tolkien: Artist and Illustrator*. Boston, MA: Houghton Mifflin, 1995.

Hammond, Wayne, and Christina Scull. *The Lord of the Rings: A Reader's Companion*. Boston, MA: Houghton Mifflin, 2005.

Hammond, Wayne, and Christina Scull, ed. *The Lord of the Rings, 1954–2004: Scholarship in Honor of Richard E. Blackwelder*. Milwaukee, WI: Marquette University Press, 2006.

Isaacs, Neil D., and Rose A. Zimbardo, eds. *Tolkien and the Critics: Essays on J. R. R. Tolkien's The Lord of the Rings*. Notre Dame, IN: University of Notre Dame Press, 1968.

Isaacs, Neil D., and Rose A. Zimbardo, eds. *Tolkien: New Critical Perspectives*. Lexington, KY: University Press of Kentucky, 1981.

Johnson, Judith A. *J. R. R. Tolkien: Six Decades of Criticism*. Westport, CT: Greenwood Press, 1986.

Kocher, Paul H. *Master of Middle-earth: The Fiction of J. R. R. Tolkien*. Boston, MA: Houghton Mifflin, 1972.

Lobdell, Jared C., ed. *A Tolkien Compass*. 2nd edn. LaSalle, IL: Open Court, 2003.

Marquette University, Patrick and Beatrice Haggerty Museum of Art. *The Invented Worlds of J. R. R. Tolkien: Drawings and Original Manuscripts from the Marquette University Collection*. Milwaukee, WI: The Museum, 2004.

McIlwaine, Catherine. *Tolkien: Maker of Middle-earth*. Oxford: Bodleian Library, 2018.

Pearce, Joseph, ed. *Tolkien, A Celebration: Collected Writings on a Literary Legacy*. London: Fount, 1999.

Petty, Anne C. *Tolkien in the Land of Heroes: Discovering the Human Spirit*. Cold Spring Harbor, NY: Cold Spring Press, 2003.

Priestman, Judith. *J. R. R. Tolkien: Life and Legend*. Oxford: Bodleian Library, 1992.

Purtill, Richard L. *J. R. R. Tolkien: Myth, Morality, and Religion*. San Francisco, CA: Harper & Row, 1984.

Reynolds, Patricia, and Glen H. Goodknight, ed. *Proceedings of the Tolkien Centenary Conference 1992*. Altadena, CA: Mythpoeic Press, 1995.

Rosebury, Brian. *Tolkien: A Cultural Phenomenon*. Houndsmills: Palgrave Macmillan, 2003.

Scull, Christina, and Wayne G. Hammond. *The J. R. R. Tolkien Companion and Guide*. 2 vols. Boston, MA: Houghton Mifflin, 2006.

Shippey, Tom. *J. R. R. Tolkien: Author of the Century*. London: HarperCollins, 2000.

Shippey, Tom. *The Road to Middle-earth*. Rev. and expanded edn. Boston, MA: Houghton Mifflin, 2003.

Sibley, Brian, and John Howe. *The Maps of Middle-earth*. 2 vols. Boston, MA: Houghton Mifflin, 2001.

Solopova, Elizabeth. *Languages, Myths, and History: An Introduction to the Linguistic and Literary Background of J. R. R. Tolkien's Fiction*. New York: North Landing Books, 2009.

Strachey, Barbara. *Journeys of Frodo: An Atlas of J. R. R. Tolkien's The Lord of the Rings*. London: George Allen & Unwin, 1981.

Tolkien, John, and Priscilla Tolkien. *A Tolkien Family Album*. London: HarperCollins, 1992.

Tolkien Society, *Leaves from the Tree: J. R. R. Tolkien's Shorter Fiction*. London: The Tolkien Society, 1991.

Vaccaro, Christopher, and Yvette Kisor, ed. *Tolkien and Alterity*. Cham: Springer Nature/Palgrave Macmillan, 2017.

West, Richard C. "A Tolkien Checklist: Selected Criticism 1981–2004." *Modern Fiction Studies* 50(4) (2004): 1015–1028.

West, Richard C. *Tolkien Criticism: An Annotated Checklist*. 2nd edn. Kent, OH: Kent State University Press, 1981.

Zettersten, Arne. *J. R. R. Tolkien's Double Worlds and Creative Process: Language and Life*. New York: Palgrave Macmillan, 2011.

Useful Websites

Council of Elrond, councilofelrond.com.

The One Ring, theonering.com.

The One Wiki to Rule Them All, lotr.wikia.com.

Tolkien Gateway, tolkiengateway.net.

The Tolkien Society, www.tolkiensociety.org.

Best Journals

Journal of Tolkien Research. Valparaiso University.
Mallorn. The Tolkien Society.
Mythlore: A Journal of J. R. R. Tolkien, C. S. Lewis, and Charles Williams Studies. Mythopoeic Society.
Parma Eldalamberon. Elvish Linguistic Fellowship.
Tolkien Studies: An Annual Scholarly Review. West Virginia University Press.
Vinyar Tengwar. Elvish Linguistic Fellowship.

Future Tolkien Research

Students of Tolkien owe a great debt to writers and scholars such as Humphrey Carpenter, Verlyn Flieger, Wayne Hammond, Carl Hostetter, Christina Scull, and Tom Shippey. Their work has been thorough, accurate, well written, and clever. Some of Tolkien's legacy has been thoroughly studied—his work as a philologist comes to mind. Some of his legacy has been less well charted and assessed. Three parts of that legacy come to mind here as badly in need of further attention: his biography, his oeuvre, and critical theory's application to his work.

The first is obvious from the fact that we have only one useful biography: Carpenter's "official" biography. That, however, is now more than forty years old, and it was always a slight work. The idea that the life of one of the most important writers of the twentieth century could be represented by fewer than 300 pages is, frankly, absurd. However, that greater biography will not be forthcoming unless the Tolkien family and the Trust make available in an unmediated way all of Tolkien's journals and letters. Carpenter occasionally quotes from the journals and co-edited a small selection of Tolkien's letters (assisted by Christopher Tolkien), but that is all. Yet, if one looks carefully at the letters he wrote one can see that Tolkien was not the placid and unremarkable and untroubled man that the official biography suggests. In 1972, Tolkien wrote to his son Christopher some deeply insightful comments about how hard his early life and Edith's had been ("dreadful sufferings" is the phrase he uses). How much their childhood trauma had never entirely healed in either of them. How often it had "proved disabling" in later life. How much their love saved them through the power of memory, for they could always recall how that love had first blossomed. How much that love was a talisman against the inevitability of death (Tolkien 2000: 420–1). Deeply moving. Remarkable. Heartbreaking. Not the carefully airbrushed portrait Carpenter gives us.

The second piece that's missing—full knowledge of the oeuvre— would only be possible if the Tolkien family and the Trust were to make available all of Tolkien's manuscripts and typescripts. Ever since Tolkien's death we have had volumes by him (usually edited by his son Christopher) released every couple of years and sometimes more often. The introductions are helpful; Christopher Tolkien has worked hard and assiduously in preparing the texts. However, again and again he refers to manuscripts and typescripts that only he or a few select others have ever seen, let alone examined. And it is not clear to me, despite Christopher Tolkien's academic credentials, that he is the best person to be editing his father's work. He cannot be objective, and his introductions are sometimes unclear and confusing. Without access to the original materials, any reader may feel as if he is shadowboxing a mirage.

The third gap in the scholarship on Tolkien is obvious to anyone who has studied critical theory. We have little other than linguistic analysis (some of which quickly becomes arcane and abstruse to those not trained in the discipline), belletristic discussion, historical approaches, genre studies, sketchy cross-disciplinary research, and myth studies. Where are the deconstructive readings, the postmodern analysis, the psychoanalytic approaches? No Russian Formalism, no Formalism, no New Historicism, no phenomenology, few feminist readings, almost no queer theory. It is hard to explain this absence. Is it just that Theory is hard? Is it that theorists are not attracted to Tolkien's work? Is it that they take as gospel Tolkien's comment to C. S. Lewis in 1948: "I am *not* a critic. I do not want to be one" (2000: 126)? Do critics take to heart Tolkien's dismissal of criticism: "I think 'criticism'—however valid or intellectually engaging—tends to get in the way of a writer who has anything personal to say. A tightrope walker may require *practice*, but if he starts a theory of equilibrium he will lose grace (and probably fall off)" (Tolkien 2000: 126, footnote)? Of course, that is nonsense, but it does rather sound like a request for critics not to be, well, too critical, to dig too far beneath the surface glitter of the text. And Tolkien's texts do glitter beautifully!

REFERENCES

Alexander, Michael (1991), "The Battle of Maldon," *The First Poems in English*, London: Penguin Classics, [92]–104.

Anderson, Douglas A. (2002), *The Annotated Hobbit*, rev. and expanded edn, Boston, MA: Houghton Mifflin.

"The Battle of Maldon" (2009), https://web.archive.org/web/20090109124524/http://www8.georgetown.edu/departments/medieval/labyrinth/library/oe/texts/a9.html (accessed June 2, 2019).

Carpenter, Humphrey (2000), *J. R. R. Tolkien: A Biography*, Boston, MA: Houghton Mifflin. First published 1977.

The Christ of Cynewulf (1964), ed. Albert S. Cook, Hamden, CT: Archon Books/The Shoe String Press. First published 1900.

The Fellowship of the Ring (2001), dir. Peter Jackson, USA: New Line Cinema/WingNut Films, 2001.

Fonstad, Karen Wynn (1991), *The Atlas of Middle-earth*, rev. edn, Boston, MA: Houghton Mifflin.

Grotta, Daniel (1992), *The Biography of J. R. R. Tolkien: Architect of Middle Earth* [*sic*], Philadelphia, PA; Running Press. First published 1976.

Hammond, Wayne G., and Christina Scull (1995), *J. R. R. Tolkien: Artist & Illustrator*, Boston, MA: Houghton Mifflin.

Hammond, Wayne G., and Christina Scull (2005), *The Lord of the Rings: A Reader's Companion*, Boston, MA: Houghton Mifflin.

The Hobbit (1966), dir. Gene Deitsch with Jiri Trinka and Adolf Born, USA: Rembrandt Films.

The Hobbit (1977), dir. Jules Bass and Arthur Rankin, Jr., USA: Rankin/Bass Productions.

The Hobbit: An Unexpected Journey (2012), dir. Peter Jackson, USA: New Line Cinema/WingNut Films/MGM.

The Hobbit: The Desolation of Smaug (2013), dir. Peter Jackson, USA: New Line Cinema/WingNut Films/MGM.

The Hobbit: The Battle of the Five Armies (2014), dir. Peter Jackson, USA: New Line Cinema/WingNut Films/MGM.

The Lord of the Rings (1978), dir. Ralph Bakshi, USA: Bakshi Productions.

The Lord of the Rings (2001–3), dir. Peter Jackson, USA: New Line
Cinema/WingNut Films.

The Return of the King (1980), dir. Jules Bass and Arthur Rankin, Jr.,
USA: Rankin/Bass Productions.

The Return of the King (2003), dir. Peter Jackson, USA: New Line
Cinema/WingNut Films.

Salu, Mary, and Robert T. Farrell (1979), *J. R. R. Tolkien, Scholar and
Storyteller*, Ithaca, NY: Cornell University Press.

Santayana, George (1953), "Reason in Common Sense," pt. I of *The
Life of Reason; or, The Phases of Human Progress*, rev. by George
Santayana and Daniel Cray, New York: Charles Scribner's Sons,
pp. 3–86.

Scull, Christina, and Wayne G. Hammond (2006), *The J. R. R. Tolkien
Companion and Guide*, 2 vols. (1 *Chronology*; 2 *Reader's Guide*),
Boston, MA: Houghton Mifflin.

Shippey, Tom (2003), *The Road to Middle-earth*, rev. and expanded edn,
Boston, MA: Houghton Mifflin.

Tolkien (2019), dir. Dome Karukoski, USA: Fox Searchlight Pictures.

Tolkien, J. R. R. (1922), *A Middle English Vocabulary*. Oxford:
Clarendon Press, 1922.

Tolkien, J. R. R. (1949), *Farmer Giles of Ham*, London: George Allen &
Unwin.

Tolkien, J. R. R. (1954–5), *The Lord of the Rings*, London: George Allen
& Unwin.

Tolkien, J. R. R. (1961), *The Adventures of Tom Bombadil and Other
Verses from The Red Book*, London: George Allen & Unwin.

Tolkien, J. R. R. (1962), *Ancrene Wisse: The English Text of the Ancrene
Riwle*, London: Oxford University Press/Early English Text Society.

Tolkien, J. R. R. (1964), "Leaf by Niggle" in *Tree and Leaf*, London:
George Allen & Unwin, pp. 71–92. First published 1945.

Tolkien, J. R. R. (1966), "The Homecoming of Beorhtnoth Beorthelm's
Son," in *The Tolkien Reader*, New York: Ballantine Books, pp. [1]–27.
First published 1953.

Tolkien, J. R. R. (1967a), *The Road Goes Ever On: A Song Cycle—Poems
by J. R. R. Tolkien; music by Donald Swann*, New York: Ballantine
Books.

Tolkien, J. R. R. (1967b), *Smith of Wootton Major*, London: George Allen
& Unwin.

Tolkien, J. R. R. (1967c), *Sir Gawain and the Green Knight*, 2nd edn, ed.
Norman Davis, Oxford: Clarendon Press. First published 1925.

Tolkien, J. R. R. (1975), *Sir Gawain and the Green Knight, Pearl, and Sir
Orfeo*, New York: Ballantine.

Tolkien, J. R. R. (1979), *Pictures by J. R. R. Tolkien*, Boston, MA:
Houghton Mifflin.

Tolkien, J. R. R. (1980), *Unfinished Tales of Númenor and Middle-earth*, ed. Christopher Tolkien, Boston, MA: Houghton Mifflin.

Tolkien, J. R. R. (1982), *Mr. Bliss*, London: George Allen & Unwin.

Tolkien, J. R. R. (1983), *The Book of Lost Tales Part I*, vol. I of *The History of Middle-earth*, ed. Christopher Tolkien, Boston, MA: Houghton Mifflin.

Tolkien, J. R. R. (1984), *The Book of Lost Tales Part II*, vol. II of *The History of Middle-earth*, ed. Christopher Tolkien, Boston, MA: Houghton Mifflin.

Tolkien, J. R. R. (1986), *The Shaping of Middle-earth: The Quenta, The Ambarkanta, and The Annals*, vol. IV of *The History of Middle-earth*, ed. Christopher Tolkien, Boston, MA: Houghton Mifflin.

Tolkien, J. R. R. (1987), *The Lost Road and Other Writings: Language and Legend before "The Lord of the Rings,"* vol. V of *The History of Middle-earth*, ed. Christopher Tolkien, Boston, MA: Houghton Mifflin.

Tolkien, J. R. R. (1992), *Sauron Defeated: The End of the Third Age* (*The History of the Rings Part Four*), vol. IX of *The History of Middle-earth*, ed. Christopher Tolkien, Boston, MA: Houghton Mifflin.

Tolkien, J. R. R. (1993), *Morgoth's Ring: The Later Silmarillion, Part One—The Legends of Aman*, vol. X of *The History of Middle-earth*, ed. Christopher Tolkien, Boston, MA: Houghton Mifflin.

Tolkien, J. R. R. (1994a), *The Fellowship of the Ring*. Boston, MA, Houghton Mifflin.

Tolkien, J. R. R. (1994b), *The Two Towers*. Boston, MA: Houghton Mifflin.

Tolkien, J. R. R. (1994c), *The Return of the King*. Boston, MA: Houghton Mifflin.

Tolkien, J. R. R. (1994d), *The War of the Jewels: The Later Silmarillion Part Two—The Legends of Beleriand*, vol. XI of *The History of Middle-earth*, ed. Christopher Tolkien, Boston, MA: Houghton Mifflin.

Tolkien, J. R. R. (1996), *The Peoples of Middle-earth*, vol. XII of *The History of Middle-earth*, ed. Christopher Tolkien, Boston, MA: Houghton Mifflin.

Tolkien, J. R. R. (1997a), "Beowulf: The Monsters and the Critics," in *The Monsters and the Critics and Other Essays*, ed. Christopher Tolkien, London: HarperCollins, pp. [5]–48. First published 1936.

Tolkien, J. R. R. (1997b), *The Monsters and the Critics and Other Essays*, ed. Christopher Tolkien, London: HarperCollins. First published 1983.

Tolkien, J. R. R. (1997c), "On Fairy-Stories," in *The Monsters and the Critics and Other Essays*, ed. Christopher Tolkien, London: HarperCollins, pp. [109]–161. First published 1939.

Tolkien, J. R. R. (1998), *Roverandom*, ed. Christina Scull and Wayne G. Hammond, Boston, MA: Houghton Mifflin.

Tolkien, J. R. R. (1999a), *The Silmarillion*, ed. Christopher Tolkien, 2nd edn, London: HarperCollins. First published 1977.

Tolkien, J. R. R. (1999b), *The Father Christmas Letters*, ed. Baillie Tolkien, rev. edn as *Letters from Father Christmas*, London: HarperCollins. First published 1976.

Tolkien, J. R. R. (2000), *The Letters of J. R. R. Tolkien*, ed. Humphrey Carpenter with the assistance of Christopher Tolkien, Boston, MA: Houghton Mifflin. First published 1981.

Tolkien, J. R. R. (2002), *Bilbo's Last Song (at the Grey Havens)*, rev. edn, New York: Alfred A. Knopf. First published 1990.

Tolkien, J. R. R. (2006), *Finn and Hengest: The Fragment and the Episode*, ed. Alan Bliss, London: HarperCollins. First published 1982.

Tolkien, J. R. R. (2007a), *The Hobbit or There and Back Again*, Boston, MA: Houghton Mifflin. First published 1937.

Tolkien, J. R. R. (2007b), *The Children of Húrin*, also titled *Narn I Chîn Húrin: The Tale of the Children of Húrin*, ed. Christopher Tolkien, Boston, MA: Houghton Mifflin.

Tolkien, J. R. R. (2009), *The Legend of Sigurd and Gudrún*, ed. Christopher Tolkien, Boston, MA: Houghton Mifflin.

Tolkien, J. R. R. (2013), *The Fall of Arthur*, ed. Christopher Tolkien, Boston, MA: Houghton Mifflin.

Tolkien, J. R. R. (2014), *Beowulf: A Translation and Commentary together with Sellic Spell*, ed. Christopher Tolkien, Boston, MA: Houghton Mifflin.

Tolkien, J. R. R. (2016a), *The Lay of Aotrou and Itroun together with the Corrigan Poems*, ed. Verlyn Flieger, London: HarperCollins.

Tolkien, J. R. R. (2016b), *The Story of Kullervo*, ed. Verlyn Flieger, Boston, MA: Houghton Mifflin.

Tolkien, J. R. R. (2017), *Beren and Lúthien*, ed. Christopher Tolkien, Boston: Houghton Mifflin.

Tolkien, J. R. R. (2018), *The Fall of Gondolin*, ed. Christopher Tolkien, Boston: Houghton Mifflin.

Tolkien, J. R. R. et al. (1963), *Angles and Britons: O'Donnell Lectures*, Cardiff: University of Wales Press.

The Two Towers (2002), dir Peter Jackson, USA: New Line Cinema/WingNut Films.

White, Michael (2003), *Tolkien: A Biography*, New York: New American Library. First published 2001.

INDEX